NATIONAL ACCOUNTS
AND
ENVIRONMENTALLY SUSTAINABLE NATIONAL INCOME

National Accounts
and
environmentally
Sustainable National Income

Roefie Hueting and Bart de Boer

http://www.sni-hueting.info

Eburon Academic Publishers
Utrecht, 2019

Supported by the Foundation for research on Sustainable National Income

ISBN 978-94-6301-252-2

Published by Eburon Academic Publishers, www.eburon.nl

JEL Journal of Economic Literature codes

E01 Measurement and Data on National Income and Product Accounts and Wealth • Environmental Accounts

O44 Environment and Growth

Q01 Sustainable Development

Q50 Environmental Economics – General

H43 Project Evaluation • Social Discount Rate

F64 Economic Impacts of Globalization – Environment

E61 Policy Objectives • Policy Designs and Consistency • Policy Coordination

H23 Externalities • Redistributive Effects • Environmental Taxes and Subsidies

I30 Welfare, Well-Being, and Poverty – General

O11 Macroeconomic Analyses of Economic Development

A10 General Economics - General

NUR

781 Algemene economie

947 Internationale ontwikkelingsstudies

943 Omgevingswetenschappen

944 Natuurbeheer

Preface

In this book Hueting reviews and re-evaluates his earlier work on environmental functions and environmentally sustainable national income (eSNI). This book is not merely a copy of earlier work, and one can recognise the learning over time, though the authors tend to emphasize the continuity.

This book has particular importance for the current mainstream of the "capital approach" for linking the economy and the environment. Hueting´s approach and the mainstream have the same analytical structure – see Section 6.12 – but the definition of the environment here and the concept of environmental functions, leading to the concept of eSNI, are more informative, effective and efficient.

eSNI is defined as the maximally attainable level of production, using the technology of the year under review, whereby the vital environmental functions (possible uses) of the not-human-made physical surroundings remain available for future generations. eSNI provides information and is only a normative target if chosen as such. Environmental sustainability – defined in Section 8.6 – is only possible at the world scale, think of global warming. Environmental standards are derived from global conditions. Calculation of an eSNI for one country requires the assumption that other countries and the world are environmentally sustainable too.

In economic theory, producing is called the adding of value. National income is the sum of value added, so it measures production. When the growth of production is called "economic growth" then this is in conflict with economic theory. Recently natural scientists had a conference to redefine the kilogram, and this book proposes that economists have a meeting of minds to reserve "economic growth" for welfare and to speak about "production growth" for production. Let us call GDP growth "production growth", that is wat it is.

When this book is going to press there is the IPBES report on biodiversity and extinction. Changing weather patterns are alerting the world that something is happening indeed. While the Netherlands are raising the dikes, this is still measured as raising "income" and "productivity" and "economic growth" – while higher national income also causes a higher contribution to the EU – and all this is erroneously presented as a success of economic policy making. This book clarifies the conceptual error and provides a better way to use the economic indicators.

The abbreviation NI is used for *standard* national income. For comparison of NI and eSNI the relevant indicator is the distance eΔ = NI – eSNI. [1]

We will also use NI = GDP and eGDP = eSNI, though conceivably NI and eSNI may also refer to other definitions of income, like NNI and eNNI = eSNNI.

Since the distance eΔ is the key variable to look at, it should be obvious that NI is not abolished but maintained as a relevant variable, and that NI and eSNI are looked at jointly, alongside each other. There are economists who call for an abolition of NI yet this would be counterproductive.

---

[1] See Section 1.15 on notation.

This book focuses on income, production and production growth. The computer model for eSNI also generates much output on the various environmental issues, for which this book is not a useful place to report about. Hueting has proposed research on also other assumptions on preferences than only for environmental sustainability, but there were no funds to do so in the past.

The major news is that CBS Statistics Netherlands (2018), as editors of the Dutch "Monitor Broad Welfare" (MBW) (actually a pleonasm), have decided to refer to eSNI, which is the first official support of the measure, though CBS does not calculate it itself, see Section 11.15. Other major news is that William Nordhaus received the Nobel Prize in Economics in 2018 "for integrating climate change into long-run macroeconomic analysis". This is a long overdue recognition for the economic research into the relation of the economy and the environment.

Hueting and De Boer have collaborated for about three decades. Hueting & De Boer (2018, 2019) made a preliminary estimate of eSNI for the Netherlands 2015. Colignatus assisted in structuring this book, suggesting improvements in didactics, collecting the Appendices, and writing drafts for the Summary Overview and parts on Misunderstandings and Comparisons. We thank Thomas Colignatus, Thea Sigmond, Peter Stauvermann and the Stichting Wetenschappelijke nalatenschap Jan Tinbergen for their permission for reproducing the articles in the Appendices.

We thank CBS Statistics Netherlands where Hueting started in 1969 and De Boer in 1991. CBS supported the development of eSNI and supported the calculation of eSNI by IVM. We thank our many colleagues at CBS Statistics Netherlands for their involvement. Our special thanks are for Peter Bosch and Henk van Tuinen for their enduring engagement and comments on drafts of this book.

We thank again the team at IVM that did the study and/or calculation on eSNI for the Netherlands for 1990, 1995, 2000 and 2005: Harmen Verbruggen, Marjan Hofkes, Rob Dellink, Reyer Gerlagh, Wietze Lise, Huib Jansen, Onno Kuik, Vincent Linderhof.

We thank again Ekko van Ierland, Jan van der Straaten and Herman Vollebergh for their editing of the 1999 conference book, Van Ierland et al. (eds) (2001). We want to thank all participants in that volume: Paul Ekins, Herman Daly, Richard Norgaard, Astrid Scholz, Sarah Fleisher Trainor, Wilfrid Beckerman, Kirk Hamilton, Giles Atkinson, Sylvie Faucheux, Martin O'Connor. A paper was sent in by Karl-Göran Mäler but he did not finalise his contribution for that conference book. Already departed from us in warm memory are David Pearce (1941-2005), Robert Goodland (1939-2013) and Salah el Serafy (1927-2016). For the organisation of the conference, Steven Keuning contributed to the scientific committee and operational support was by Theo Potma (1932-2017), Fred Kromhout and Jacques Bron. Joy Hecht made a fine report of the discussion at the World Bank seminar, see Chapter 17.

We thank Roeland Bosch for organising a colloquium at the Dutch Ministry of Economic Affairs on June 3 2013. We thank Albert Steltenpool for his comments on the estimate of eSNI 2015.

We thank Jan Pronk, Jan Terlouw and Herman Wijffels for their support and Frans Rooijers at CE Delft for hosting and supporting the Foundation SNI (FSNI).

Contents in brief

Contribution of this book

Overall: Extending welfare economics for the new scarcity of the environment, creating the concepts of environmental functions and environmentally sustainable national income (eSNI), with the development of a new theory for statistical measurement of national income, namely by using conditionality in measurement of both standard NI and eSNI, in order to respect the precautionary principle and the management of risk on economy and ecology.

Components are:

(1) Integration of economics and ecology by defining the notion of environmental functions (possible uses) and empirical description of their properties for practical application.

> Within this area also:
>
> Identification of *vital* environmental functions. Clarification that the distinction between weak and strong (environmental) sustainability is irrelevant for those vital functions. More obviously, other factors in welfare like work and leisure are secondary to ecological survival.
>
> Recognition of *revealed supply* via elimination costs and *revealed demand* via compensation and damage costs, to allow for standard cost-benefit analysis; yet, also recognising that major costs cannot be adequately measured when such CBA has limited relevance.

(2) Awareness that using national income as one of the factors influencing welfare, requires the conditionality of making assumptions on preferences, resulting in (i) both a better understanding of standard NI and (ii) the design of the concept and definition of environmentally sustainable national income (eSNI) as: the maximally attainable level of production, using the technology of the year under review, whereby the vital environmental functions of the not-human-made physical surroundings remain available for future generations. Crucial then is the development over time of $e\Delta = NI - eSNI$.

> Within this area also:
>
> Formulating the conditions for an economic model, collecting standards for environmental sustainability, overseeing the actual calculation of an eSNI for the Dutch economy, and explaining what the outcome means.
>
> Finding a practical approach for asymmetric bookkeeping, and identifying NI minus asymmetric bookkeeping = NI-A, located between NI and eSNI.

(3) Developing this theory and practice upon the old and tested foundations of economics and national accounting, thus enhancing both scope and depth of economics, and thus making for ready acceptance by fellow economists, and thus supporting economic policy makers with key concepts and tools to deal with the very real current risk of global warming and other threats to the economy and environment and ecology.

About the authors

For some fifty years dr. Roefie Hueting (1929) has worked on a framework for the estimation of an environmentally sustainable national income (eSNI) as an indicator of the production level that does not threaten living conditions for future generations. He graduated in 1959 at the University of Amsterdam with Pieter Hennipman, worked in accountancy in 1959-1962, and then in 1962-1969 on labour market studies at both the Ministry of Social Affairs and Public Health and the Ministry of Housing and Spatial Planning. In 1969, he was asked to create the Department of Environmental Statistics at CBS Statistics Netherlands. In 1974, he published his cum laude thesis, under supervision by Jan Pen, *New Scarcity and Economic Growth. More welfare through less production?,* a seminal study about the greening of national income, with an English translation in 1980. He assisted the Dutch Ministers of Health and Environment with their first environmental legislation, introducing the principle that *the polluter pays*. He did a cost-benefit analysis on the construction of a polder in the Waddensea, an estuary of international environmental importance, which resulted in the plan being abandoned. He was offered a professorship but declined for his family. The Dutch environmental accounts that he developed had great influence upon the development at the UN Statistical Division (UNSD or UNSTAT) at the onset and later also UN SEEA 2003, and that are currently included in the satellite accounts there. In 1991 Jan Tinbergen and Roefie Hueting published a first rough estimate of Sustainable World Income in a paper for the 1992 Rio conference. In 1992, CBS Statistics Netherlands and the World Wildlife Fund (WWF) published his *Methodology for the Calculation of eSNI*. Hueting retired from CBS in 1994 and received a knighthood and the UNEP Global 500 Award, see page 211. He remained an official adviser to CBS till the end of 2000 and received the CBS silver medal. In 1999, an International Symposium on his work was held at the KNAW Royal Academy of Sciences in Amsterdam. In 2001 the World Bank organised a seminar on the book Van Ierland et al. (eds) *Economic Growth and Valuation of the Environment: a Debate*. That book contains an estimate of eSNI for the Netherlands, which also forms a *proof of concept*. Hueting presented papers on eSNI at seminars sponsored by the World Bank, OECD and WSSD where delegates have strongly recommended that eSNI estimates be developed for more countries. Before mid 2007 the abbreviation "SNI" is used but henceforth "eSNI" is to be preferred since "sustainability" has been collecting all kinds of other aspects that are irrelevant for ecological survival and that are not included in Hueting's definition. In 2018 CBS Statistics Netherlands included a preliminary estimate of eSNI 2015 as an element in its monitor on well-being, which is the first official recognition by CBS itself of the actual relevance of the indicator.

Hueting has a dual life as a jazz pianist. He founded the Down Town Jazz Band in 1949, that performed in major European halls and theatres, and with which he recorded around 250 tracks on 78 rpm, LP and CD. His last CD of 2005 consists of own compositions, mainly played as a piano solo. In 2007 he had the Trad Jazz Duo (piano and bassax) and in 2019 he still performs solo weekly.

Ir. Bart de Boer (1947) graduated in electrotechnical engineering and specialised in automatic control engineering and environmental management at Technical University Twente 1973. He remained at TU Twente as researcher, worked on systems analysis of water quality management at Gelderland Province in 1974-1978 and returned to TU Twente till 1982. Subsequently he was with DHV Consulting Engineers, joined CBS Statistics Netherlands in 1991-2005, and then moved to CE Delft till 2007, remaining active on topics related to environmental sustainability. De Boer provided for essential steps for the calculation of eSNI, with support in deriving environmental sustainability standards and application in optimal control theory.

Support

The analysis on environmentally sustainable national income (eSNI) got full support by Jan Tinbergen (1903-1994), see the article Tinbergen & Hueting (1991), which article has been included in Appendix 15 here.

Though Hueting is the progenitor of eSNI, the involvement by Tinbergen in eSNI is strong. Tinbergen was a pioneer in the development of national accounting and economic modelling. At his advice, CBS in 1969 appointed Hueting specifically for the task to correct national income for the impact on the environment. Tinbergen wrote a preface to Hueting's thesis (1974, 1980). Tinbergen (1985:35) devotes a chapter to "counterproduction", which Hueting now calls asymmetric bookkeeping. The formula for non-renewables is by Tinbergen (1990). Tinbergen encouraged the UNEP award for Hueting. The World Bank invited Tinbergen and Hueting to write a joint paper for a collection, and this became Tinbergen & Hueting (1991). The two authors decided that it would be better for the reception of the analysis that Tinbergen, with his international recognition, would be first author.

Jan Tinbergen received the first Nobel Prize in economics in 1969 jointly with Ragnar Frisch (1895-1973). His brother Niko Tinbergen (1907-1988) was a biologist and received the Nobel Prize for physiology or medicine in 1973 with Karl von Frisch and Konrad Lorenz. One can imagine that Jan Tinbergen was open to the discussion about the challenges to the environment.

Jan Tinbergen studied physics in Leiden with Paul Ehrenfest. In his thesis he already made the switch to economics, and he was a leading figure in the creation of the new approach of econometrics. In 1929 he was appointed at the new department on business surveys and mathematical statistics at CBS Statistics Netherlands. There he helped create the Dutch national accounts, which effort was part of the international movement that eventually led to the System of National Account (SNA). In 1936 he presented the world's first macro-economic model, which idea has become standard in economic policy making. He was consultant to the League of Nations (1936-1938) on the issues of the Great Depression, and had a famous discussion with John Maynard Keynes about the use and relevance of econometrics. In 1945 he became the director of the newly created Central Planning Bureau (CPB), that has been important for Dutch economic policy making since then. In 1955, with CPB running smoothly, Tinbergen turned his attention to the more pressing problem of the developing world. Other contributions were on education, income distribution, the optimal social order, the Cold War and disproportional defence expenditures.

Contents

Part 1. Introduction

1. *Summary overview*

1.1 *Definitions*

The United Nations developed the System of National Accounts (SNA). Eurostat developed the European System of National and Regional Accounts (ESA 2010), based upon the Council regulation EU (1996). The figure for *National Income* (NI) is important for government policy, for example for establishing tax bases or for monitoring budget deficits in the European Economic and Monetary Union (EMU). NI is a multi-purpose figure that perhaps cannot be praised enough. NI is also important for welfare economics, since production is one of the key contributors to economic welfare, e.g. with food production, medicine and so on.

However, our planet is threatened by a wrong belief in wrongly formulated growth. This book develops *environmentally Sustainable National Income* (eSNI) defined as the maximally attainable level of production, using the technology of the year under review, whereby the vital environmental functions (possible uses) [2] of the not-human-made physical surroundings remain available for future generations. This book looks at the economic aspects of the environment – it does not look at the use of NI for other purposes – and shows that proper judgement requires that both NI and eSNI are looked at jointly, alongside each other.

1.2 *UN SEEA*

The UN *Handbook of National Accounting – Integrated Environmental and Economic Accounting 2003* (UN SEEA) gives an overview of methods to relate national income to the environment, see UN, EU, IMF, OECD (2003). In sections 10.199-214, p453-457 there, the editors of UN SEEA, refer to Hueting & De Boer (2001b), and give their evaluation. Section 10.199 states:

> "Much of the initiative to look for an alternative path for the economy rather than a different measure of the existing economy came from the work of Hueting in the late 1960's and early 1970's. He introduced the concept of environmental function referred to throughout this manual, explaining how pressure on functions leads to scarcity or competition for these functions. As with any economic good or service, this scarcity gives rise to an economic value due to the opportunity costs involved in their use or appropriation. The concern is then to define aggregate indicators to characterise a sustainable economy which ensures the maintenance of key environmental functions in perpetuity. Such an economy may be described as a 'greened' version of the existing economy where typically an increase in national income is secured at the expense of worsening environmental degradation. Interest then focusses not on the new aggregates themselves but the gap between the existing economy and the greened version."

Apart from this evaluation by the editors, Hueting and De Boer also contributed the method of *environmentally sustainable national income* (eSNI) directly, and this was included in UN SEEA 2003 Section 11.163-171, p504-507. The estimate by Verbruggen et al. (2001) at IVM obviously was important for this inclusion.

---

[2] See Chapter 6 and overview Section 1.7.

1.3 *Key graph of the empirical finding*

The following graph summarises the empirical finding for the Netherlands 1990-2015, see **Figure 1** and the data in **Table 1**.

(1) Dutch GDP in 1990 is set at 100 and over 25 years it rose to 164.4 in 2015, with an average growth of 2.0% per year. This is relatively low compared with the 1950-1970 period. It includes a rise in population.
(2) In 1990, eGDP = eSNI was 53% of GDP, close to the Tinbergen & Hueting (1991) rough estimate of 50%. However, eSNI has been growing by 3.1% per year, and thus has been catching up with GDP to an estimated 69% in 2015. This growth was caused by a switch to the service sector, deliberate policies for environmental improvement, and the global financial crisis in 2007-2011.
(3) The level distance eΔ = GDP – eGDP has increased from 47.4 to 50.4 percentage points of GDP 1990. The Dutch environmental pressure increased.
(4) The figure of eGDP = eSNI has a larger range of uncertainty though there are no sensitivity analyses yet. These outcomes thus are only indicative.

Figure 1. GDP and eSNI of the Netherlands in 1990-2015, 1990 = 100

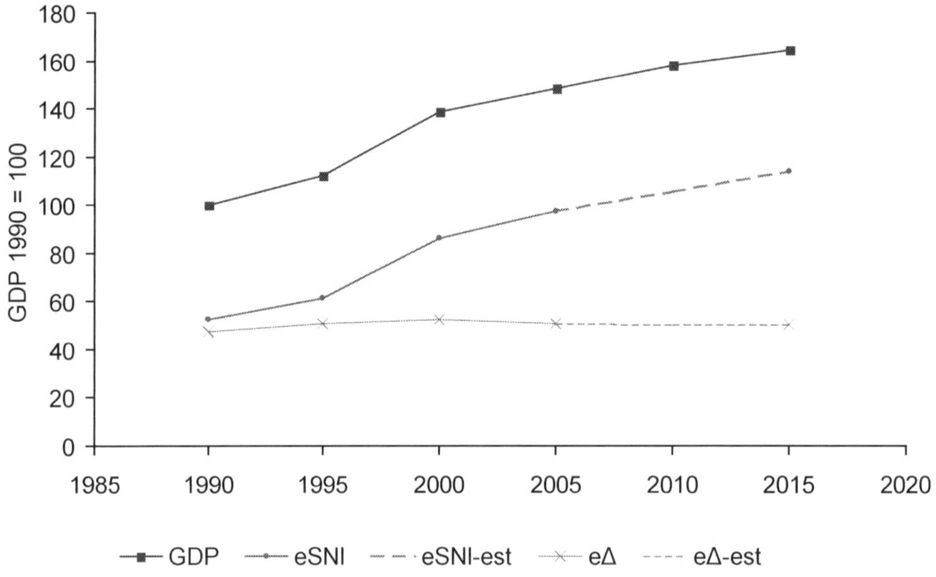

Table 1. Data for Figure 1. Italics: rough estimate

	1990	1995	2000	2005	2010	2015	per year
GDP	100	112.2	138.8	148.3	157.9	164.4	2.0%
eGDP = eSNI	52.6	61.3	86.2	97.4		*114.0*	3.1%
Distance, eΔ	47.4	50.9	52.6	50.9		*50.4*	0.2%
%	53%	55%	62%	66%		*69%*	1.1%
eFootprint	1.9	1.8	1.6	1.5		*1.4*	

Hueting & De Boer (2018, 2019); eΔ ≈ NNI – eSNNI (Section 12.3); eFootprint = 100 / %.

The inverse ratio is an *environmentally sustainable footprint* = eFootprint = GDP / eSNI, which is a "footprint" with a methodology from welfare economics. It has dropped from 1.9 in 1990 to 1.4 in 2015.

It is encouraging for the Netherlands that the ratio between GDP and eSNI has been improving. The key information for policy making concerns the level distance. The distance eΔ between the two variables increased in absolute terms, and this is not encouraging. The Dutch economy is still far removed from environmental sustainability. Economic processes are not only still damaging environmental functions (incl. depleting resources) in a manner that affects the survival conditions and the well-being of future generations, but they do so increasingly.

For a perspective on this development, **Figure 7** on page 93 contains a hypothesis of a country reaching environmental sustainability in 2080.

Apart from the distance eΔ = NI – eSNI, there is also information from the dynamic development over time, where the unyielding laws of growth come into play. Suppose that, with NI at 100 and eSNI at 50, NI grows by 5% to 105 and eSNI drops from 50 to 49: then it is obvious that such growth is unsustainable. Suppose that policy makers want a change so that the burden remains constant. Then target eSNI = 105 – 50 = 55, and thus eSNI must grow by 10%, thus twice as fast, which is quite an objective. In this way, eSNI provides information on the direction and speed of the sustainability of economic development.

PM. The Stern Review (2006) estimated that societies would have to invest 1% of GDP annually to avoid the worst effects of climate change. In 2008 professor Nicholas Stern raised to 2% because of faster than anticipated climate change. How do his outcomes compare with the 40% distance between NI and eSNI? The Stern Review concerns the transition path from NI to eSNI. If the distance of 40% is to be covered in 20 years, then this arithmetically becomes 2% per annum. Economically, the cost would be higher because investments in abatement would meet with diminishing returns and anyway no longer go into factories that produce consumer goods. eSNI is also wider than climate change. The Paris Agreement of 2015 – "keeping a global temperature rise this century well below 2 degrees Celsius above pre-industrial levels and to pursue efforts to limit the temperature increase even further to 1.5 degrees Celsius" [3] – may well mean a reduction of real incomes compared with the decades of rising incomes, measured wrongly because of unsustainable use of the environment.

1.4 *Purpose and result*

The purpose of this book is to review the economic theory and practice behind this approach – environmental functions and eSNI. According to us, economics and statistics as sciences have an important role: to provide information for society. Building upon the results of predecessors, like Jan Tinbergen (1903-1994) and so many others, prevents repeating mistakes. Closer consideration of the subject matter of economics and the new scarcity allows us to be more precise. [4]

---

[3] https://unfccc.int/process-and-meetings/the-paris-agreement/what-is-the-paris-agreement

[4] See Section 4.5.

The subject of this book is *welfare economics* with an application to *statistical measurement of national income* in the National Accounts. This book describes the connection between economics, economic growth, production and the environment. The key result is the awareness from welfare economics that *the statistical measures on national income are conditional to assumptions on preferences.* Economics and statistics *as scientific endeavours* only generate adequate information for policy making on both production and environment *when there is a distinction between two conditions* that are assumed for doing the actual accounting, and that guide the measurement modelling:

- the common assumptions behind standard national income (NI or GDP)
- the assumptions for environmental sustainability, that generate environmentally sustainable national income (eSNI or eGDP).

Under the hypothesis of a preference for environmental sustainability part of NI is *not* income but only *expenditure.* Mistaking NI as income means living above the available means. Consequentially there is the distinction between *sustainability* and *environmental sustainability.* Since it is unknown which set of assumptions holds true, each indicator by itself can be misleading, and both are needed, including their distance, for adequate information about the state of the economy with respect to the environment and the path towards environmental sustainability.

These assumptions are not of a political but of a theoretical nature, and of a practical nature for national accounting. Politicians do not decide what constitutes information. Without such assumptions measurement is impossible. Outcomes have only a meaning conditional upon their assumptions. The assumptions concern the generation living today since their views pertain to future generations. Hueting (2001d:367):

> "(...) even in a country with high standards of democracy such as The Netherlands, a lack of information can result in fatal decisions being made. Without economic information on the very crux of environmental problems – the conflict between the environment and production growth as measured in national income (population times volume of economic activity) – well-founded decisions on environmental conservation cannot be made. Besides opportunity cost data, data on (individual) preferences are indispensable for such information. If one takes as an established fact that the latter data can be deduced only very partially from market behaviour or surveys, then making assumptions *vis-à-vis* preferences is inevitable (...)."

The world has seen a range of proposals of Green-GDPs or related indicators but in our analysis eSNI is the only measure or statistic with a *proper* foundation both within economic theory and the practice of national accounting, so that it can be used alongside standard NI or GDP indeed.

eSNI is a historical, statistic figure just like standard NI. Estimating an eSNI is a comparative static exercise using a model with a hypothesis on the future, yet the result is not a forecast but the use of a model for the past.

While the environmental data are already collected in the satellite accounts, it costs 0.25% (or a quarter of a percentage) of the budget of CBS Statistics Netherlands to additionally integrate these data into a figure for eSNI – or if done each 5 years then 0.05% per year – compared with 1.3% of the budget to produce the Consumer Price Index or 6.6% for the National Accounts including NI.

This book summarises the work by the authors over many years, which work is partly to be found in their publications, partly in unpublished notes. [5] [6] Hueting developed the Dutch environmental statistics at CBS Statistics Netherlands starting in 1969, that had basic influence upon the development at the UN Statistical Division (UNSD or UNSTAT) and UN SEEA, and that are included in the satellite accounts there. The concept of eSNI was originated by Hueting in 1986b while De Boer provided both essential steps for its implementation and support in development of sustainable standards and application in optimal control theory. [7]

1.5 *Asymmetric bookkeeping and the notion of NI-A*

Asymmetric bookkeeping can best be introduced by an example: when an oil spill pollutes a beach, then the costs of cleaning up tend to be entered into NI as expenditures in final demand but the damage standardly is not entered. Other terms are "defensive expenditures" or "double counting" or "counterproduction" (Tinbergen (1985)) but "asymmetric bookkeeping" is the better term. Chapter 7 will discuss NI-A = NI corrected for asymmetric bookkeeping = NI minus asyms = NI ex asyms. Arithmetically the total value of asymmetric bookings is A = NI – NI-A. The proper comparison concerns NI-A and eSNI, with distance NI-A – eSNI.

1.6 *Correcting NI versus comparing NI, NI-A and eSNI*

Early texts about eSNI – like Tinbergen & Hueting (1991), here reproduced in Appendix 15 – spoke about "correcting NI". This term borrowed from the continuous effort to improve the relevance and accuracy of the System of National Accounts (SNA). However, when NI is compared with eSNI, then NI is taken as it is, and there is no correction of it. The term "correcting NI" then distracts, because the focus is on the comparison and looking at the distance. A better expression is "to correct *the use* of NI".

Hueting (1974a, 1980:164-165) was already cautious about the notion of "correcting NI" and suggested to use figures alongside each other:

> "All these shortcomings of the measurement of national income, (...), call for strong relativization of the results and form reasons for the further development of statistical work, but they do not seem to be urgent problems. What is urgent is the problem of environmental deterioration.

[5] The first author published around 150 articles, essays and papers on this subject, starting in the mid sixties. While his thesis Hueting (1974a, 1980) concluded that no measure could be found, eSNI is a correction on this thesis. The thesis and the theory developed there still forms an integral part of this analysis and also the present book.

[6] The second author has been involved in the subject area since 1976 and co-authored some ten articles with Hueting.

[7] Due to limitations of time, these latter contributions using optimal control theory are only indicated in this book. See e.g. Zeelenberg, De Boer, Brouwer (1997) on sustainability in growth models.

The losses of function form a considerable and rapidly increasing aspect of new scarcity that is not allowed for in the figures of national income. On the contrary, when measures of elimination and compensation are taken by private persons or the government, the costs contribute to the increase in national income. By the identification of these results with the concept *economic growth* and the strong emphasis on growth in economic policy the danger is thus created of growth rates that, like a whirling compass, indicate that the national economy is proceeding along the desired course, whereas in reality society is drifting off in a different, undesired direction. It is therefore urgently necessary to calculate the size of environmental deterioration as far as possible in terms of money and to compare the results of these calculations with the figures of national income. It is definitely *not* the intention to replace the present figures by others, but merely to introduce alongside the current calculation an alternative one, in which the costs of measures of elimination and compensation are interpreted as intermediate deliveries. If this proves possible, insight into growth, interpreted as increase of the availability of economic goods, can at least be somewhat improved."

1.7 *Integrating economics and ecology by environmental functions*

It is common knowledge that air pollution affects the quality of life, otherwise it would not be called "pollution" in the first place. When mapping the environment and collecting statistics on it, around 1970, it appeared necessary to develop a systematic description. This resulted into the identification of environmental functions. [8] Reference to environmental functions may result into pedantic language, e.g.: when traffic uses the function 'air as medium to get rid of waste' then this disrupts the function 'air for physiological functioning'. It was a key step to identify environmental functions but this book will try to use common language.

The recognition of environmental functions allows the integration of economics and ecology. When Hueting started the department of environmental statistics at CBS Statistics Netherlands department he started by hiring biologists, physicists and chemical engineers. This aspect is part and parcel of Hueting (1969a) (1974a, 1980) and later work, and is reflected in collaboration by Hueting with biochemical researcher Lucas Reijnders. For an appreciation of Hueting's work by a biologist and environmental scientist see Robert Goodland (2001). All this will be presupposed here in the background, and this book continues with a focus on economics, while incorporating the awareness about vital environmental functions.

1.8 *Finding proper integration*

We concur with this observation by El Serafy (2001:201):

---

[8] The environmental functions (possible uses) of an environmental resource j (e.g. water), with level x_j (stock, state), are the possible uses i, for $i = 1, ..., n_j$, having actual usage u_{ij} (flow). With p_{ij} the purity or availability, and q_{ij} the relevant optimal (e.g. fishing) or maximal (e.g. water quality) purity, for example q_{ij} = 100% (e.g. no pollution), then purity after usage is $p_{ij} = q_{ij} - u_{ij}$. Norms on resources and their availability give norms on their usage. In Figure 5 on page 79 only a single function is depicted with purity or availability p. See Section 10.5 for formal details.

> "Recall the title of the United Nations guidelines for the compilation of the satellite accounts: *'Integrated environmental and economic accounting'*. This kind of language gave the impression that the conventional estimates could continue to stand unadjusted, being viewed as *economic*, whereas the environmentally amended magnitudes, insulated in satellite accounts, are implicitly held to be extraneous to the economic calculus, bereft of merit for economic description, analysis or policy."

No doubt the data in the satellite accounts are relevant and must be accurate. Hueting has worked hard to get sound environmental data and quality statistics also at the level of UN SEEA. The objective here is to integrate them within economic theory, and produce the eSNI estimate, that can be compared with NI and NI-A. The SNA then can be extended with the methodology for constructing the eSNI estimate.

A first step in this integration is, and we may again quote El Serafy (2013:5):

> "Economically viewed – and a narrow view at that – it is not in fact the natural resources per se that need protection, but their services. In an effort to reduce the complexity of the issues involved and to form a bridge connecting the environment with economics, the work of the Dutch economist Roefie Hueting is remarkable. Imaginatively, he coined the concept of 'environmental functions' which are services provided by Nature and are being progressively stressed [Hueting, 1974a, 1980]. From my perspective, the cost of safeguarding, repairing and maintaining these environmental functions should be recognized explicitly in the national accounts simply by invoking the fundamental maxim of 'maintaining capital intact' (El Serafy, 1998)."

El Serafy unfortunately associates environmental functions (possible uses, state variables) with services (uses, flow variables), but otherwise the analysis is valid. The second step in this integration of the environmental accounts into the SNA is (i) either à la El Serafy by keeping monetary capital intact – see Section 12.4 – or (ii) as in this book via environmental sustainability by keeping the functions of resources available for future generations.

This integration of the economy and the ecology has the same analytical structure as the modern mainstream "capital approach" – see Section 6.12 – but the approach presented here is parsimonious and more effective and efficient.

1.9 *National accounting and risk*

Hueting (1974a, 1980) refers to the finding by E.P. Odum that ecological collapse cannot be predicted and can be observed only when it is too late. This causes the essential insight that national accounting in our times changes from the more legal context into an issue of information management concerning risk too. For economics in general the key question becomes whether the field is open to the current ecological risk, thus open to extending the foundations of economic theory, and, by implication for national accounting whether it will be open to the notion of extending the national accounts with variables of sustainability that compared to capital have an even longer horizon above one accounting period.

eSNI is part of a wider movement amongst economists and international bodies of governance to deal with this issue, and Chapter 12 does comparisons.

1.10 *Welfare, income and standards*

The notions of welfare, income and standards can be clarified with the use of **Figure 2.** The figure gives a conventional graph from an *introduction to economics* with convex Production Possibility Frontier (PPF) and concave indifference curves of a Social Welfare Functions (SWF). There are two sets of these two: (i) one with unsustainable reality (U) with income NI measured by SNA, and (ii) another with environmentally sustainable target (S) with income eSNI. The axes mention two uses of environmental functions: [9] (1) exhaust of CO_2, (2) use of fresh water. The use reduces the availability. The production of more fresh water by e.g. distillation, and thus the increase of more possibilities to pollute it, causes an increase in the output of CO_2, and thus a reduction of the remaining possibilities to exhaust CO_2. Point S assumes natural absorption of CO_2 and natural generation of fresh water. Point U assumes additional measures to make the functions available, for example by taking from future generations.

Figure 2. Welfare, income and standards

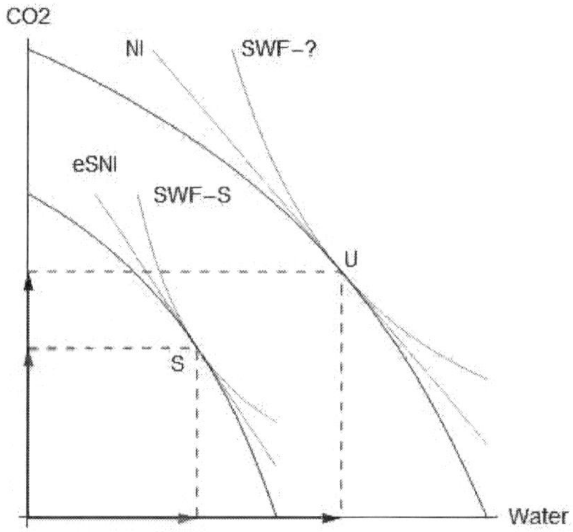

Properties are:

- NI is a weighted sum of the use of functions at current market prices at U, and eSNI is a weighted sum of the standards at shadow prices at S. [10]
- Whether SWF-? or SWF-S is *highest* is determined by *hypotheses*.

The observations of NI, actual use (long arrows) and market prices allow the estimation of production functions and demand curves. Assuming unsustainable optimality, they imply a SWF with indifference curve SWF-?. This optimality is unrealistic (hence the question mark), and it is not suggested that use is optimal

[9] The environmental functions will be more specific than used in this diagram. The relation between availability of a function and its actual use is discussed in Section 10.5.
[10] Additionally there is the decomposition in aggregate price and volume change.

because it is observed. The standards at S (short arrows) can be substituted in these production and demand functions. The diagram at point S assumes that all standards are binding and that the lower PPF and indifference curve SWF-S still are tangent, with unique shadow prices. The latter thus follow from the condition of a social preference for environmental sustainability, and render eSNI.

The diagram also shows the interpretation of outward or inward moves:

- A move outward is the conventional thinking that "more is better" but comes with the implicit assumption that there are additional measures for more availability of functions, for example by taking resources from the inheritance of future generations.
- A move inward is the precautionary principle that "less is better", with the explicit observation that there actually are no real additional measures for more availability.

The distinction between availability versus use of an environmental function is discussed in Section 10.5. The diagram above refers to *use* and can be compared with the diagram of the vertical demand curve in **Figure 6** that refers to *availability*. The latter has the schedules of elimination and damage *to the left of* the vertical demand curve at *standard* S – because resources are actually taken from future generations and not really "useable" as **Figure 2** suggests here. **Figure 6** gives the proper economic perspective, when natural abundance is reduced to scarcity, and when standards must be derived. However, a figure that refers to availability is less easy to combine with the numerical outcome that actual *use* is higher than the standard of maximal use (and minimal availability), and that NI at U has a higher value (by accounting costs as income) than eSNI at S.

Figure 2 may clarify that both NI and eSNI are part of reality and of statistics, though with different properties. NI is an estimate following current practices in SNA, and eSNI is an estimate that relies upon standards and model.

Of course, eSNI is work in progress. There is discussion of what can be done for new research. If we want to deal with the uncertainties then we need more and not less research. Whatever those uncertainties, given the conventional use of NI it is best to have both NI and eSNI available for decision making under risk for future generations.

The diagram uses concepts from a basic course in economics. It is remarkable that the key notions can be presented so, with the actual underlying complexity.

1.11 *On the definition of the term "economic growth"*

Section 1.1 made the statement that *our planet is threatened by a wrong belief in wrongly formulated growth*. Section 2.3 derives *from the subject matter of economics*:

> "The central idea of this study is as follows. Economic theory does not call for continuing growth of *production*. Economic growth can mean nothing other than an increase in welfare – i.e. the level of satisfaction of needs or wants. This depends not only on goods and services produced but also on factors such as employment, income distribution, labour conditions and most certainly on environmental goods that have become scarce."

In economic theory, producing is called the adding of value. National income is the sum of value added, so it measures production. When the growth of production is called "economic growth" [11] [12] [13] then this is in conflict with economic theory.

1.12 *Advice that eSNI is calculated by national statistical bureaus*

Because of the mission of national statistical bureaus to provide adequate information, the authors advise that eSNI is calculated and published by them on a regular base. Environmental sustainability standards can be derived from the scientific literature, and thus are *recorded* in statistics and *referred to* and not *set*. One would also use the (for this purpose) best available economic model. There is uncertainty in the standards and the model, yet see the comments on sensitivity analysis below, and in particular the on validity in Section 11.6.

1.13 *Repetition but also a nutshell*

This book restates what already has been presented in the past. There is nothing new here other than the selection, composition, rephrasing, summarizing and also presenting an overview. However, there has also been learning from the past, and we have also been re-evaluating what we wrote in the past.

The advantage of this book is that it provides a nutshell of the theory that was developed from 1967 to 2018, which theory itself builds upon the development of the System of National Accounts (SNA) since the 1930s.

The book starts with a synopsis of Hueting's thesis "*New scarcity and economic growth: more welfare through less production?*" (1974a, 1980) (online PDF). This thesis originally had the negative conclusion that there is no good way to correct NI for the new scarcity of the environment. The book then continues with a synopsis of the introduction in 1986b of the vertical demand curve found by the assumption of environmental sustainability. While the definition of eSNI forms a dramatic break with the pessimism of *New Scarcity,* the theoretical and empirical foundations by *New Scarcity* provide the bedrock upon which eSNI is possible, and the reader can enjoy seeing how the same arguments from welfare economics, cost benefit analysis and statistical measurement permeate the whole edifice.

While we have been writing about the subject for all these decades and have repeated ourselves numerous times, we are amazed ourselves that we did not present this nutshell overview before, though Hueting & De Boer (2001b) is a good effort. We hope that this book then contributes to a better general understanding of the analysis as a whole. With the overview provided in this book, readers will also have a better guide to the details that are still provided in our earlier work.

---

[11] For example, the website of CBS Statistics Netherlands defines "economic growth" as "The growth of the volume of GDP (frequently in market prices)."

[12] https://web.archive.org/web/20190116194524/https://www.cbs.nl/nl-nl/onze-diensten/methoden/begrippen?tab=e#id=economische-groei

[13] https://web.archive.org/web/20190111105726/https://www.cbs.nl/nl-nl/reeksen/economische-groei

1.14 *Outline of the book*

Part 1 gives an overview and introduction. Part 2 is a synopsis of *New Scarcity* enlarged with more details about asymmetric bookkeeping. Part 3 is a synopsis of eSNI. *New Scarcity* already discussed the valuation of the environmental functions by means of revealed demand and revealed supply. This discussion is now moved from Part 2 and put into Part 3, so that this discussion is fully integrated with the eventual assumption of the vertical demand curve. Part 4 discusses misunderstandings about eSNI and compares with other environmental indicators. Part 5 is a short Epilogue that reviews what is not discussed here: some work already done and some work to do.

The first Appendix is the article by Tinbergen & Hueting (1991), by which Jan Tinbergen, as one of the founding fathers of SNA, expressed his full support and active engagement with Hueting's solution for the measurement problem. Two appendices are by Thomas Colignatus whose outsider overview of our work might be refreshing for readers who are new to our jargon. Peter Stauvermann reviews Frequently Asked Questions and Thea Sigmond alerted the Stiglitz, Sen, Fitoussi commission on how eSNI provides answers to some of their main problems. Appendix 17 gives a lively report on the World Bank Seminar of 2001.

1.15 *On notation*

Variables in formulas are defined per Chapter and not uniform in the book.

Many symbols have an origin in abbreviations. Before 2007 the term "sustainable national income" (SNI) was used, but the notion of sustainability got so much burdened with other aspects that it became better to emphasise the relevance for the environment by using "eSNI". Issues of welfare on work and leisure and such are of a different order of relevance than ecological survival of mankind with respect to climate change and other environmental challenges.

It is advisable to shift from abbreviations to using indicators. Some concepts have so many words that the acronym becomes unusable too. For example, NI will stand for "standard National Income", and we better maintain NI and avoid the abbreviation "sNI". A lower-case prefix "e" will mean "environmentally sustainable", like in eGDP and eΔ. We might write eNI instead of eSNI, but we are used to eSNI. Puristically, we might write eSGDP and eSΔ, comparable to eSNI, but this appears to read akwardly, and eGDP and eΔ are best.

2. *Introduction to the book*

2.1 *Abstract*

From the viewpoint of welfare economics both NI and eSNI are conditional upon assumptions. Policy making needs both figures – and their distance – in order to assess the current location w.r.t. environmental sustainability. When the System of National Accounts (SNA) produces only one of these indices then it provides a wrong compass.

2.2 *Why this book is needed*

The problem of the environment has been anything but solved in recent years and in our expectation will increase in severity in the years to come. After all, the *a priori* of continuing growth of *production*, which is arguably the cause of the problems, is still adhered to by the governments of all countries in the world, their international organizations and the whole of business. The old same arguments are still used for this. These arguments are disputable from the point of view of economic theory or quite simply incorrect. They include the proposition that the *production* must grow in order to earn the means to safeguard the environment. There are also seductive expressions such as 'green growth'. A painstaking refutation of these misconceptions in a form accessible to everybody therefore seems no less necessary in this day and age than 20 or 40 years ago. The heart of the study is the concept of environmental functions, introduced by Hueting in 1969a.

2.3 *Economic growth refers to welfare and not production*

The central idea of this study is as follows. Economic theory does not call for continuing growth of *production*. Economic growth can mean nothing other than an increase in welfare – i.e. the level of satisfaction of needs or wants. This depends not only on goods and services produced but also on factors such as employment, income distribution, labour conditions and most certainly on environmental goods that have become scarce.

The simplest economic datum is the following: when goods are scarce, more of one means less of another. Investing in energy-saving measures, in the development of clean, riskless forms of energy or in treating plants, switching to a kind of agriculture offering better chances of survival to plant and animal species and changing to methods of production and patterns of consumption (usually on a smaller scale) that spare the environment thus slow down the growth of production or lead to a lower production level. They are measures for the preservation of non-market goods which by definition have no return in market terms but are quite certainly justifiable from the economic point of view, insofar as people attach greater importance to these goods for themselves and for coming generations than to continuing cumulative growth of production. All these measures create very considerable employment but – again by definition – are at the expense of (growth of) the real wage rate. For wage is a claim to produced goods; non-market goods do not come under it. Since a shadow price can be constructed for environmental goods only exceptionally, it cannot be established whether our activities still lead on balance to economic growth or already to economic decline (increase or decrease of welfare).

2.4 *The new scarcity of the environment*

The present study may be summarized as follows. The deterioration of the environment is described as a rapidly spreading new scarcity. This scarcity is caused by the increasing calls made on the *functions (possible uses) of the not-human-made physical surroundings,* the environment, the carrier of the functions, on which humans are entirely dependent. A conflict is being waged between use of environmental functions for the increase of production on the one hand and, with great plausibility, the future use of these functions and the present and future use of other functions on the other hand. More simply stated, there is a conflict between growth of production and population on the one hand and the environment on the other. So, the new scarcity is manifesting itself in increasingly severe competition between the activities utilizing the various environmental functions, leading to loss of function. The environmental functions now in short supply are *by definition* economic goods. Deterioration of the environment may be defined as the occurrence of losses of function. The latter should be regarded as costs.

In the study "*New scarcity and economic growth*" (Hueting, 1974a, 1980) the functions and the losses of function are classified per environmental component (water, soil and air). A distinction has been made between quantitative, spatial and qualitative competition of functions. This makes quantification possible in physical units and, with the aid of an assumption, in monetary units, since the extremely complex whole of environmental deterioration is subdivided in this way into a large number of sub-problems. Both the classification and the quantification have been worked out by the multidisciplinary team of the Department of Environmental Statistics Netherlands under the direction of one of the present authors.

2.5 *Pioneer works*

New Scarcity forms an integral part of the present analysis. Its Chapter 3 discusses pioneer works on environmental deterioration and economic growth. It suffices to refer to the discussion there, but those pioneers may still be mentioned: A. Marshall (1890), A.C. Pigou (1920), K.W. Kapp (1950,1963), K.E. Boulding (1966) (1950) (1971), E.J. Mishan (1967), W. Isard (1968) (1969), A.V. Kneese (1970), R.U. Ayres (1969), R.C. d'Arge (1969), W.W. Leontief (1970), J.W. Forrester (1971), D.H. Meadows et al. (1972), D. Arthur et al. (1972), B. Commoner (1972). Undoubtedly this list is incomplete.

2.6 *Difference with the literature on external effects*

Losses of function differ among other things on the following points from external effects. External effects are defined in the literature, briefly, as unintended side-effects outside the market. By the definition of the market process the government cannot cause any external effect because the government actions occur outside the market, but *can* cause losses of function, even when interests are weighed perfectly against one another. For external effects, a common distinction is between ´main´ and ´subsidiary effects´. For losses of function, we cannot, speak of 'main functions' and 'subsidiary functions'. There are no 'positive gains of function' on the analogy of positive external effects: scarcity in the environment does not occur until functions are in competition with each other. In the concept of function the environment occupies the central position, and not production, which is dependent on the functions (possible uses) of our not-human-made physical surroundings as set out above.

2.7 *Shadow prices*

In the attempt to establish the shadow prices of the environmental functions, the *costs* of elimination of the agent are plotted against the resultant *benefits*. The point of intersection of the marginal cost curve and the marginal benefit curve yields the shadow price of the function. At this point the social costs are minimum, whereas the difference between benefit and cost is maximum. The point indicates the optimal degree of availability of the function concerned.

It will be shown that in general the costs of elimination can in fact be estimated. Great difficulties occur on the benefit side. Part of the benefits can be established by estimating the reduction in compensatory costs (desalination canals, facilities at waterworks, building dikes etc.) and in financial damage (losses suffered by erosion, by flooding, by droughts, by corrosion, etc.) as a result of elimination measures. These costs are engendered by losses of function and disappear upon restoration of function. The expenditure on compensatory measures and the financial loss reflect needs for the environmental functions. These amounts may be derived from market data. However, the greater part of the needs for environmental functions cannot be expressed in market quantities. Also with the aid of simulated market behaviour (contingent valuation, questionnaires) the needs for environmental functions can be quantified in terms of money in only a few cases (e.g. recreation).

2.8 *Preferences at micro or macro scale*

On a micro scale the preferences for environmental functions cannot be established. The utility of the two categories of goods (produced goods and environmental functions) should be directly weighed the one against the other, with due observance of their production costs – the costs of elimination measures are the 'production costs' of the functions. The prices of market goods are irrelevant here, because they do not give the slightest information on the ranking of the needs with regard to market goods and environmental functions; they may even be misleading.

On a macro scale, which is the subject of this study, information can be given by making an assumption about the – unknown – preferences. To give an example, environmentally sustainable national income (eSNI) is based on the supposition that people have a preponderant preference for preserving the availability of essential environmental functions for future generations. In other words, preferences are assumed for sustaining these functions for the future. The carrier of environmental functions is our physical surrounding. Therefore, whether a function is sustainably used has to be established by means of physical limit values or standards, established by scientists; the reliability of these standards increases as research progresses. If the use of a function does not meet a standard, either technical measures have to be taken or a direct shift to alternative use has to be put into effect in order to meet the standard; this forms the elimination costs. Without physical standards environmental sustainability is indeterminate. Since the standards are derived on the basis of scientific knowledge, environmental sustainability is as objective as science: it is an objective concept insofar science is objective. Of course, the preferences, and the decisions thereupon, for *completely, partly or not at all* meeting the standards, are subjective.

2.9 *Statistical measurement of economic growth*

Proceeding from the subject matter of economics the term 'economic growth' can mean nothing other than increase in welfare, defined as the satisfaction of wants derived from our dealings with scarce goods. Welfare is not a quantity that can be measured directly 'from outside'; it is a category of individual experience. It is for this reason that the statistician focuses in practice on charting trends in factors that *can* be measured and that can plausibly be argued to influence welfare. Some important welfare-influencing factors are: (1) the package of goods and services produced, (2) scarce environmental functions, (3) time, i.e. leisure time, (4) the distribution of scarce goods, i.e. income distribution, (5) the conditions under which scarce goods are acquired, i.e. labour conditions, (6) employment casu quo unemployment, (7) future security, to the extent that this depends on our dealings with scarce goods, and specifically the vital functions of the environment. *These factors cannot be combined into one figure that indicates the welfare.*

These factors are often in conflict with one another, although this is not always the case. For scarce goods it holds by definition, however, that more of one is less of another, for a good is scarce when something else has to be sacrificed in order to obtain it (sacrificed alternative, opportunity cost). Nowadays environmental functions have become scarce goods. All other things remaining equal (including the technological state of the art), more production therefore means less environment and vice versa. Ceteris paribus, it is therefore misleading to identify the growth of *production* as measured in national income (or GDP) with an increase in welfare, or with economic growth and economic success, as is still common practice even today.

All human action – breathing, drinking, producing, consuming, recreating etcetera – depends on the possible uses (functions) of the not-human-made physical surroundings, the environment. Essential functions have become obviously scarce and consequently economic goods.

- Producing is, according to standard economic theory, adding (economic) value. National income (NI) equals the sum of the values added. So NI measures – the fluctuations in the level of – *production*. Consequently scarce environmental functions, the most fundamental economic goods at human's disposition, remain outside the measurement.
- The heart of the concept of environmental sustainability is the precautionary principle. In the just mentioned dissertation the many objections to interpreting growth of NI as increase of welfare are enumerated and

discussed. The conclusion made both there and in later publications that actually define eSNI, is that in view of the scientific literature that mentions serious threats as a result of human activities, the most urgent complement to the statistical measure of NI is a statistical measure of an *environmentally sustainable* production level.

Environmentally sustainable national income (eSNI) is defined as the maximally attainable level of production, using the technology of the year under review, whereby the vital environmental functions of the not-human-made physical surroundings remain available for future generations. It is based on the assumption of strong preferences for environmental sustainability. Because of drastic changes in the price ratios resulting from internalising the sustainability costs, eSNI will comprise a consumption package differing from the present one.

Because of the precautionary principle, future technological progress is not anticipated in the calculation of eSNI. When constructing a time series of eSNI's, technological progress appears only after it has been realised. eSNI is a historical, statistic figure just like standard NI. Estimating an eSNI is a comparative static exercise. It is evidently not forecasting, but the use of a model for the past.

The greater the distance that has to be bridged between the present production level and the desired more environmentally benign production level, the higher the costs of the elimination measures are. These measures, consisting of (i) technical means to reduce the use of the environment, (ii) direct shifts to less environment-damaging products and (iii) birth control, are interacting with deliveries of all products, including services. When putting these measures into practice, the interdependences between the producers, consumers and the environment cause changes to all commodity flows and prices. For a correct approximation, such calculations have to be done by a general equilibrium model, which also generates the prices for produced goods in a sustainable economy. The level of sustainable national income follows from such a model as well.

2.10 *NI, eSNI and their distance*

Statistically correct information about the current situation is provided by current production at NI and environmentally sustainable production at eSNI, and the distance between these figures. When this distance increases, society is drifting farther away from environmental sustainability, if this distance decreases, society is getting closer to environmental sustainability.

3. *Principles and consequences*

3.1 *Abstract*

This provides a summary overview of this book but now with the logical distinction between principles and consequences. Taken from Hueting & De Boer (2001b).

3.2 *Principles*

1. In our approach to eSNI we are engaged in statistics, a science of the past, not in forecasting the future. Concerns about future generations, which are justifiable, are recognized as being an important element of the preferences of the current generation. In observing and measuring the past, it is relevant to take these preferences into account; doing so is not forecasting but the use of a model simulation for the past.
2. We remain within the traditional methods of the System of National Accounts (SNA), but provide another national income figure, eSNI, for use alongside the standard figure. Our figure is based on assumptions regarding preferences that differ from the assumptions implicitly made when standard national income (NI) figures are used as one of the indicators for welfare, namely that the current package of goods and the state of the environment perfectly reflect the preferences of the economic subjects, implying that the current path of the economy is optimal. The latter is questionable (see Principle 3, iv). Changes in the volume of NI are nonetheless still taken universally as the key indicator for economic success. The main purpose of the eSNI research is to improve the statistical information about our economic success (increase in welfare).
3. Estimation of eSNI rests on four pillars.
   i. The formal or indifferent concept of welfare, as introduced probably by Rosenstein-Rodan (1927) and elaborated further by Robbins (1932) and particularly by Hennipman (1940, 1962, 1995), from which it follows immediately that if there exist strong preferences for the environment, conservation measures will lead to a decline in NI and an increase in welfare (Hueting, 1974a, 1980). Thus, when strong preferences for sustainable use of the environment are assumed, as is the case when constructing eSNI, satisfying these preferences has a positive effect on welfare, borne of the knowledge that future generations will have freer disposal over the functions of their (not-human-made) physical surroundings, which outweighs the negative effect on welfare due to the resultant decline in instantaneous consumption. As Hueting (1996) emphasizes, this assumption can be neither proved nor refuted on empirical grounds.
   ii. The concept of possible uses of our physical surroundings, referred to as environmental functions, or simply functions. Competing functions are economic goods (Hueting, 1969, 1970a, 1970b, 1974a, 1980).
   iii. The position that environmental sustainability is an objective, scientific concept that must be clearly distinguished from whether or not there exist

preferences for such. This implies that it is indeed possible to establish sustainability standards, even though these may sometimes be bracketed within high margins of uncertainty. Standards for sustainability must thus be sharply distinguished from subjective preferences for attaining such standards, or for not doing so.

iv. The position that there exist certain 'blockages' (or 'barriers') as a result of which preferences for environmental conservation are *incapable* of being fully expressed through the market and budget mechanisms. This justifies making assumptions about preferences that differ from those underlying NI figures, when used as an indicator of economic success (see Principle 2).

4. For the valuation of environmental functions or losses of function (which amounts to the same thing) data are required on both preferences (demand) and costs (supply). Data on the costs of restoring and maintaining vital functions can, in principle, always be obtained. Preferences for such measures can be only very partially estimated, however, because of the existence of blockages (see Principle 3, iv). This is particularly true of preferences for maintaining vital environmental functions for the future, that is for sustainability. Making assumptions about preferences for the present and future availability of functions is therefore inescapable.

3.3 *Consequences*

1. *The eSNI according to Hueting is the maximally (net [14]) production (income) which can be sustained on a geological time scale, with future technological progress assumed only in the development of substitutes for non-renewable resources, where such substitution is indispensable for sustaining environmental functions, in turn essential for sustaining income.* The modelling exercise to estimate eSNI can only be consistent if the vast majority of the subjects in the model are assumed to have an absolute preference for sustainability. This eSNI concept is theoretically sound as well as operational, although it involves considerable statistical effort. Its theory is in line with so-called general growth theory.
2. When applying the concept of 'environmental function', the distinction between weak and strong sustainability cannot be made: non-renewable resources must gradually be substituted by other elements of our (not-human-made) physical surroundings, whereas substitution of a large class of renewable resources is impossible, particularly life support systems, including ecosystems. Economically speaking, we find no essential difference between renewables and non-renewables: the only thing that matters is that their functions must remain available.
3. The environment is defined as the not-human-made elements of our physical surroundings, on which elements we are entirely dependent and which can be described as a collection of possible uses or functions. In accordance with standard theory, producing is defined as adding value by labour. Goods can be produced solely by using and changing the environment. This process has

[14] The original definition concerned net production, but under some conditions it can be gross, see Section 12.3. Keeping capital depreciation the same, the relevant distance eΔ is the same.

an exclusively positive effect on welfare, and consequently adds exclusively positive value to our surroundings, as long as functions are not rendered scarce in the same process. When functions start to compete, however, they become scarce and their price rises from zero to an ever-greater positive value, which constitutes an impoverishment, and consequently an increase in costs. On this view it follows that in moving from NI to eSNI or some other green national income only negative corrections can be made, and no additions.

4. Proper comparison of eSNI is not to NI but to NI-A = NI minus asymmetric bookkeeping. There is lack of awareness of the relevance of NI-A. Maintaining a record of eSNI leads to greater awareness of the effect of asymmetric bookkeeping with respect to the use of environmental functions on NI.
5. We seek the maximum (net) national production (income) at which the environmental functions are sustained. This implies that the functions must be sustained above or at the approximated minimum levels that nature can support and that the sacrifices required to attain the associated sustainable development path are minimum. (An eSNI calculated with future function levels chosen as high as possible will probably be zero.) The goal, consistently, is to ensure that possible (potential) future uses of the environment (that is functions) are not lost. Future generations then retain their freedom of action vis-à-vis these functions, although we explicitly assume that they exercise this freedom while remaining on a specific, namely sustainable production and consumption path.
6. Because the bulk of national income is generated by those production (and consumption) activities that are most burdensome to the environment, a shift from environmentally burdensome to less burdensome activities will have a negative effect on the volume of NI (Hueting, 1981c; Hueting et al., 1992d). Calculation of this effect is a three-step process: (1) capital goods are reallocated as part of the optimization embodied in effectuating the necessary shifts among production activities; (2) the production possibilities frontier is assumed to be curved 'around' the origin; (3) prices are used that arise after internalization of the costs of the required elimination measures (including the levies to induce direct shifts) when making the step from standard to sustainable national income. Shifts from meat to beans, say, or from car to bicycle or plane to train for example are the most essential possible solutions from the environmental angle and also the most plausible (see 'Three myths', Hueting (1996)). However, the sectoral subdivisions available at Statistics Netherlands (CBS) are not yet sufficiently detailed to simulate this effect in the model, so that the effect is not yet visible in the result (see Verbruggen et al. (2001)). We hope to improve the approximation at a later stage. For the time being, less essential and less plausible shifts have been incorporated.
7. The eSNI according to Hueting is defined such that adjustment of NI in the successive years of investigation is based on the technology of the year in question, including technology that is operational but not yet on the market. This precludes the risks of extrapolated technological progress subsequently proving unattainable (precautionary principle). An inevitable exception is

substitution of non-renewables, see Section 9.9.2. This position implies that eSNI may be expected to increase over time.

8. The above has mentioned the comparison of the levels of NI, NI-A and eSNI. The relevant comparison is by taking the differences. These differences or distances are monetary measures (in real values, in prices of a base year), and they concern what this analysis boils down to. The difference eΔ = NI – eSNI forms, under the assumption of strong preferences for environmental sustainability, the costs that currently are mistaken as income. The distance eΔ-A = NI-A – eSNI is a monetary measure for the distance between the current and the sustainable development path. Observe that the total flow NI and the base material found in statistical observation are kept intact, but only accounted differently for environmental sustainability, as NI = eSNI + eΔ.
9. Sustainability standards for environmental pressure are – in theory – the levels of environmental pressure on the sustainable development path that is associated with eSNI and that includes both the economy and the environment. These standards reflect the regeneration capacity of the environment with respect to the various forms of environmental pressure and, with the exception of those relating to the consumption of non-renewables, are constant.
10. In practice it is and will probably remain unfeasible to compute the sustainability standards, the costs associated with attaining these standards and eSNI in a theoretically consistent manner, that is with a single, comprehensive, dynamic environmental-economic model. Instead, the standards are calculated with the aid of environmental models and eSNI according to Hueting with a general economic equilibrium model. This requires introduction of additional rules as well as several ad hoc choices. The principal rule is the assumption that sustainability is guaranteed if human activity and the resultant environmental pressure do not accelerate the extinction of biological species at the global level. Because of these rules, the practical sustainability standards for environmental pressure and the practical eSNI are probably lower than their theoretical counterparts were they to be computable.
11. As a very rough estimate of sustainable world income Tinbergen and Hueting (1991) arrive at a figure of 50 per cent of current world income. The provisional results of the study on an eSNI for the Netherlands are of similar magnitude (Verbruggen et al., 2001). This means that roughly half our present production and consumption depends on unsustainable use of the environment.
12. We are concerned here with a comparative, static exercise in which time plays no role. The model imposes environmental sustainability instantaneously. The rate of discount is zero, see Section 9.7.1. This way of calculation differs from reality in which time will play a role. A transition to a lower, sustainable level of economic activity free of shock to the social fabric will require considerable time. The transition route to a sustainable level must itself also be sustainable, that is, insofar that it doesn't involve irreparable damage to vital environmental functions. The quest for such a route would be the obvious sequel to the present eSNI study. Assuming a preference for environmental sustainability, welfare will increase by pursuing this route as rapidly as possible.

Part 2. Foundation in economic theory

4. *The subject matter of economics*

4.1 *Abstract*

Classical economics started with a focus on material production. Neoclassical economics "studies human behaviour as a relationship between ends and scarce means which have alternative use" (Robbins, 1932). A possible reformulation is to be more precise on what those means actually are, in the light of ecological survival.

4.2 *Scarcity*

Briefly formulated,[15] economic problems are born of the scarcity of means compared with the wants. It follows immediately from this definition that deterioration of the environment is also an economic problem. After all, humans are dependent on the not-human-made physical surroundings, the environment, in all their doings, such as breathing, consuming, producing et cetera. Resources such as oil and copper with their numerous functions, clean water, fresh air, a properly functioning soil and space for agriculture, industry etc. as well as for natural ecosystems are all essential to human life. But at the same time they are scarce and they are becoming scarcer with great rapidity. If the environment were abundantly available in undamaged form, it would not present any economic problem and the marginal value (the price) of environmental goods would be nil. Unfortunately, reality displays a different picture. The new scarcity is impinging painfully on more and more people.

In the light of these simple truths it is remarkable that some authors with great obstinacy construe a contrast between 'economics' and 'the environment'. This misunderstanding, which can adopt a variety of forms, may be traced back to two main causes: an outmoded idea of what constitutes the subject matter of economics and an outmoded diagnosis of the environmental situation. The first occurs more frequently than the second.

4.3 *Classical economics*

The old-fashioned idea of the subject matter of economics has its roots in the eighteenth and nineteenth centuries. Adam Smith was interested in material, marketable goods – after all, in his opinion they form the 'Wealth of Nations'. Even services – they are 'immaterial' – fall outside this category (Mill, 1876),[16] as does the environment. The material goods are valued in accordance with the costs of production – the value is created by production, thus by the input of labour. In

[15] See Hueting (1974a:6) for a full definition.

[16] John Stuart Mill makes a distinction between directly productive, indirectly productive and unproductive work. Mill describes as indirectly productive that work which causes the productivity of the directly productive sector to increase (e.g. the government's work insofar as this contributes to the proper functioning of industry and the – medical – work devoted to saving a productive worker). This is reminiscent of the view sometimes heard today that measures on behalf of the environment are 'economically justified' only if they further productivity.

other words, this is a productivistic point of view, and one in which the concept of production is interpreted very narrowly, viz. as the production of material goods.

4.4 *Neoclassical economics*

In the course of the nineteenth century three changes occurred in this point of view.

- In the first place it came to be seen that the distinction between material goods and immaterial services is not relevant to an overall economic viewpoint. Government services also come under this category.
- In the second place the concept of wealth was replaced by that of welfare (utility). This means the satisfaction of wants evoked by the scarce means. In other words, it is a psychical and subjective quantity. This is the period of the "marginal revolution". When economists presume that 'welfare has to be maximized', they simply mean that scarce resources have to be used in such a way that the resultant satisfaction of wants is as great as possible.
- In the third place, the concept of value – the labour theory of value – evolved. The subjective value is caused by the discrepancy between want and the means of satisfying want, i.e. by scarcity. Of course the marginal utility school, which brought about this shift in thought, did not forget that there are also such things as the costs of production; their relevance to value is that the costs help to determine the volume of production, and thus the ultimate scarcity of the goods and services produced.

As a result, production acquired a more modest place in the overall economic picture than with Adam Smith and the English classicists. Welfare can be increased (or in other words scarcity can decrease) by production, but also by a reduction in the level of wants. Welfare can even be increased by reduced production, for instance when leisure time is valued more highly than the produced good sacrificed for it. In this way the productivistic idea has been abandoned. Increase of welfare, by whatever cause, is economic growth by definition.

4.5 *A possible reformulation of the subject matter of economic theory*

Given the meaning of the environmental functions, the subject matter of economic theory could be formulated as follows: the problem of choice with regard to the use of the scarce, alternatively applicable, dead and living matter of our physical surroundings for the satisfaction of classifiable wants. Or, very briefly: arranging the dead and living matter of the environment according to our preferences. [17]

4.6 *Criticism of neoclassical economics*

Criticism of neoclassical economics was present from the start, as the notion only arose from the discussion itself. There are various competing schools now, like on behavioural economics or "ecological economics" (that is more oriented on thermodynamics and entropy and less on economics, see Røpke (2004:310)). For our purposes, neoclassical economics suffices as a framework for discussion. Economists with a background in neoclassical economics share common

[17] Originally proposed in Hueting (2011b) "five ways".

knowledge about definitions and implications. When someone highlights some assumption then others can follow the reasoning because of the common knowledge base. Welfare economics has been a perfect vehicle for the development of the analysis in this book. By this, there is no claim that all assumptions of neoclassical and welfare economics satisfy empirical truth. The theory is important to derive workable approaches that are empirically relevant and that can be tested in econometrics. The choice of this approach does not imply that other approaches like behavioural economics or other would not be relevant. The neoclassical approach combined with econometrics is only how the present analysis has come about.

There is a view that nature may have an intrinsic value, and that neoclassical economics has an anthropocentric approach since it looks only at the values attached by humans, see e.g. Lintsen et al. (2018). This view is expressed by humans though, and authors who refer to such intrinsic value are actually humans who express their own value. As humans we cannot avoid this anthropocentrism simply because we are humans. Thus this line of reasoning cannot be used to reject the analysis that leads to the development of eSNI.

4.7 *Comment on happiness*

For a long time, there have been objections of a spiritual and religious nature about the pursuit of worldly and material possessions, because this interferes with more essential properties of the human spirit, see Hueting (1974a, 1980). Closely bound up with this criticism are the ideas of Marcuse (1964), who states that man has lost his freedom through industrial capitalism and has become a slave of consumer goods imposed upon him, while his 'real needs' are not fulfilled. Easterlin (1972 and 2003) does not discover (in inquiries) a connection between happiness and the growth of production. Layard (2005), reviewing the literature on happiness, states that happiness is related to the activity level in different parts of the brains. Dependent on the country and the specific research it appears that after the 1960's or 1980's the level of happiness has not increased while the level of GDP increased substantially. Based on this research the following remarks can be made on the relationship between production (one of the factors influencing welfare) and happiness.

(1) Scarcity, which demarcates the economic discipline, and welfare are defined precisely (see above). None of the present authors has found an exact definition of happiness. (2) Happiness includes, apart from economic items such as income and employment, a series of items that are not submitted to a budget restriction and therefore do not force us into making a choice as in the case of scarce goods. Consequently, in this respect happiness falls outside the economic discipline. Layard (2005) mentions love, friendship (both not for sale according to the saying), social relations, acknowledgement, creativity, marriage and personal freedom. However, we concur with the comment by Colignatus that human decision making upon these items can meet with scarcity in the (mental) resources for decision making and personal utility optimisation, and then meets with aspects of scarcity in a fundamental economic manner, comparable to the handling of satiation (like the choice of one apple from a basket of apples). (3) According to the spiritual and Marcusian criticism mentioned above, happiness and welfare can develop

opposite to one another. (4) The results of the above-mentioned inquiries suggest that when economic agents attain a level of wealth at which they grow satiated, then produced goods are no longer scarce. This would mean that the reduction of National income (NI) that results from attaining environmental sustainability does not involve costs and will be easily accepted. In practice, however, the resistance to this is considerable. Hueting (1980a) gives arguments why it is plausible that the increase of production by itself contributes to welfare and refraining from it involves costs, although the existence of a macro variant of the law of diminishing utility is plausible too. (5) Starting from the 1960's or 1980's the level of happiness seems not to have been affected by NI growth. However, simultaneously the emission of greenhouse gases, the loss of biodiversity, the loss of landscape, droughts and floods increased considerably too, without affecting happiness. Nowhere in the literature is an explanation provided for this phenomenon, it is not even mentioned.

5. *Environmental changes as economic phenomena*

5.1 *Abstract*

After the step to neoclassical economics, the development of the new scarcity comes with misunderstandings still relating to views from classical economics. There remains a true conflict between material production and the environment.

5.2 *A false opposition of economics versus environment*

Those who construe a contrast between 'economics' and 'environment' are often still assuming that the production of material goods is the only concern of economics. They believe that economics calls for more and more production, whereas in fact economics assumes that man aims at an increasingly high level of welfare (that is, the satisfaction of wants).

Now it must immediately be remarked that greater production and increased welfare are often positively correlated. If great poverty prevails, it may safely be assumed that additions to production increase welfare within broad limits (though allowance should definitely be made here for the fact that inhumanly long working hours, child labour, etc. reduce welfare). But as soon as production has attained a certain level and the injurious side-effects of production make themselves felt, this parallelism may cease. It is extremely difficult to say when exactly this is the case. A sound 'scientific' answer cannot be given; it is a matter of a subjective appraisal, which may differ from person to person. But everything points to the fact that continuing growth of production in a finite world leads to increasingly serious bottlenecks in the environment and to catastrophes. As a result, the environmental problem is above all one of the needs by the present generation for a world fit for future generations to live in. This thorny problem turns up at various points in the study.

The view that the 'environment' contrasts with 'economic interests' may for the greater part be explained by a misplaced identification of 'economics' with production. In part, however, the view challenged here may perhaps be a hangover from the time when the environment seemed to be a free good, abundantly available in respect of the existing wants, with a marginal value equal to nil, and therefore not relevant to economic discussion.

5.3 *Neoclassical economics*

The transition to the theory of subjective value opened the way to the development of welfare economics. For in the subjectivistic view it is the greatest possible satisfaction of wants, the maximum welfare of individuals, not the maximization of national product, that is of primary importance. True, as a result economic theory loses the objective criterion against which the result of economic effort may be judged, but it does gain in realism to a considerable extent. Scarcity, interpreted as the discrepancy between wants and means, [18] now occupies a

[18] Ricardo describes scarcity – in addition to the amount of work required – as a determining factor for the value in exchange of goods. From the context of his argument scarcity proves to

central position in the definition of the subject matter of economics and thus as an explanation of the value phenomenon. Following the above reasoning, the subject matter of economics may be defined as the problem of choice with regard to the use of scarce, alternatively applicable means for the satisfaction of classifiable wants.[19]

This definition is an obvious widening of the earlier theory. In principle the one-sided coupling of economics to the phenomenon of production has been abandoned. In modern economic theory production is regarded as only one of the means that can contribute to the satisfaction of wants – the welfare – of man. Production thus ceases to be the central objective of economic action and is regarded as only one of the means of attaining a given end.

Of the authors who have constantly reflected on the points of departure of economic theory, P. Hennipman occupies a special position. He defines the view referred to here as the point of view that 'the common heart of the problems concerning economic science lies in the relations between relatively scarce, alternatively usable goods and the whole of the wants or purposes, whatever their nature, served by the goods' (Hennipman, 1962, 1995). It emerges from the context of Hennipman's view that this definition contains a broad concept of goods which in fact can better be designated by the term 'means'. The ends themselves are meta-economic and are not for economists to judge. Ends or wants are given, and are discussed only insofar as their achievement or satisfaction depends on the use of scarce means. Maximizing or even just increasing the size of the social product is no longer a necessary aim that can lay claim to a logical priority. All objectives desired by individuals which are in conflict with this maximizing, form also a logical part of economic policy. When they are given preference above production this does not mean a sacrifice of welfare on the strength of 'non-economic' considerations (Hennipman, 1962, 1995).

Of course, this view does not mean a denial of the importance that production may have to society's welfare (satisfaction of wants). But the fundamental difference from the old productivistic interpretation is that the modern approach likewise regards the use of scarce means for the satisfaction of wants outside production, or at the expense of production, as an economic choice that can contribute to welfare.

It is L. Robbins (1932) in particular who has pointed to the importance to human activity of the phenomenon of scarcity. 'Scarcity of means to satisfy ends of varying importance is an almost ubiquitous condition of human behaviour', Robbins writes. The economist studies the disposal of scarce means. He is interested for instance in the way different degrees of scarcity of different goods give rise to different ratios of valuation between them. He is also interested in the way in which changes in conditions of scarcity – whether coming from changes in ends or changes in means – affect these ratios. Robbins: "Economics is the science which studies human behaviour as a relationship between ends and scarce means which have alternative uses."

---

mean to him the degree of availability. There is no question of a subjectivistic explanation of the value phenomenon in Ricardo (D. Ricardo. The Principles of Political Economy and Taxation. London, 1969, p. 3 et seq.).

[19] See the definition using environmental functions as the base for human life in Chapter 9.

5.4 *Formal concept of welfare*

The view now accepted by the mainstream of economic thought is that the phenomena emanating from scarcity, irrespective of the end for which the scarce means are used, form a logical entity. This view is designated as the formal or indifferent concept of welfare. This nomenclature was probably introduced for the first time in the essay *Grenznutzen* by P.N. Rosenstein-Rodan (1927). "The subjective state of welfare or the aggregate economic benefit that people aspire to when they consider issues economically, is determined in modern economic theory in a purely formal manner: it includes all aspirations – of course only to the extent of which economic goods are required for such purpose – regardless of whether they are selfish or altruistic, ethical or unethical motives, 'really existing' or just 'imaginary' needs", Rosenstein-Rodan writes. [20] Robbins states: "There are no economic ends as such; there are only economic problems involved in the achievement of ends" (Robbins, 1939, pp. 116-117).

In the Netherlands a clear-cut definition of the formal concept of welfare is given in P. Hennipman's work – not only in the already mentioned essay *'Doeleinden en criteria'*, but also in his dissertation *'Economisch motief en economisch principe?'* (Hennipman, 1940, pp. 71-82). According to Hennipman, when the field of economics is demarcated by means of the scarcity criterion, it is only logical and consistent to interprete welfare, the end and result of the economic process, in a corresponding sense, i.e. like any satisfaction of wants pursued or obtained with economic goods or, more precisely, as the balance of the positive utility over the negative utility caused by external effects or productive efforts.

5.5 *The new scarcity*

In the light of the modern definition given above of the subject matter of economics, there can be no doubt that the problem of environmental deterioration has a clearly economic facet. In view of the great social importance of the problem, the resultant problems of choice deserve the full attention of economic theory. For it is clear that the development in the industrialized countries on the one hand makes some scarce goods less scarce (and creates new wants alongside existing ones), but on the other hand makes certain originally free goods scarce and other scarce goods scarcer than before.

As regards the environment, a considerable degree of new scarcity has occurred. Large groups of people consider it unacceptable for ethical, religious and other reasons that human activities are impoverishing the Earth, with species of animals or plants dying out and remaining natural areas being damaged or even destroyed. For instance, Hueting (1987d), referring to the ecological risks by production growth, postulates: "Man derives part of the meaning of existence from the company of others. These others include in any case his children and grandchildren. The prospect of a safer future is therefore a normal human need, and dimming of this prospect has a negative effect on welfare." The restoration of

[20] 'Der subjektive Wohlfahrtszustand oder der Gesamtwirtschaftsnutzen, den die wirtschaftenden Menschen anstreben, ist in der moderne ökonomischen Theorie rein formal bestimmt: er umfasst alles Erstrebte – natürlich nur soweit für dessen Erreichung Aufwendungen wirtschaftlicher Güter erforderlich sind –, gleichviel ob es aus egoistischen oder altruistischen, ethischen oder unethischen Motiven, 'wirklich bestehenden' oder nur 'eingebildeten' Bedürfnissen entsteht'

a proper quality of our environment calls for measures and provisions of many kinds or, to put it another way, for the utilization of scarce means. A problem of choice thus occurs with regard to the use of scarce means, either in the direction of the further increases in the amounts of goods and services becoming available, or of improvements to the environment. This problem comes under the subject of economic study.

5.6 *A true conflict between production and environment*

As a result of the deterioration of our environment we are now faced with a problem of choice or conflict between production and environment.[21] Since both contribute to our satisfaction of wants (welfare), the renunciation of a further increase in production cannot be defined as the weighing of an economic disadvantage (the abandonment of potential production) against a non-economic advantage (improvement of the environment). When, for whatever reason, it becomes the general feeling that the situation of our environment is unacceptable and the government proceeds to lay down measures relating to production processes and consumption habits leading to a smaller quantity of available goods and services, but to improvement in the environment, then the overall satisfaction of wants obtained from economic goods is enhanced as a result. In that case, less production leads to greater welfare.

The problem of environmental deterioration is, from the economic point of view, an allocation problem. This is the case in a dual respect. In the first place some products impose a greater burden on the environment than others. This fits in entirely with the traditional concept of allocation: allotment of scarce means to products. In the second place the total level of production – which traditionally is regarded in detachment from allocation – may be viewed as an allocative problem, in the sense that more production may entail a greater burden on the environment. Here again the rule is that more of the one means less of the other – the heart of economics. The well-known difficulty is finding the optimal combination.

5.7 *Aggravation of market imperfections*

That difficulty already exists with individual goods distributable via the market mechanism. For, as we know, the market mechanism operates imperfectly and prices are often a deficient indicator of scarcity. The problem is all the greater when decisions on the collective and unpriced goods of our environment must be taken via the budget mechanism. We come up against even greater difficulties when we have to take decisions about the most desirable total level of production in relation to the overall state of the environment.

5.8 *False opposition of material versus immaterial*

After the above clarification on the subject matter of economics, which has been undertaken with the aim of clarifying a number of persistent misunderstandings about environment and economics, it will be clear that the contrast between 'material welfare' and 'immaterial well-being', made repeatedly in the discussions, obscures the harsh problem of choice confronting society. In this contrast, material

---

[21] Part of the production, such as treatment plants, are on behalf of the environment. These so-called asymmetric entries will be dealt with in Chapter 7.

welfare designates the goods produced, or 'economies', while immaterial well-being relates to the environment.

Of course, this is not right at all. It emerges from the above that welfare is in the economic theory a psychical quantity (an aspect of one's personal experience) and therefore 'immaterial'. In addition, from the economic point of view it makes no difference whether man's wants are met by material goods or 'immaterial goods'. But the remarkable thing is that precisely the new scarcity in the environment resulting from the growth of production, consumption and population relates to material goods par excellence. Birds and fish, for instance, are material things. When they lie on the beaches in their thousands as victims of oil or float dead in the rivers, you can take hold of them. A forest is a material thing. As long as the trees are still standing you can bump your head against them; as proof of their hard matter a lump develops. Clean and polluted air is no less material than manufactured perfume. Polluted and unpolluted soil is likewise material. Noise nuisance is a physical phenomenon (vibrations in the air) and damage to hearing is a physical thing. It is odd to consider a tree as immaterial and the chair made of it as material. Irrefutably, the new scarce goods are no less material than the goods that are produced at their expense.

5.9 *Well-being*

The following may be said in addition to the comment on happiness, in Section 4.7. For an economic approach to the environmental problem the use of the term well-being alongside welfare may merely add to the confusion. Nevertheless, the contrast between well-being and welfare may be meaningful if well-being is defined as the psychical state of mind which is not influenced by the use of scarce resources. In this definition well-being is not an economic category. It may relate to love and friendship, which after all money can't buy. Insofar as the environment is still abundantly present and functions perfectly, well-being can be derived from it. But unfortunately the days when the saying ‘the best things in life are free’ also applied to the environment are gone for future generations.

6. *Environmental functions*

6.1 *Abstract*

Definition of environmental function, and some examples. Scarcity arises also by competition. Scarcity and competition provide us with guides for measurement. Dimensions are quantity, quality and use of space. Because of the complexity of the environment and its functions, models must be used to determine the (longer run) effects. Economically there seems to be no essential difference between renewables and non-renewables.

6.2 *The concept*

In the theoretical basis for environmentally sustainable national income (eSNI), the environment is defined as the not-human-made physical surroundings: water, air, soil, plant and animal species and the life support systems (including ecosystems) of our planet, on which humanity is entirely dependent whether producing, consuming, breathing or recreating. It is true that our observable surroundings are largely human-built. However, houses, roads, machines and farm crops are the result of two complementary factors: labour, that is technology, and elements of the physical surroundings as here intended.

The possible uses or functions of our physical surroundings (see below) have come into being largely via processes proceeding at a geological or evolutionary pace. For the life support systems it is unfeasible ever completely to be replaced by technology, as is shown by Goodland (1995), see also Dasgupta & Heal (1979). It is largely thanks to these life support systems, which are under threat of disruption, that indispensable (or vital) environmental functions remain available. Life support systems are understood to mean the processes that maintain the conditions necessary for life on Earth. This comes down to maintaining stable conditions within narrow margins. The processes may be of a biological or physico-chemical nature, or a combination thereof. Examples of biological processes include the carbon and nutrient cycles, involving the extraction of such substances as carbon dioxide, water and minerals from the a-biotic environment during creation of biomass, and the return of these substances to the a-biotic environment during decomposition of the biomass. Examples of physico-chemical processes include the water cycle and regulation of the thickness of the stratospheric ozone layer. These examples show that there is interaction between the processes, whereby equilibrium may be disturbed. The water cycle, for example, may be disturbed by large-scale deforestation. Climate change is largely due to disturbance of the global carbon cycle. In our physical surroundings, a great number of possible uses (*possibilities* to use) can be distinguished, which are essential for production, consumption, breathing, et cetera, and thus for human existence. These are called *environmental functions*, or in short: functions (Hueting, 1969a, 1974a, 1980).

6.3 *Competing functions*

As long as the use of a function does not hamper the use of an other or the same function, so as long as environmental functions are not scarce, an insufficiency of labour, in this context intellect and technology, is the sole factor limiting production growth, as measured in standard NI. As soon as one use of a function is at the expense of another or the same function (by excessive use), though, or threatens to be so in the future, a second limiting factor is introduced. This *competition of functions* leads to partial or complete loss of function. An example of excessive use of one and the same function, leading to its loss, is overfishing resulting in decreased availability of the function 'water to accommodate fish species'; then the catch of some species decreases or species become extinct. Competing functions are economic goods, for more of one functions means less of another.

6.4 *Examples of environmental functions*

It may be instructive to give some examples of environmental functions. As regards water, a distinction has been made between the following functions: 'water for drinking', 'water for cooling', 'water for flushing and transport', 'process water', 'water for agricultural purposes', 'water for recreation', 'water in the natural environment', 'navigable water', 'water as an element in the social environment', 'water for construction', and 'water as a medium for dumping waste'.

In the elaboration the functions have been further subdivided. Thus 'recreational water' can be further broken down into 'water for swimming', '- fishing', '- boating', '- skating', and '- waterside recreation'. Each of the further subdivided functions evidently again satisfies separate wants and makes its own specific qualitative requirements. Thus 'water for fishing' makes quite different requirements of the quality of the water than does 'water for swimming'; 'process water' makes requirements that are different from and stricter than those of 'cooling water'. As regards air, mention may be made of 'air for physiological functioning' (loss of function manifests itself for instance in irritation of the respiratory organs upon inhalation of polluted air), 'air as a factor in agriculture', and 'air as a medium for storing matter' (loss of function here may lead to accelerated corrosion).

6.5 *Quantity, quality and space*

An environmental component always has three aspects, a quantitative one (the amount of matter), a qualitative one (the degree of pollution) and a spatial aspect. The decreased availability of a function may relate to each of these three aspects. The competitive use of functions is therefore, as a first approximation, divided into quantitative, qualitative and spatial competition (Hueting, 1974a, 1980).

At first sight, it may not seem obvious to include space and amount of matter in an environmental study. However, this study is concerned principally with the economic consequences of environmental deterioration. Now, the consequences of a shortage of space and matter caused by the increase in production and population prove comparable to those of environmental pollution in the usual sense. Both, therefore, come to the fore in this project as losses of function. Thus the availability of the recreational function of a piece of land may decrease as a result of noise nuisance but also by its being taken up by roads; the consequences of space being taken up by all kinds of activities are probably at least as serious for the natural environment function as the consequences of pollution. The losses of function occupy a central position.

A situation in which the quantity of a component of the environment is inadequate for its use or intended use may be described as *quantitative competition of functions*. Here the functions directly confront one another. Quantitative competition is absolute; the part of a resource withdrawn on behalf of a certain function entirely excludes use of that part for other functions. With regard to water, this takes place by actual withdrawal of water from the environment. In the case of air, quantitative competition occurs in air traffic. In soil, quantitative competition includes the current or expected future shortage of so called non-renewable resources such as oil, metals, mineral phosphate and a renewable resource: groundwater. When there is not enough space for the use or intended use of the functions, *spatial competition of functions* occurs. Worldwide competition exists between use of space for production of food, production of bio fuels, natural ecosystems and the survival of species, road building, building of houses, traffic and possibilities for children to play and discover their surroundings. This occurs above all on soil. Especially the function 'space for the existence of natural ecosystems' is threatened. Spatial competition is probably the main cause of species extinction, through loss and fragmentation of habitats. Everything points to this process continuing in accelerated tempo unless drastic measures are taken. Conservation of natural species is a key criterion for estimating Environmentally Sustainable National Income according to Hueting (see Part 3). Like quantitative competition, spatial competition is direct, i.e. without intermediate processes; one use is directly at the expense of an other.

In *qualitative competition*, overburdening the function 'medium for dumping waste' by chemical, physical or biological 'agents' has caused partial or total loss of all other possible uses of the environment; examples are the function 'resource for the production of drinking water' or 'air for physiological functioning of humans, plants and animals (breathing)'. By agent, in this context, is meant a constituent or amount of energy (in whatsoever form) which may cause loss of function either by its addition to or by its withdrawal from the environment by man. An agent could be a chemical, plant, animal, heat, radioactivity etc.

In an environmental component qualitative changes may be caused by human actions. These can be brought about in two ways. Firstly, as the result of direct introduction of waste into the soil, direct dumping or discharging of waste into the water, direct emission of substances or the causing of sound vibrations in the air. Secondly, they may be the result of an unintentional or 'unavoidable' side-effect in the utilization of other functions. In both cases the environment is used in its function 'getting rid of waste'. When, as a result of this use, a component of the environment becomes less suitable for other possible uses, we speak of qualitative competition of functions. In the case of the component water, this function is described as water used as 'medium for dumping waste'. As regards air, the term 'air as a medium into which to release waste matter' has been opted for; this includes not only the emission of injurious substances but also noise nuisance. Qualitative competition thus includes pollution, disturbance of ecosystems by exotics and phenomena such as climate change.

Utilization of this function therefore decreases the availability of other functions, such as 'drinking water' and 'air for physiological functioning'. Competition occurs between the function 'medium for dumping waste' and all other functions. In this case, the competition between the functions is indirect. It occurs via the qualitative change, which is the vector of the competition. Both change and loss of function may be described in scientific or technical terms, as may also be measures of elimination and compensation required for restoration or replacement of functions. In tracing the losses of function, it has been found that the use of water and air as media for accommodating the waste products of human activities now leads to decreased availability of all other functions.

6.6 *Economics and ecosystems*

All kinds of competition relate to the use of labour and capital for the use of a resource for the purpose of increasing the production on the one hand and for the development of substitutes in order to safeguard the functions of the resource for future generations on the other.

It may be useful to give some examples of severe competition between functions. Worldwide competition exists between use of space for production of food, production of bio fuels, natural ecosystems and the survival of species, road building, building of houses, traffic and possibilities for children to play and discover their surroundings. In many regions of the world the quantity of ground and surface water is insufficient to meet the needs for both raining on agricultural crops and industrial processes and drinking water and the survival of species. The function 'soil for cultivating crops' may be damaged by unsustainable use of the function 'supplier of timber' of a forest, leading to loss of its function 'regulator of the water flow' and subsequent erosion; it may also be in conflict with itself, when unsustainable farming methods lead to erosion and salinization of the soil. Loss of the function 'regulator of the water flow' of forests leads to flooding and subsequent drought. The many functions of natural resources that threaten to get lost as a result of exhaustion of the resource are in competition with use by future generations. This competition of functions leads to partial or complete loss of function.

In the course of time, continuing use of environmental functions, especially of non-renewable resources such as space and renewable resources like fish, wood and groundwater cause gradual changes of the quantities and the qualities of these resources, including ecosystems. The thus changed state of the environment determines the (remaining) availabilities of the functions. These dynamic processes are inherent elements of the competition of functions.

6.7 *Practical classification*

For a further clarification of the interactions between human activities and environmental functions, a first rough breakdown of the environment is made into the components water, soil and air. The classification into environmental functions by component has been inspired by the idea that each use makes certain qualitative requirements of an environmental component that often differ greatly. Each function of an environmental component thus on the one hand satisfies specific human wants and on the other makes specific requirements of the quality of a component. The concept of environmental function is based on the general concept of function of a good. Thus, every loss of a good as a unique 'individual' is definitive; the function of a good remains available as long as the good can still be reproduced.

6.8 *Renewables and non-renewables*

When using the concept of environmental function, the only thing that matters in the context of environmental sustainability is that vital functions remain available to an extent that supports its use. Those are the functions that are essential for human activities like breathing, production, consumption, recreation etc., and for people to be ensured of the survival of mankind and all other species in the long run. As for renewable resources, their functions remain available as long as the regenerative capacities of the processes that provide the functions remain intact.[22] Regeneration of 'non-renewable' resources such as crude oil and copper that are formed by slow geological processes is close to zero. A sustainable availability of the functions of these resources can be achieved by the development and production of substitutes. The possibilities for this are promising (Brown et al., 1998; Reijnders, 1996). So, economically speaking, there seems to be no essential difference between renewables and non-renewables. The difference is only of a practical nature.

6.9 *Scarcity and competition as guides for measurement*

As long as the space, the quantity and the quality of an environmental component are such that a claim laid to a function is not at the expense of availability of that function or the availability of other functions for the existing needs thereof, there is no question of an economic problem. If, for instance, in a certain region the burden of biodegradable organic matter on the water can be handled by the water's capacity for self-purification, without invalidating its use as recreational water, drinking water, etc., nor its function of providing information about the state of the aquatic ecosystem, this is not interpreted in this study as environmental deterioration. The recreational water can then meet the existing wants undisturbed and to the same extent as before; the supply of drinking water can proceed normally, the costs being confined, for instance, to distribution costs or simple filtering through a sand bed, depending on the local situation. But as soon as the claim to a function of an environmental component leads to reduced availability of another function, we may speak of environmental deterioration in the economic sense. For then there is a loss of usefulness and, consequently, a reduction in satisfaction of wants that was possible before.

Environmental deterioration is in this study defined as decreased availability of functions of an environmental component. Or, more briefly, as loss of function. Loss of function has apparently occurred because, as a consequence of the increasing burden on the environment, so great a claim is laid to the various functions of the environment that these functions have come to compete with one another. In other words, the claim laid by a human activity to a certain function is at the expense of the availability of an other function. It is therefore self-evident to classify the losses of function occurring by investigating where competition of

[22] See Section 9.9.1 for a precise formulation.

functions is to be found in an environmental component. This has been done in Hueting (1974a, 1980).

6.10 *Competition of functions*

The great variety of environmental functions and the effects of their use on the availabilities of the functions suggest a systematic representation of their relations. As **Figure 3** shows, the use of a function leads to changes in the state of the environment, that in turn reduce the possibilities to use other environmental functions, except when the function is in competition with itself, such as in the case of overfishing.

Figure 3. Basic elements of the competition of environmental functions

use of an environmental function

↓

changes of the state of the environment

↓

effects on the availabilities of functions, especially for future generations

Presenting the relations between all relevant variables would result in a vast table system. Hueting (1974a, 1980) provides such a system for qualitative competition in water and air. To show this is not necessary now for the purposes of the present book. A simple example is, that when oil is used then the *change of the state of the environment* is depletion of oil reserves, and the *effects* are on the functions for energy and synthetic materials.

6.11 *Estimating effects by models*

The effects of the use of a function (use of resources, emissions of refuse matter etc.) on the state of the environment occur with delays which are characteristic for the processes involved. For instance the effects of emissions of greenhouse gases on global warming persist during many centuries. As a result, the effects of global warming on biota and ecosystems persist centuries as well. From this it follows that the effects on the availabilities of the functions occur on the same time scale. These effects cannot be predicted exactly. With the aid of the body of knowledge on environmental processes which has been built up since the sixties, it appears possible to make 'proxy predictions' of these effects. Usually these predictions make use of environmental models of the involved processes. Additionally, it may be assumed that certain social preferences for environmental functions correspond with levels of environmental state variables that may not be exceeded. Using the aforementioned models, these levels may then be connected to availabilities of functions. Thus the competition of a number of functions with some other functions may be estimated for environmental equilibria.

6.12 *Natural capital and ecosystem services*

Economic theory distinguishes capital (stock, state) and income (flow, use). Capital (a stock) associates with investments (a flow), and both of these pertain to the same kind of commodities (e.g. machines). In the same manner, an environmental function (a state variable, to be transferred to next period or generation) associates with the actual use of the function (a flow).

Hueting (1967, 1969a, 1974a, 1980) developed his concepts and analysis at a time when the terms "capital" and "services" had a well-formulated meaning in the System of National Accounts (SNA), namely for human-made goods and human-provided services. Hueting used the terms of "natural resources" and new phrases like "not-human-made physical surroundings" and "possible uses" c.q. "environmental functions" to allow a clear reasoning about the relationship between production as defined in the SNA and the environment, see for example Hueting (1974a, 1980:167 footnote). [23] This was also recognised in the recommendations for an UNEP award. [24]

Other authors have preferred later not to introduce new terms but to extend the meaning of the existing terms of *capital* and *services*, see Ahmad et al. (eds) (1989), Pearce et al. (1989:3), Pearce & Atkinson (1993) and Hamilton (1994). In their view, the natural resources including ecosystems, and their environmental functions (possible uses, with their capacity depending upon the resource level and composition), can be seen as items of *"natural capital"* (stocks, states). The use (flow) of environmental functions, relevant for income accounting, can also be seen as *"(ecosystem) services"*. What has been identified as vital environmental functions are called elsewhere "critical natural capital". **Table 2** gives an overview of the terminology.

Table 2. Terminology in the literature

	State variable	*Flow variable*
System of National Accounts (SNA)	Capital	Goods and services, national income
Environment, in this book	Natural resources, (vital) environmental functions	Use of environmental functions, environmentally Sustainable National Income
Environment, "capital approach" still not in the SNA	(Critical) natural capital	Ecosystem services

The reference in the literature to "ecosystems services" caused Hueting et al. (1998a) to distinguish between services and 'services': "Environmental functions are defined as possible uses of our natural, biophysical surroundings that are useful for humans. Uses can be either passive or direct and practical. The 'services' of environmental functions are defined as their possibilities or potential to be used by humans for whatever end. Some functions can be conceived as consumption goods, others as capital goods." For example, the value of a fish in the shop differs from the value of a fish in the water.

[23] In only this single statement, Hueting (1974a, 1980:127) uses the term "services of the environment" but without clarification whether this concerns use or potential use: "After all, the whole of production depends on the services of the environment. This well-known fact (...) does not lead to special individual behaviour as long as the functions are available to a sufficient degree."

[24] http://www.sni-hueting.info/EN/Others/2019-05-02-Tinbergen-1990-UNEP-Sasakawa-Hueting.pdf

The World Bank (at some distance of SNA) has tended to refer to natural capital while simultaneously looking at (genuine) savings and depletion, see Section 12.5 on comparisons. An early reference to the distinction between produced, human, natural and social capital is O'Connor et al. (1995). A critical discussion is by Hueting and Reijnders (2004a).

The methods have an underlying structural identity and a quite different practical implementation. For example World Bank (2006:123) provides this explanation (though beware that income is not the same as the change in wealth):

> "Consistent with Hicks's notion of income (Hicks 1946), sustainability requires nondecreasing levels of capital stock over time or, at the level of the individual, nondecreasing per capita capital stock. Indicators of sustainability could be based on either the value of total assets every period, or by the change in wealth and the consumption of capital (depreciation) in the conventional national accounts."

Authors who recognise the identical meanings in **Table 2** are e.g. UN SEEA (2003) quoted in Section 1.2 and El Serafy (1998) and El Serafy (2013:5) quoted in Section 1.8. Herman Daly (see page 156) has the comment that the calculation of income requires that capital is kept intact, so that income already would be sustainable by itself, and so that "sustainable national income" is a pleonasm, that is, if one approaches the issue from the angle of "capital theory". In Hueting's terminology it is no pleonasm, since capital belongs to SNA, and sustainability is a condition imposed from the environment.

At the fundamental level of economic theory, with the methods of accounting for capital and income, this book thus doesn't differ from the method used at the World Bank. We maintain the terminology of Hueting (1974a, 1980) not only for comparison with our earlier work but also for the same reasons of clarity. When we speak about capital and services then these would be recognised in the SNA; and when we speak about resources and functions and their use then they may not be recognised in the SNA.

Apart from theory there are relevant practical differences. A weak point of the World Bank "capital approach" is the reliance upon indicators instead of the use of a full-fledged model that describes the relationship between the economy and the environment. Also, there is often a lack of environmental standards to judge the level of such indicators. The "capital approach" tends to require that natural capital is valued in terms of money as well, which tends to come with tedious questions, while the approach of environmentally sustainable national income (eSNI), discussed below, is parsimonious in its requirements.

eSNI was part of the official Dutch national strategy of sustainable development for Johannesburg 2002, see Ministry of VROM (2002). The cabinet instructed the national planning bureaus to continue with the research on the indicators for sustainable development. eSNI obviously is an indicator too. Subsequently, the World Bank "capital approach" was adopted by the new generation of researchers at CBS Statistics Netherlands in the Dutch "sustainability monitor", see CBS, CPB, MNP, SCP (2009). Later, by advice of CBS, also the Conference of European Statisticians (CES, 2013) adopted this approach. Both CBS et al. (2009) and CES (2013) mention eSNI but refer to Hueting (1974, 1980), in which eSNI is not mentioned since it was introduced by Hueting (1986b). This gives the impression that the new generation of researchers at CBS did not study both thesis and eSNI.

While UN SEEA and El Serafy alerted economic researchers to the issue of terminology, there was the remarkable development that various researchers were not aware of it. For example, CBS et al. (2009) present the "capital approach" as alternative to eSNI, so that the new generation may not be aware that the same economic theory is being used. The practical difference concerns the implementation and calculation of eSNI.

7. *Asymmetric bookkeeping*

7.1 *Abstract*

The issue is discussed in Hueting (1974a, 1980) though the name *asymmetric bookkeeping* was adopted only later. Part of this discussion also appeared in Dutch in ESB, Hueting (2011f). [25]

Restoration costs are a special type of elimination costs. When an oil tanker pollutes a beach, then the loss of environmental functions is not entered as a cost but the primary inputs of capital and labour involved in the cleaning up are conventionally accounted as value added in national income: this is asymmetric.

For notation: NI minus asymmetric bookkeeping = NI – *A* = NI-A. This is the level of national income that fits with the intentions of the developers in the 1930s. Part 3 below discusses eSNI, and finds that the proper comparison of eSNI is to NI-A instead of NI.

7.2 *Introduction*

Producing is defined, in accordance with standard economic theory, as the adding of value. National income (NI) equals the sum of the values added. So NI measures production – and the fluctuations in the level of this. It does so according to its definition and according to the intention of the founders of its concept to get an indicator for one of the factors influencing welfare – and a tool for quite a few other purposes.

As mentioned just now, producing is adding value. This value added has another dimension than the not-human-made physical surroundings have. Consequently, environmental functions (the most fundamental economic goods at human's disposal) remain outside the measurement of standard NI. This is logical and easy to understand, because water, air, soil, plant and animal species and the life support systems of our planet are not produced by humans.

The calculation currently is:

- Losses of functions, caused by production and consumption, are correctly not entered as costs in the definition of SNA.
- However, expenditures on measures for their *restoration* and basically also compensation *are* conventionally entered as value added, which happens structurally when produced by the government and partly also by private firms. This is *asymmetric*. These expenditures should be entered as costs, notably as intermediate deliveries.

7.3 *Example with accounting tables*

The following gives an example. **Table 3** has the conventional setup for a NI = 100 + 20 = 15 + 90 + 15 = 120 units, intermediate deliveries of 30 and thus output of 150. There are sectors X and Y and a sector for elimination, repair and compensation (ERC). The expenditures for ERC exclude direct damages that people might accept without spending funds on them.

[25] http://www.sni-hueting.info/NL/Publicaties/2011-05-13-Hueting-ESB.pdf

Table 3. Accounting of elimination, repair and compensation (ERC) in NI

	Intermediate			Final		Total
	X	Y	ERC	Cons	Gov	
X	15	10	5			30
Y				100		100
ERC					20	20
NI	15	90	15			120
Total	30	100	20			150

Table 3 presents the situation that the government spends 20 units on the ERC sector, e.g. financed by taxes *T* = *Gov*. When accountants identify sector Y as the polluter, then the government expenditures can also be identified as pseudo final demand, and then we get **Table 4**. We find that NI-A = 100 = 15 + 70 + 15.

Table 4. Accounting of ERC in NI → NI-A, using intermediate deliveries

	Intermediate			Final		Total
	X	Y	ERC	Cons	Gov	
X	15	10	5			30
Y				100		100
ERC		20				20
NI	15	70	15			100
Total	30	100	20			150

These tables have been taken from Hueting (1974a, 1980:172-173, tables 5.1 and 5.3). The discussion there tells the story of a government that first did those outlays in final demand indeed, as booked in **Table 3**, and that switches to imposing the costs to the particular sector, as booked in **Table 4**. The proper issue however concerns mere accounting, and not government regulation. These two tables provide the analysis in a nutshell. Above bookkeeping is done in real terms, so that the allocation of value added between labour and capital can change.

7.4 *Time and asymmetric bookkeeping*

This asymmetry is sometimes defended by the statement that these expenditures contribute to welfare and generate income, see De Haan (2004) and Heertje (2006). This is of course self-evident, counting from the moment at which the loss of environmental functions and the consequential adverse effects have already occurred. However, the production factors, used for the measures, do not add any value counting from the moment that the functions were still available.

With respect to that original situation these measures consequently cause no increase in (1) the quantity of final goods produced and (2) the availability of environmental functions. In other words:

- Income, to be spent on the market or to be transferred to public authorities, is a claim on goods and services produced by industries and public authorities, it is not a claim on the functions of the not-human-made physical surroundings.

- By entering these expenditures as final instead of intermediate, the growth of production is overestimated, thus obscuring what is happening with both environment and production.

Asyms are clearly in conflict with the original intention of the creators of NI as an indicator of the fluctuations in the level of the volume of production. The information about the development of production is improved by estimating a NI-A = NI ex asyms, alongside NI. With NI-A there are no changes in prices and behaviour (as is the case with simulated eSNI). So there is no change in the consumption and production package. The asyms can thus be simply deducted. By way of supporting this point it is useful to mention: if expenditure on elimination, compensation and restoration of damage were entered as costs instead of value added, then one arrives at the same level NI-A as in the case of deduction.

One first sight, it may not be evident what is and what is not an asymmetric entry. Thus the national statistical bureaus have to develop criteria (standards and protocols) when to avoid asymmetric bookkeeping with respect to environmental damage. The definition and measurement of elimination, compensation and restoration costs will help to develop these criteria.

7.5 *Choice of the accounting period*

Undoing the asymmetry does not require special conditions for the accounting period. The costs can be entered when they occur. The basic principle remains that neutralising a damage (basically caused by production) should not be regarded as contributing to production. The main point is to distinguish common expenditures and those that are targeted at elimination, repair or compensation of environmental damages – and this distinction requires the development of standards and protocols.

When traffic uses the function 'air as medium to get rid of waste' then this disrupts the function 'air for physiological functioning'. Expenditure on medical help for patients with asthma or COPD largely takes place in the same financial year, though we shouldn't overlook longer run costs for patients who move to cleaner areas and still require a period of recovery. The same simultaneity of accounting period often applies to the loss of the recreational function of beaches through oil washed ashore and the cleaning up. The latter is a measure to repair the damage, while the use of particular chemicals still uses the oceans as a dumping ground for waste so that this hasn't included all elimination costs yet.

Emissions of greenhouse gasses cumulate and disrupt the life support systems. Expenditures on this are partly in the same year and partly later years, like on elimination measures to reduce these emissions at home and abroad (by buying emission rights), expenditures on measures to compensate for the repercussions of loss of function such as construction of water reservoirs and the raising of dikes, and expenditure on repairing damage resulting from loss of function.

7.6 *Time sequence of events and accounting*

Figure 4 shows the relevant variables involved in the occurrence of loss and repair of environmental functions. The Left Hand Side (LHS) shows the actual events of damage and repair and the Right Hand Side (RHS) shows the assumption that everything takes place within one financial year.

Figure 4. Damage and repair, events (LHS) and accounting (RHS)

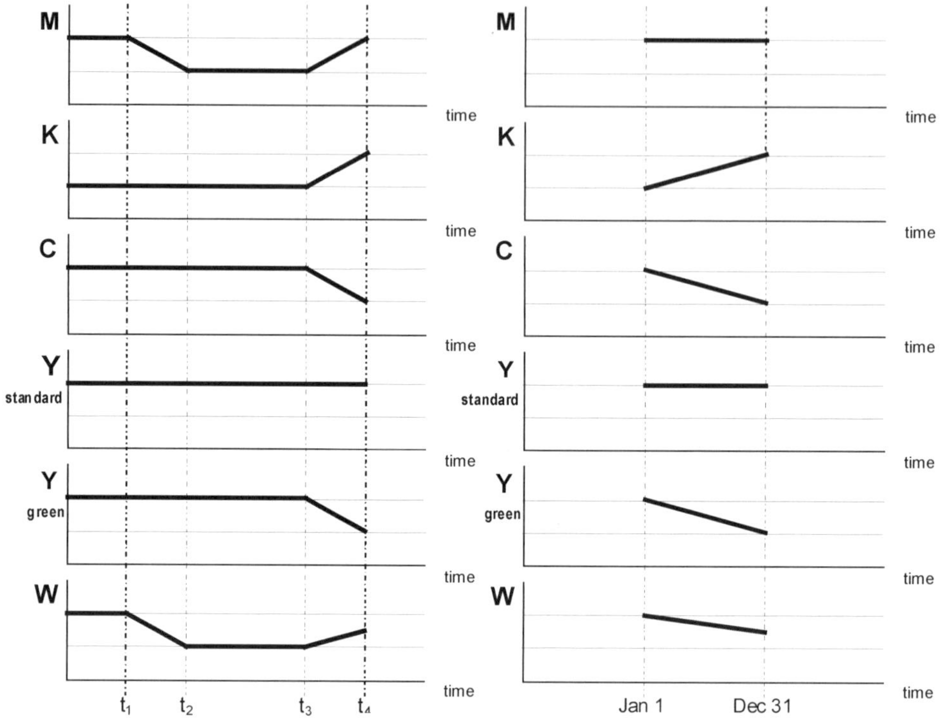

Legend: LHS = actual events, RHS = financial accounting year

Time	*Variables*
t_1 before the damage	M = environmental function in a physical unit
t_2 damage	K = repair costs in money
t_3 repair starts	C = (government) consumption in money
t_4 repair finished	Y = NI = standard national income
	Y green = NI-A = NI minus asymmetric bookkeeping
	W = welfare, ordinal, thus we only know that $W[t_4] < W[t_1]$

Two comments may be made here. Firstly, an economic activity always has a balance of a positive and a negative effect on welfare. Secondly, an indicator in cardinal units must always have the same direction as ordinal welfare.

- The Left Hand Side (LHS) gives the moments: 1 before the damage, 2 at the damage, 3 when the repair starts, 4 when the repair is completed.
- The Right Hand Side (RHS) gives M = environmental function in physical units, K = costs of environmental measures in monetary units, C = volume of consumable produced goods – also by the government – in monetary units, Y = NI = national income, Y green = NI-A = national income minus asymmetric bookkeeping (Y minus asyms) and welfare (W).

Since consumers have spent funds on repair, they accept that scarce environmental functions must be recovered. Thus we observe a fall in *proper* consumption (without the pseudo element). Consumption decreases due to the withdrawal of production factors for environmental measures. Welfare is an ordinal, immeasurable variable. Welfare declines on balance, both on the LHS and the RHS. Because welfare is an ordinal quantity, the exact amount can not be displayed. However, we know that $W[t_4] < W[t_1]$.

On the LHS, when the damage is occurring, welfare first diverges from NI and NI-A. Welfare reacts immediately to the damage. NI only responds via the costs K when the damage is repaired. NI-A responds then too. People do not respond immediately, and the period t_2 to t_3 can be termed as an incubation period. NI-A, or here Y green, shows the course of welfare eventually correctly and standard NI does not. When NI does not change then this suggests that welfare does not change either, while in fact welfare declines.

7.7 *Conclusions for this chapter*

Some conclusions specifically for this chapter are:

(1) Given the attention for global warming and the (likely insufficient) objective of maximally 1.5 degrees Celsius above pre-industrial levels, we can expect that many measures will be taken for repair (reverting earlier damages) or compensation (like raising dikes). Their conventional inclusion in NI would send the wrong signal that (wrongly defined) "economic growth" continues. Those expenditures are excluded from NI-A.

(2) When in reality productivity has decreased because production factors have been re-allocated from producing consumption goods to elimination, repair and compensation of loss of environmental functions, then this decrease in productivity has to be shown in the national bookkeeping.

(3) SNA should include the publication of both NI and NI-A.

7.8 *Looking ahead to NI-A and eSNI*

Below we shall deal with environmentally sustainable national income (eSNI). NI-A is important for comparison to eSNI as well.

eSNI is intended to gauge the distance between the achieved and the environmentally sustainable level of production. Because expenditures on elimination, repair and compensation are booked as contributions to NI, NI is no good yardstick of the level of production.

During a transition to the sustainable path the distance between NI and eSNI may increase while the gap between the sustainable and the present level of production (NI-A) decreases. Hence the gap that has to be bridged to achieve a sustainable level of production (eSNI) is eΔ-A = NI-A – eSNI and not eΔ = NI – eSNI. On occasion and for convenience we refer to eΔ when we actually mean eΔ-A. See De Boer and Hueting (2010) for details.

The next part introduces eSNI.

Part 3. The concept of eSNI

8. *Environmentally Sustainable National Income*

8.1 *Abstract*

Since NI is a wrong compass, the precautionary principle causes the need for eSNI. We get information only by keeping these two figures alongside each other. The precaution comes with uncertainty in scientific estimates but this uncertainty should not be confused with different views about preferences. The calculation of the Dutch eSNI is a proof of concept.

8.2 *A wrong compass*

Economic growth, wrongly defined as increase of production as measured in standard national income, enjoys top priority in the economic policies pursued by every country of the world. The economic success of government policy and even success *tout court* is measured primarily against the yardstick of production growth, above unemployment and inflation. In doing so, we are steering by the wrong compass, however, for production growth – that is to say, a decrease in the scarcity of man-made goods – is accompanied by an increase in the scarcity of environmental goods. This is not a new phenomenon. Hueting (1974a, 1980) provides a brief historical survey, which includes Plato (about 400 BC) on erosion, Juvenal (about AD 100) on noise nuisance in Rome and Erasmus (around 1500) on the unhygienic conditions prevailing in European cities, with their open sewers and waste-strewn streets. In earlier ages it was a local phenomenon, though, which proceeded slowly. The world had only a small population, moreover, and space was abundant: if need be people could simply move on. According to Tinbergen, even in the 1930s the environment did not play any substantial role in the economy, and it was consequently ignored when the System of National Accounts (SNA) was established (Hueting, 1974a; Tinbergen and Hueting, 1991). Since about the middle of the twentieth century environmental degradation has become a global phenomenon, with pressure on the natural environment increasing rapidly, together with production and population, the doubling rates of which have declined markedly, showing up as a veritable explosion on long-term time charts.

8.3 *An unprecedented challenge for humankind as a whole*

Starting in the second part of the twentieth century we see a phenomenon entirely new in the history of humankind. Humanity is capable of destroying its civilizations and perhaps even the human species as such. This may be through nuclear war and the ensuing nuclear winter, but it may also be by way of an insidious process that eats away at the very foundations of our existence: *the vital functions of our (not-human-made) physical surroundings.*

Over the past half century, the latter possibility has been the subject of a wealth of literature that has signalled the very real risks being posed to future generations by our actions here and now. One of the first reports to review the issue was the Study of Critical Environmental Problems (SCEP) *Man's Impact on the Global Environment* carried out by the Massachusetts Institute of Technology (Wilson et al., 1970). As the main threats to life on Earth the study identifies climate change and large-scale disturbance of natural ecosystems. According to Odum (1971) the impact of the extinction of biological species, particularly predators, on life on Earth can only be established with certainty after the 'point of no return', that is after recovery of equilibrium is no longer possible. This whole process is occurring at breath-taking speed, when viewed on an evolutionary time scale. There is a high risk of irreversible effects occurring, and the further the process continues the more difficult and of longer duration recovery will be. According to *The Limits to Growth* (Meadows et al., 1972), if population and production continue to grow, catastrophes are probably inevitable. Hueting (1974a, 1980) provides a synopsis of these publications.

8.4 *Caring about descendants*

The principal justification for an eSNI lies in the following: there are solid, rational grounds for being concerned about the conditions under which our children's children will have to live if we maintain current levels of production and consumption, because of the cumulative nature of many of the processes involved. In particular, a wide variety of poorly degradable toxins and greenhouse gases are accumulating in the environment and human encroachment on undeveloped land – the main cause of species extinction – continues apace. In the now six decades-long debate on growth and the environment, there are two diametrically opposed opinions. Given continued gross economic growth, taken as per capita production multiplied by population, some hold that the situation will improve, others that it will deteriorate. We ourselves hold the latter position (Tinbergen and Hueting, 1991; Hueting, 1996). Ultimately, though, the response of ecosystems, life support systems and other natural processes to human activity is unpredictable, and will always remain so, as will the potential – or otherwise – of future technologies to alleviate the environmental impact of an ever-growing volume of produced, material goods. We see the future as a race between environmental technology and production growth, the outcome of which cannot be predicted (Hueting, 1997).

8.5 *Definition of eSNI*

Environmentally sustainable national income (eSNI) is defined as the maximally attainable level of (net) production (including consumption), using the technology of the year under review, whereby the vital environmental functions, that is possible uses, of the not-human-made physical surroundings remain available for future generations.

In such discussions concerning what is possible and what is not possible in the future, eSNI appears to provide a welcome *statistical resting point.*

In this approach, sustainability is formulated as the maintenance of vital environmental functions *ad infinitum* (Hueting and Reijnders, 1996a, 1996b, 1998b). The difference between standard and environmentally sustainable national income reflects the *distance,* expressed as costs, which must be bridged in order to attain sustainability; this is our debt to future generations. Any politics concerned with safeguarding the foundations of human existence should surely give first priority to bridging this gap, and then wait and see whether, and how much, production growth then results.

8.6 *Precaution, scientific uncertainty, different preferences*

As elaborated in Chapter 9, from the perspective of preferences there exist as many shadow prices for environmental functions as there are possible assumptions about demand for uses of the environment, that is for environmental functions; *ergo,* there are also as many 'green' national incomes, but only one of them is eSNI.[26] Given the future perils stemming from our activities now, sustainability is viewed by many as the crux of the environmental problem (IUCN et al., 1980; [27] World Commission on Environment and Development (WDED), 1987; IUCN et al., 1991). Sustainable development has been properly defined by IUCN (1980), but the term "sustainability" has been watered down and thus it is better to speak about "environmental sustainability". The environment is defined as the not-human-made physical surroundings which can be conceived as a collection of possible uses, i.e. environmental functions.

The eSNI points the way for application of the so widely recommended precautionary principle. This principle asserts that, given the inherent unpredictability of the future and the real risk of human activity having unprecedented effects, that activity should be governed by avoidance of such effects. When informing people on the issue of environment and growth, economists, in particular, have a responsibility that is of a different order than that involved in informing them on any other issue, *because the possible consequences of misjudgement are of an entirely different order.*

Among other possible green national incomes eSNI consequently enjoys a special status. To this may be added that in some regions in the South the future already appears to have begun: many thousands have already lost their lives or livelihoods as a result of floods, droughts and poisoned water resources, the result of neglecting the importance of nature's functions for humanity. This is obviously not to say that calculation of one or more green national incomes alongside eSNI would not contribute substantially to the information flow.

8.7 *Dutch eSNI is a proof of concept*

The calculation of Dutch eSNI is a proof of concept. In the eSNI study the estimate for the Netherlands is seen as an indicator for what is occurring at the global level. The picture is growing clearer as an eSNI is calculated for more nations. In the Dutch case, the extent of the measures required to achieve sustainability is determined by and proportional to the contribution of the Netherlands to global environmental pressure (or to regional pressure in the case of regional problems). With an import and export quote of around 50 per cent, the

---

[26] In calculating the eSNI, often choices must be made because of existing scientific uncertainties (see Hueting and Reijnders, 1999). From both the preference side and the cost side, a whole spectrum of outcomes can result, from which a choice must be made for the purpose of presentation. This uncertainty derives from science and must not be confused with different views about preferences.

[27] J.C. Van Noordwijk-Van Veen, who has been involved with IUCN, was also chairperson of the subcommission, of the Central Commission of Statistics of CBS Statistics Netherlands, that kept oversight of the environmental statistics, that has been founded by Hueting in 1969.

Netherlands is solidly interlinked with the rest of the world and the environmental degradation occurring there. Importation of tapioca livestock feed and tropical hardwood, to take but two examples, has serious environmental consequences in the respective countries of origin. The Netherlands is one of the most densely populated countries in the world and is among the nations with the highest per capita production. In the study *The Ecological Footprint* (Wackernagel and Rees, 1996) the Netherlands scores high: the 'ecological footprint' of the Netherlands is almost 15 times higher than its land mass warrants. Conversely, the Dutch are exporting their – or rather the world's – environmental resources for a price below sustainability costs, as the exporters of tapioca and hardwood are doing with their environment. As a worked example, the Netherlands does not seem such a bad choice.

8.8 *Information arises when NI and eSNI are alongside each other*

Right from the start, it has been argued that an income corrected for the environment should be estimated alongside rather than instead of standard national income (Hueting, 1967, 1974ab, 1980). The latter course of *replacing* NI would, in the first place, disrupt a key macroeconomic time series that is employed for a wide variety of other purposes besides estimating production growth. Secondly, a green national income derives its informative value precisely from establishing the *distance* from standard national income, measured in terms of costs. As is familiar knowledge, a national income, standard or green, is itself a meaningless figure: only when a comparison is made over time, or with other incomes, does meaningful information arise (see, for example, Hueting et al. 1992d).

9. *Valuation of environmental functions: A practical approach for an unsolvable problem*

9.1 *Abstract*

Hueting (1974a, 1980) derived a shadow price using revealed demand, but also inferred that this was unrealistic since the market mechanism did not function adequately for the environment, because of external effects like the tragedy of the commons. Hueting (1986b) found the solution in the vertical demand curve.

9.2 *Definitions of shadow price and value of a function*

A prerequisite for eSNI is its comparability with the standard net NI; comparability is understood here to be that the figures of these quantities are expressed in the same units and can be added and subtracted: they must be additive. For this purpose the prices of environmental functions must be found which are comparable with market prices. A way to achieve this, is to search for the minimum of the sum of the demand and supply curves of the functions. From this follow the shadow prices of the functions. These prices are used in the present project to estimate the costs which constitute the distance between NI and eSNI.

The shadow prices can only be established with the aid of data on supply and demand for environmental functions. Because functions are collective goods, they fall outside the market mechanism, and therefore a supply and a demand curve must be construed for each function. Data of *both* demand and supply are needed. For, if there are no preferences for a good, its value is zero, irrespective of how important, or even indispensable, that good may be for humankind. If a good can be obtained without sacrificing an alternative, its value is likewise zero. In valuing environmental functions, both preferences and costs must be quantified. These are therefore two inseparably linked elements of the valuation of environmental functions and their loss. Valuations that are, ultimately, based on estimates of only preferences (demand) or costs (supply) are here viewed as techniques forming part of the single valuation method presented here. See also "The parable of the carpenter" (Hueting and De Boer, 2001b).

Value is understood to be here price times quantity of a good, thus excluding the consumers surplus (what one is prepared to pay above its price, whether it is a market price or a shadow price). Knowing the shadow prices of the environmental functions is necessary for knowing which production factors (labour and capital) are needed for preservation of the functions which are essential for human life, including production and consumption. The sum total of the values of the production factors equals the distance between NI and eSNI.

The availability of functions depends on the state of their carriers: our physical surroundings. If the latter become less suitable or unsuitable for the use of some functions by the excessive use of other functions, mostly for production and consumption, then the physical surroundings have to be restored. To what extent this has to be done, depends on the urgency of the preferences for the availability of the impaired functions. See the schemes in Section 6.10.

9.3 *A stylized discussion*

For the sake of simplicity it is assumed below that one given function is impaired by one agent, like a function of a natural resource that can only be affected by the use that is made of it. This function is not influenced by other agents (see Section 6.2), and the agent in question does not impair any other functions. Of course, this situation occurs rarely if ever in practice. The assumption is made solely to simplify the following explanation. Apart from this, the calculation of the supply and the demand curve is part of a comparative static exercise.

9.4 *Scissors of supply and revealed demand*

In **Figure 5** *function availability p* (purity) is recorded on the horizontal axis, in physical units, while the vertical axis gives the *preferences* and *annual costs.* Going from the origin to the right, the burdening of the function decreases and its availability p increases. With fixed reference q, actual usage $u = q - p$ is read from the right to the left, see footnote 8. The figure connects ecology and economics.

Two cost curves are constructed. The *abatement* or *elimination costs* $E = E[p]$ constitute a **supply**. The *compensation costs* $C = C[p]$ and the *willingness to pay for damages* $D = D[p]$ sum into the curve $C + D$. By summing the two curves a U-shaped curve $C + D + E$ is obtained. The minimum of total costs then reflects the position of optimum function recovery.

The increase by one unit of availability of the function corresponds to a reduction of the burden in terms of $C + D$. This reduction is actually a benefit. Thus $C + D$ can be mirrored along the horizontal axis and we can interpret $-(C + D)$ as benefits. Thus $-(C + D)$ has the economic meaning of **demand**. This recognition provides for a link with cost-benefit analysis. By subtracting the elimination costs E we find the *benefits minus costs* as the curve $-(C + D + E)$. Maximising the difference between benefits and costs gives the optimum again.

9.5 *Deduction on the extremum*

The aim, now, is to find the optimum. The optimum condition can be stated using marginal quantities, see **Figure 5 (b)**. The annual sum of money per additional unit of availability of the function appears on the vertical axis. The first derivative of the $-(C + D)$ curve w.r.t. the availability p of the function is: $-(d/dp)(C + D) = c + d$

In the graph the following then happens. Curve $c + d$ lies in the first quadrant, where it runs from top left to bottom right. The mirror is $(d/dp)(C + D)$ which lies in the fourth quadrant, where it runs from bottom left to top right. At the point where the **demand curve** $c + d$ intersects the **supply curve** e the above-mentioned optimum is to be found. The minimum of total costs is thus given by the intersection of the marginal curves:

Total costs of elimination: E
Marginal costs of elimination: $dE/dp = e$
Total costs of compensation and damage: $C + D$
Total benefits: $-(C + D)$
Marginal benefits: $-(d/dp)(C + D) = c + d$
For U-shaped $C + D + E$ the minimum has $(d/dp)(C + D + E) = 0$
Whence $e = c + d$

Figure 5. Costs of elimination and revealed preferences for an environmental function: (a) total cost curves; (b) marginal supply and demand curves. p = *purity = availability of the function,* $E = E[p]$ = elimination costs, $C + D = C[p] + D[p]$ = compensation and (financial) damage costs, $T[p]$ = *total costs,* $e[p]$ = marginal elimination costs, $c[p] + d[p]$ = marginal compensation and damage costs. Taken from Hueting (1974a, 1980:119). Actual usage is read from the right to the left. The sum of purity p and usage u give a fixed reference point $q = p + u$, e.g. q is at M (e.g. 100% no pollution). See Section 10.5. NB. For comparison with **Figure 6**, point W actually equals K on the horizontal axis.

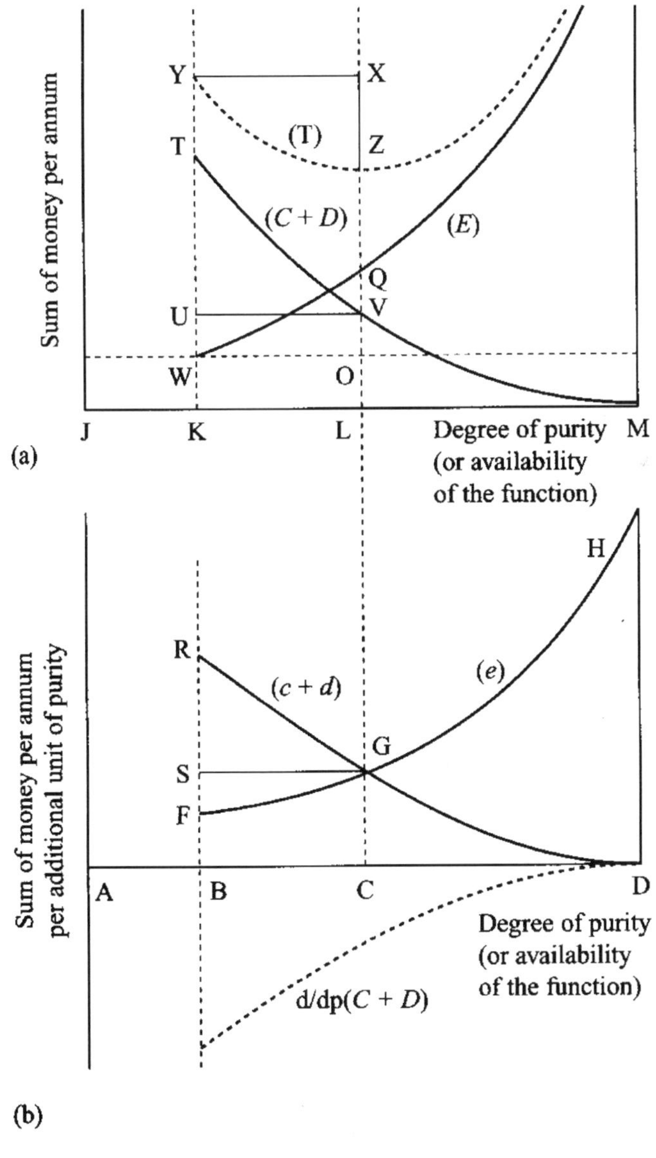

This defines the optimal degree of function recovery. For a shadow price we want that it reflects social costs. The adage is that it must be equal to the marginal costs. However, here we set marginal costs to zero, as $(d/dp)(C + D + E) = 0$. At first this is a conundrum but the solution is found by recognising that $-(C + D)$ actually are benefits from elimination. The marginal costs for cost-benefit analysis may be found on the *e* curve, i.e. the distance from the horizontal axis to the *e* curve. *The (optimal) shadow price of an environmental function is therefore equal to the marginal costs of elimination at optimal restoration of function.*

9.6 *Supply of an environmental function*

The elimination cost or abatement cost curve in **Figure 5** is built up from expenditures on measures, to be taken by whatever party from the year of investigation onwards, which increase the availability of the original functions. This can only be achieved by eliminating the cause of loss of function and, where necessary and feasible, by neutralizing the accumulated impact of earlier environmental burdening in situ (for instance, sanitizing the contamination of the soil by toxic substances). The measures involved thus eliminate the source of the loss of function, that is the environmental burden, permitting partial or complete restoration of the function in question. Elimination is thus defined as removing the burden. The elimination measures are, of course, arranged such that the total elimination costs up to each regained availability of the function are minimal, i.e. arranged by increasing costs per unit of function restored. This results in a progressively rising curve, which can be seen as a supply curve, because it supplies the function. We call this the elimination cost curve, because it refers to measures that eliminate the pressure on the environment. Except in the case of irreparable damage, the elimination costs can always be estimated by consulting environmental technical expertise. So this curve can always be constructed. The measures consist of:

(1) technical measures, including process re-engineering, redesign, developing and applying (renewable) substitutes for non-renewable resources (for example solar energy, glass fibre) and rearranging space to create more space for ecosystems
(2) direct shifts from environmentally burdening to less burdening activities (reallocation)
(3) a decrease in the size of the population.[28]

No pronouncement is made as to the time frame within which these measures are to be implemented. Yet the elimination measures are based on the technology and the size of the population in the year of investigation.

From how the curve is built up it follows that it is a collective supply curve. The sum of the elimination costs is equal to the sum of the costs of the production factors that must be withdrawn, by a variety of routes, from the production of consumption goods and collective goods in order for functions to be restored. Of

[28] In principle, a shrinkage of economic activity, with employment remaining unchanged (more leisure time) could be one of the measures. However, production and consumption will decrease considerably by taking the measures 1, 2 and 3 for reaching an environmentally sustainable level. It is highly improbable that people will agree with a much lower level of disposable income and therefore one cannot avoid a discussion about the size of the population.

course, this reduces the production level as measured in national income. As just explained, the curve rises progressively from bottom left to top right.

9.6.1 *Supply of renewable natural resources*

This type of resources are the carriers of many functions, for instance 'surface water as basis for ecosystems', which conflicts with 'surface water to catch fish from', 'soil as basis for ecosystems', which conflicts with the function 'supplier of timber' and so on. The functions of (such a) renewable resource remain available as long as the regenerative capacity of the resource remains intact. For that purpose the use of the resource must be limited to a level below which the regeneration is not endangered. This, in turn, requires maintenance of a 'sufficient' size of the resource (Odum, 1971). If the use of a resource exceeds these limits, the excess use has to be eliminated.

Restoring and preserving the function 'fresh surface water as carrier of ecosystems', for instance, basically means to stop eradicating species which are important for supporting ecosystems. This calls for techniques to reduce by-catch and to control of a number of water quality variables, such as the concentrations of various groups of substances in the water body and the sediment, among which biologically degradable organic matter, nutrients like phosphates and nitrates, and toxic substances such as various heavy metals and biocides. Elimination measures directed towards limitation of discharges and seepage containing these substances include installation, extension and improvement of waste water treatment plants, improvement of agricultural methods and control of sewer overflows and surface run-off. The effects and the costs of these elimination measures necessary for the preservation of the function are then arranged in the supply curve of the function.

The function 'fresh surface water as a source of organisms for consumption by humans' can only be sustained by protecting the just mentioned function, 'fresh surface water as carrier of ecosystems', and additional elimination measures such as reduction of the catch of fish and other species and improvement the ways of catching these organisms. In order to avoid double counting of the elimination cost of the first mentioned function in eSNI (to be discussed below), the elimination cost curve for the function 'fresh surface water as a source of organisms for consumption by humans' must be built-up from only the cost effectiveness data of the just mentioned additional measures.

Protection of the function 'soil as a basis for cultivating crops in agriculture', is partly profiting from the protection of the two just mentioned functions, but demands extra measures such as improvements of cultivation methods, which vary from reducing the application of manure to measures for realising so-called biological culture, or still further, biological-dynamic culture. The latter two systems respectively minimise and exclude the use of synthetic biocides and artificial fertilisers. Again, for calculation of eSNI the measures must be arranged in order of increasing cost-effectiveness (costs per unit availability of the function, expressed physically), resulting in the supply curve of the function.

9.6.2 *Supply of non-renewable resources*

The functions of very slowly forming natural resources such as crude oil and copper, which are to all intents and purposes non-renewable, 'regeneration' can take three forms: efficiency improvements, recycling and, over the longer term, substitution of the resource by another resource or a product that can provide the same functions. Familiar examples of substitution include solar power and glass fibre for crude oil and copper wire, respectively.

Sustainability of non-renewable natural resources means that in a given period (year) only as much may be withdrawn from the stock as new potential for recycling and conserving the resource (by improvement of efficiency) and substitutes for the resource are expected to be developed. These elimination measures result in a lower level of production that prevents the resource from being exhausted prematurely, that is, when the technology does not improve fast enough. Of course, in the longer run only substitution can replace the resource and thus maintain its functions. In this way the functions of a resource available in the year of investigation can be maintained in the future.

The investment, labour and running costs of the three types of measures are specific for each non-renewable resource (as well as for the sector in which they are applied, but this aspect is preliminarily neglected). Again, the costs and effects of the measures must be arranged in an elimination cost curve for each non-renewable resource that threatens sustainability. The prospects are hopeful for energy carriers such as oil, gas and coal. For many rare metals however, the costs of their substitution, if possible at all, are extremely high (Reijnders, 1996).

9.6.3 *Supply of space*

As stated before, an important presumption in the set-up of eSNI (to be discussed below) is that biodiversity is a condition for the preservation of essential environmental functions. It is assumed that this condition is satisfied if the rate of extinction of species worldwide does not exceed the rate of coming into existence of species. As the first rate exceeds the second one many times (Hueting and Reijnders, 1998b), a sustainability standard would amount to maintaining the – remaining – biodiversity.

The simplest approach for estimating the costs of a different use of space in the long run directly applies to the Netherlands and boils down to estimating the area of undivided land (and water) surface that is needed for the survival of species and then multiply this number with the average yearly costs per square kilometre of borrowing the funds for buying the needed financial capital, starting from a ground-rent which correctly reflects the scarcity of the space needed for productive and consumptive activities. The area needed to safeguard species is related to the area needed globally, to the dissemination of species around the world and to the principle that all countries take their share in assigning space for this purpose. The thus estimated area in the Netherlands is larger than the area of the so-called "Ecologische Hoofdstructuur" (EHS, Ecological Main Structure). By replacing the too narrow corridors between nature areas by the broader ones that were proposed in the original design of the EHS, the ground-rate probably shall increase, as the corridors are generally situated close to urban areas.

A better but more complicated approach could be this one. Determine the relation between the increase of traffic and the construction of harbours et cetera on the one hand and the growth of average traditional labour productivity (= national income / labour volume), and thus with the growth of the volume of the production as measured in NI on the other. This process also causes an increase in the use and the fragmentation of space. By reversing this fragmentation and loss of space and thus creating large undivided areas, ecosystems will recover and extend, while labour productivity and thus – real – national income will drop. The decrease of NI could be approximated if the relation between labour productivity and traffic and the relation between labour productivity and harbour construction were explored. A complicating aspect is that these activities will also be diminished by the reduction of the use of other environmental functions. In order to avoid double counting, the optimal reduction of the use of space has to be calculated together with the use of other relevant functions in a general equilibrium model of production and consumption.

The use or supply of geographical space is not yet incorporated in the calculation of environmentally Sustainable National Income (eSNI).

9.7 *Revealed demand for an environmental function*

The second curve in **Figure 5** is the revealed (not necessarily sustainable) demand curve of the function. It consists of the sum total (without double counting) of all expenditures, actually made, by whatever party, resulting from loss of environmental functions. The costs actually incurred fall into two categories:

(1) expenditures on measures to compensate for loss of function, such as the raising of dikes as a result of disruption of various functions regulating hydrology and climate, or on preparing drinking water as a result of overuse of the function 'dumping ground for waste', or costs of additional travelling to more remote 'natural' recreation area instead of a lost less remote area; these are the compensation costs;
(2) expenditures, actually made relating to damage, such as housing damage and harvest losses caused by flooding due to loss of the function 'hydrological regulation' of forests and soil, the restoration of damage caused by flooding due to excessively cutting forests etc. (overuse of the function 'provider of wood' etc.) that consequently are losing their function 'regulation of the water flow' and production losses and medical costs ensuing from, say, loss of the function 'air for physiological functioning', and some other costs such as travel expenses incurred in going ever further to enjoy nature; this is the financial damage.

All these amounts can be interpreted as expressing revealed preferences for the original functions, so that the negative first derivative of the cost curve built up from these amounts can be seen as a collective demand curve for environmental functions: the first derivative lying in the fourth quadrant is reflected in the first quadrant: $-(d/dp)(C+D) = c + d$, where the symbol p represents the availability of the function, see **Figure 5**.

For category (2), this is based, strictly speaking, on the assumption that those suffering damage through loss of a function are prepared to pay at least the amount required to restore that damage in order to achieve restoration and lasting availability of the function in question. The curve *c* + *d* has the shape of a normal demand curve for a product – which confirms that this interpretation as a demand curve is correct. With decreasing availability of the function, progressively more compensation measures must be taken and progressively more financial damage occurs: the price (indicating the marginal utility) increases.

9.7.1 *Unknowns in the aspects in demand*

It can be argued that preferences for essential functions can be expressed very partially as the compensation and damage costs. As an example of compensation costs (as revealed preferences), there is no point in creating new forests or lakes so long as the process of acidification has not been halted by elimination measures, because without elimination at the source the process will acidify the newly created forests and lakes. Erosion-driven soil loss cannot be compensated. Much of the damage resulting from loss of functions will take place in the future; cases in point are damage due to disruption of climatic stability and to the loss of the functions of natural ecosystems such as rainforests and estuaries. No financial damage or compensation expenditures can therefore arise in the present. Choosing a discount rate, for instance the market interest, for calculating the net present value of future damage boils down to making an assumption about preferences for future environmental costs and benefits (Hueting, 1991). This does not, therefore, resolve the basic problem of preferences being unknown. We cannot base ourselves on observed individual behaviour, furthermore, given the working of the prisoners' dilemma. In practice, individuals do not switch to environmentally sound behaviour, because they doubt whether others will do the same, as a result of which the effect is thought to be negligible while the individual concerned causes him or herself detriment. The same holds at a meso- and macro-scale. If one company takes measures to protect the environment but others do not, it will price itself out of the market. If a given country adopts measures and others do not follow, that country will suffer damage, while the effect of those measures will be insubstantial. Finally, there is a lack of information, for example about the complex nature of life support systems and the relation between safeguarding the environment, employment and growth. All the aforementioned factors make it impossible and very difficult respectively to fully express preferences for environmental functions.

9.7.2 *Drawbacks of contingent valuation*

It is therefore logical to consider the possibilities for retrieving the demand for functions with the aid of contingent valuation, i.e. having statistical questionnaires on willingness to pay (WTP) or willingness to accept (WTA). Much research is being done to trace the preferences by asking people how much they would be prepared to pay to wholly or partially restore lost environmental functions and to conserve them. However, the method does not always provide reliable estimates for many reasons.

(1) Information on the significance of environmental functions is deficient in many cases. This is especially so for the functions that determine the future quality of the environment. With respect to the functions of life support systems there

is often a question of the risk that interrupting complicated processes, for instance ecosystems and climate, may lead to serious overshoots and collapse, versus the chance that technologies not yet invented may cope with those risks. Many people may not be able to weigh these risks and chances, and thus to answer how much they are prepared to pay for avoiding them. If individuals are not aware of the importance of an environmental function, the survey method is pointless.

(2) There is a considerable difference between saying that one is willing to spend money on something and actually paying for it.

(3) The questioning method in fact tries to approach the value of a collective good as if it were a private marketable good (by trying to find some points on the demand curve). In a market the bidder knows fairly well what quality and quantity can be acquired by different bids. In a collective situation, however, this is not possible, because it is not known how much other people are going to bid. Without a considerable amount of additional research it is also not known how much money is required to attain different quality standards for the environmental functions.

(4) In order not to make the questioning unjustifiably vague, some research on environmental accounting has to be done beforehand. For clear air, clean water, and so forth are not homogeneous goods from an economic point of view, as water and air have quite a few different economic functions. If the persons being questioned are to have a clear picture of the issues, they must be given information on the significance of the different functions, the consequences of their loss, and the measures and costs involved in their restoration. All together this constitutes a huge amount of information, which would not be easy to survey. Although the willingness-to-pay method might be justified for one or two factors affecting the immediate living conditions of people asked, it is not a sound base for estimating the value of essential functions such as 'soil to encompass forests that regulate water runoff', 'water for irrigating agricultural crop' and the functions that are endangered by climate change.

(5) Much of the damage resulting from the loss of functions will take place in the future. No financial damage or compensation expenditures, as revealed preferences, can therefore arise in the present. Choosing a discount rate boils down to making an assumption about preferences and therefore does not resolve the problem; see Hueting (1991a). Another example is that we cannot base ourselves on observed individual behaviour, given the working of the prisoners' dilemma.

(6) People may be interested in the effects of their bids, together with the (unknown) bids of others, on, for instance employment levels and consumption patterns. For answering legitimate questions about this, scenario studies have to be elaborated, and the results have to be presented to the persons questioned. This hardly seems feasible. Again, what might be justified on a micro scale is most probably not justified on a macro scale.

(7) Asking people how much they are prepared to pay, suggests that conserving the environment always requires extra provisions that must be paid for. In quite a few cases, however, conservation is a matter of refraining from doing

things rather than of doing them, and this saves rather than costs money. Thus not building a road through a mountainous area that is vulnerable to erosion is cheaper than building it, cycling is cheaper than driving, wearing a sweater and using an extra blanket is cheaper than raising the temperature, and confining the consumption of lettuce to the summer season is cheaper than eating it throughout the year. People who realize this may modify their answers because of such considerations.

(8) Some people will probably be convinced that it does not matter what they bid, because their bid will not influence environmental policy at all, and this conviction will render their bid unreliable.

(9) Some people may think they have a "right" to a healthy and safe environment and will probably react accordingly by not making a bid at all.

(10) People will probably have their doubts about the participation of others (the Prisoner's Dilemma from game theory) or prefer to wait and see (the Free Rider Principle from the theory of collective goods). Thus in developing countries, where the tropical rain forests are, the view is widespread, for a number of reasons, that people from the rich countries should pay for their conservation.

(11) In cases where the whole community is involved, the willingness–to–accept approach is pointless. For who is paying whom to accept the loss?

(12) The willingness-to-pay method also measures the consumer's surplus. In national income the total value of the goods is found by multiplying the quantity of each good by its respective price and then adding together the resulting amounts. Using this procedure, the consumer's surplus is not expressed in the level of national income. Thus, a doctor who saves a patient's life creates a value that, whatever one may think about its exact size, is certainly higher than the value added recorded in national income. The intra-marginal utility of goods, which is ignored in national income, will approach an infinite value, because it includes the utility of the first unit of food, drink, and so forth. For this reason the results of willingness-to-pay research are not suitable to be used in conjunction with the figures of national income. An additional objection to incorporating the consumer's surplus in the willingness-to-pay approach is that the results reflect the income distribution more directly than do the prices of market commodities; the differences between rich and poor in the weights of the "votes" become greater when the consumer's surplus is included. The occurrence of differences in weights of "votes" is often defended by the argument that the contribution to the national package of goods and services by the rich is greater than by the poor: their incomes are higher because of the greater relative scarcity of their abilities. This argument is not valid with regard to the environment, because it is not produced by humanity.

Because of the limitations mentioned above, the willingness-to-pay method does not present a firm enough basis for correcting national income for losses of scarce environmental functions. Consequently, it is not possible to construct a complete demand curve.

The just made observations concern the demand for the functions of both renewable and non-renewable resources, as well as the functions of space.

9.8 *Demand and supply curves without environmental sustainability*

As we move up along the elimination cost curve in **Figure 5,** we automatically move down the curve of compensation costs and damage costs: as the original functions become more available, the necessity of such expenditure decreases. It is this reduction in compensation and damage costs that constitutes the benefits accruing from the expenditures made on elimination measures; it cannot be excluded that certain benefits are not represented by compensation and damage.

By summing the two cost curves a U-shaped curve is obtained. The minimum of this U-curve then reflects the position of optimum function recovery, for here the total social costs are minimal, that is the difference between total benefits and costs is maximal. The minimum of the U-curve corresponds to the point of intersection of the first derivatives of the two curves, that is of the (marginal) supply and demand curves. This point of intersection would reflect the shadow price that can be compared directly with the market prices, provided all preferences for environmental functions were reflected in the demand curve constructed as described above. The shadow price (the length of CG) times the unaccepted function loss (the length of BC) simultaneously equals the revealed value of the environmental function *and* indicates the revealed costs of the unaccepted function loss. The residual function loss, recorded in physical terms (the length of CD), is accepted: the associated (increase in) production, which is entered in the national accounts, is valued more highly. Like any price, the shadow price of an environmental function indicates its marginal utility.

To value is to compare. In economics, there is no such thing as an absolute value; a good can only be worth more or worth less compared with another good. From the overview of conflict between functions, given in Hueting (1974a, 1980), the conclusion can be drawn that what is almost always at stake is a conflict between the environment and produced goods. The value indicated by the length of OZ in **Figure 5** equals the shadow price (CG) times the unaccepted function loss (BC), that is, the area of BCGS. This area comprises no consumer's surplus (SGR), just like market values. It is therefore directly comparable with the market price of a produced good.

The area of FGR is the monetized net increase of utility gained as the availability of a function increases from B to C and equals the length of line section ZX. This net increase equals the total increase in benefit BCGR minus the elimination costs BCGF. This must always be a positive number, because there is a change from suboptimal to optimal.

9.9 *The assumption of a preference for environmental sustainability*

As we have seen (e.g. in Sections 9.7.1 and 9.7.2) individual preferences for environmental functions can be measured only partially. Therefore, their shadow prices, which are defined by the intersection of the first derivatives of the constructed curves for demand and supply (see **Figure 5**), cannot be determined. Consequently, these shadow prices – and the value of environmental functions – remain largely unknown. This means that the *correct prices for the human-made goods* that are produced and consumed at the expense of environmental functions, and on which NI is based, remain *equally unknowable*.

To provide the necessary information we cannot escape from making *assumptions* about the relative preferences for environmental functions and produced goods.

One of the possible assumptions is that the economic agents, individuals and institutions, have a dominant – or absolute – preference for an environmentally sustainable development. This assumption is legitimate since governments and institutions all over the world have stated support for environmental sustainability. Furthermore Hueting (1987d), referring to the ecological risks by production growth, postulates: "Man derives part of the meaning of existence from the company of others. These others include in any case his children and grandchildren. The prospect of a safer future is therefore a normal human need, and dimming of this prospect has a negative effect on welfare." The environmentally sustainable income (eSNI), described in Chapter 8, is therefore based on the assumption of dominant preferences for environmental sustainability (for example Hueting et al., 1992d, 1998b; Hueting and Bosch, 1994).

Another possible assumption is that the economy is currently on an optimal path that is described by standard NI.

So *both eSNI and standard NI are fictitious* in the context of what is at issue in economic theory and statistics, namely to provide indicators of the effect of our actions on our welfare. This holds true apart from the fact that measuring NI likely has smaller uncertainty margins than measuring eSNI has.

The assumed absolute social preferences for sustainable use of a (vital, essential) environmental function become apparent as a very steep (inelastic) part of the demand curve of the function at the minimal sustainable level of its availability. The demand curve then reaches the abscissa practically vertically at that minimally sustainable availability. The steep part of the curve may be approximated by the vertical line representing the sustainability standard, defined as the minimal availability of the function. This assumption thus also provides a definition for the standards for environmental sustainability.

The thus defined sustainability standards can only be established by the natural sciences, not by economists, provided the economic context of the application of the standards is clear. They are objective insofar natural sciences are objective. They must of course be distinguished clearly from the subjective preferences for whether or not they should be attained. Over time, science will advance and change standards to likely greater accuracy, and this will cause revisions in eSNI and not in NI. Such revisions will generate better information and thus cannot be a reason for objection. Without standards, environmental sustainability is indeterminate.

In establishing sustainability standards, as the basic point of departure is taken the natural regeneration capacities of the concerned environmental processes: as long as these remain intact, environmental functions will remain available. These processes determine the state of the environment on which the functions and consequently the standards depend. The standards have to be chosen thus that these processes are in dynamic equilibrium, see Hueting and De Boer (2001b) and Hueting and Reijnders (2004a). For instance, the growth and mortality processes of algae or fish populations determine their age distribution, and consequently the availability of the function 'water as a habitat for fish'.

Figure 6. Translation of costs in physical units into costs in monetary units

s = supply curve or marginal elimination cost curve;
d = incomplete demand curve or marginal benefit curve based on individual preferences (revealed from expenditures on compensation and willingness to pay for damages);
d' = 'demand curve' based on assumed preferences for sustainability;
BD = distance that must be bridged in order to arrive at sustainable use of environmental functions;
area BEFD = total costs of the loss functions, expressed in money;
the arrows indicate the way in which the loss of environmental functions recorded in physical units is translated into monetary units.
NB. The availability of the function (B) does not need to coincide with the level following from intersection point (E). The coincidence of B and E, shown here, holds under the assumption that the market prices are the result of the costs and the preferences. (The latter cannot be measured, see the body of the text.)
PM. If the optimal elimination is not executed then the next period may show a larger distance to environmental sustainability.
Taken from Hueting (1986b) and Hueting et al. (1992d).

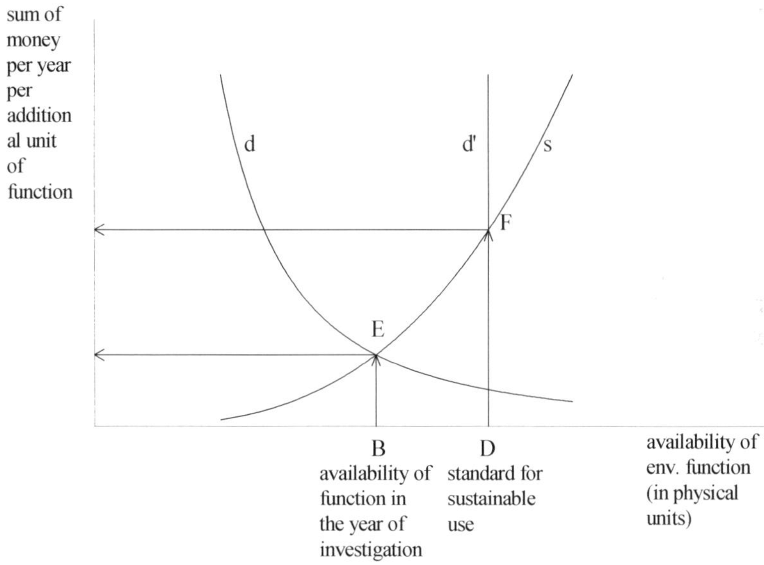

Again, the shadow price for environmental functions – and their value – based upon the assumed preferences for sustainability follow from the intersection of the vertical line and the marginal elimination cost-effectiveness curve. The following examples illustrate how these quantities and the acceptable, that is sustainable, burdens can be established.

9.9.1 *Renewable resources*

In the absence of drastic human intervention, the quantity and quality of renewable natural resources such as groundwater or biomass (including wood) generally show a substantial degree of constancy or even increase.

With respect to how sustainability relates to species, then, the standard holds that the rate of human-induced extinction should not exceed the rate at which new species come into existence. This boils down to preserving all the species still alive today, for it is assumed that during the past several thousand years conditions have been such that, leaving aside drastic human intervention for the moment, the number of new species must certainly have at least equalled the number of species lost to extinction (Raup, 1986; Hawksworth, 1995). However, in contrast to the situation prior to human intervention, the rate at which natural species are becoming extinct is today at least a factor 10000 higher than the rate at which new species are evolving (Raup, 1986). There is obviously a level, defined as a number of individuals of a species, below which the species is threatened with extinction; arriving below that level is unsustainable, remaining above that level is sustainable. Together with the condition that harvesting a species should not disrupt the ecosystem of which it forms a part (see Odum, 1971), this yields the sustainability standard for the species. No more than a rough indication of the conditions can be given under which plant and animal species are able to survive (Hawksworth, 1995; Den Boer, 1979).

When a species is close to the limit of survival, the size of its population is very small, then the chance of survival is close to zero. The sustainability standard for the preservation should therefore be determined at a distance of this limit. Also because of the precautionary principle a safe distance to this limit must be maintained.

With regard to pollution, too, criteria can be established (Hueting and Reijnders, 1996ab, 1998b). Acid precipitation, for example, should not exceed the neutralizing capacity of the soil. Likewise, there should be no exportation of risks to future generations through pollution of groundwater that is to serve as a source of drinking water for those generations. In many cases, the accompanying environmental burden can be determined with some accuracy.

As for erosion, it can be established that the rate of erosion of topsoil may not exceed the rate of formation of such soil due to weathering. Similar consumption standards can be set for other natural resources. There is a wealth of data on the rate at which new fertile soil is naturally formed and on the neutralizing capacity of natural soils, and these data enable a reliable indication to be given of the admissible environmental burden due to erosion and acid rain (Reijnders, 1996).

On the basis of the best available global circulation models it can be calculated that worldwide emissions of carbon dioxide must be reduced drastically to achieve stabilization of the global warming process. With an early version of the model IMAGE it was estimated that the total global CO_2-equivalent emission of 'greenhouse gases' has to be reduced to 22% of the emission in 1990, in order to constrain the future warming during the next centuries to 1.5°C. This has been used in the calculation of eSNI. [29] Likely, though, 1.5°C is still too high for environmental sustainability.

Shortcomings in our toxicological knowledge mean that we cannot fully analyse the risks associated with polluted groundwater. However, this does not detract

[29] Part of this standard is, by the way, that the CO_2-emission steadily diminishes further to a level of ca. 5% of the 1990 emission within ca. 10 centuries.

from the fact that improved scientific knowledge can lead to a more precise establishment of standards for sustainability.

9.9.2 *Non-renewable resources*

The principle of estimation of an environmentally sustainable level of production is to use the technology available in the year of estimation, or shortly thereafter. In the case of very slowly forming natural resources such as crude oil and copper, which are to all intents and purposes non-renewable, this principle runs into a problem. Application of this principle to non-renewables would cause depletion of the resource and a collapse of production at some time in the future. The option to pass on stocks untouched to future generations makes no sense since it would stop production here and now. Thus we must make an exception to the principle on technology. This does not imply that the principle itself is invalid. It is the exception that proves the rule. The exception does not occur with the other environmental functions. The exception is the only way to arrive at a sustainability standard for non-renewable resources.[30]

In the case of very slowly forming natural resources 'regeneration' can take three forms:

(i) efficiency improvements
(ii) recycling
(iii) substitution: over the longer term, substitution of one form of environmental element by another that can provide the same functions. Familiar examples of substitution include solar power and glass fibre for crude oil and copper wire, respectively.

This leads to the following rule to attain a numerical value:

> Environmental sustainability of non-renewable natural resources means that in a given period only as much may be withdrawn from the stock as substitutes for the resource as well as new potential for recycling and conserving the resource (improvement of efficiency) are expected to be developed in the long run.

In this way the functions of a resource available in the year of investigation are maintained at the same levels in the future. In practice this can be worked out by, for instance, taking from a period in the past the quantity of possible uses (for example heating, transportation, and so on expressed in effective energy) that has become available through efficiency improvement, substitution and recycling and then assuming that the relative rate (percentage per year) of these processes will be the same the years to come.

There follows from this a maximum permissible annual rate of extraction that can be used as a sustainability standard. In a formula: $e(t_0) \leq r(t_0).S(t_0)$, in which $e(t_0)$ is the extraction rate e in year t_0, $r(t_0)$ the relative reduction of consumption of the resource as a percentage per year (i.e. its relative rate or rate coefficient) at a constant level of production in year t_0, and $S(t_0)$ the stock in year t_0 (Tinbergen, 1990).

---

[30] The sustainability standard is re-established for each year in which the eSNI is calculated, as is the case with the cost functions themselves. Thus technology can adapt in-between.

This formula is applied at the global level, for each year of the eSNI calculation. Standards for individual countries can be subsequently derived by applying the general rule that a country's share in meeting the global standard should be equal to its share in total extraction.

The rate at which efficiency improvements, new recycling methods and substitutes become available may be so low that this method leads to a very low level of eSNI. Then it has been proposed to take additional measures for the development of substitutes (Tinbergen and Hueting, 1991) in order to "maximize" eSNI. To this end the following procedure has been proposed by Bosch (1994). For each resource, statistical data are used to establish the rate at which substitution (the ultimate solution) has taken place over the past 10 to 20 years and the annual cost this has entailed. It is then calculated how long it would take, at this rate, to completely replace the resource (1). Next, it is calculated how long it will take for the resource to be depleted, at the *current* level of production (2). Then (1) divided by (2) yields a rough approximation of the required 'acceleration factor' for the development of substitutes in time for them to replace the functions of the resource when it is depleted. This factor multiplied by the statistically established annual cost of substitute development yields the sum that needs to be reserved for this purpose.

The figures thus found can be no more than rough estimates, of course. In the context of non-renewable natural resources, though, this is an approach that does justice to the principle of environmental sustainability, which is the principle for our estimates. Our approach would be comparable with that of Solow (1974), Hartwick (1977, 1978) and others, if the latter were to exclude infeasible substitution of renewable resources by other resources and by capital (see below), that is if they were to abandon their faith in the extreme areas of formal production functions.

9.9.3 *Strong versus weak sustainability*

Advocates of 'weak sustainability' take the line that all elements of the environment can ultimately be substituted by man-made alternatives, implying that restoration of lost elements can be postponed in anticipation of cheaper substitutes provided by future technologies. However, the life support systems of our planet, on which a number of vital functions depend, are not substitutable at all (Lovelock, 1979; Roberts, 1988; Goodland, 1995; Reijnders, 1996). The same holds for most of the functions of natural ecosystems, especially in the long term. Consequently, there can be no such thing as 'weak sustainability' for the functions of these systems.

Advocates of 'strong sustainability' hold it to be impossible for humanity to substitute many of the elements of the natural environment. In its strictest form, however, this implies that stocks of non-renewable resources should remain fully intact, an unrealistic aim. Consequently, strong sustainability for non-renewable resources seems to be impossible.

In conclusion, there seems to be *only one kind of environmental sustainability*, whereby non-renewable resources must gradually be substituted by other elements of our physical surroundings in order to guarantee the availability of functions, and substitution of a large class of renewable resources is impossible, particularly life support systems, including ecosystems.

When using the concept of environmental function, the only thing that matters in the context of sustainability is that vital (i.e. essential) functions remain available.

9.9.4 *Global versus local sustainability standards*

The question is often asked whether sustainability standards should be applied locally or globally. This depends on the scale at which the functions in question can be substituted. For instance, preservation of the function 'soil for growing crops' requires local application of the standard for erosion (the erosion rate may not exceed the soil formation rate), because exceeding the standard at one place cannot be compensated by remaining under this standard elsewhere. Crude oil, on the other hand, is a global resource, so in this case the sustainability standard, effectuated through efficiency improvement and substitute development, should be applied worldwide.

9.10 *Comparing NI, NI-A and eSNI*

The notion of asymmetric bookkeeping, discussed in Chapter 7, was discussed originally in 1974 as only a criticism w.r.t. the actual measurement of production and economic growth. It appears to be a crucial part for the analysis on eSNI too. Attaining environmental sustainability requires elimination measures, and booking those asymmetrically would raise NI, with increasingly wrong information. A proper comparison requires that we avoid asymmetric bookkeeping in eSNI and NI-A.

Figure 7 concerns a hypothetical situation w.r.t. comparing NI, NI-A and eSNI, see De Boer & Hueting (2010) in Dutch.

Figure 7. Comparing NI, NI-A and eSNI

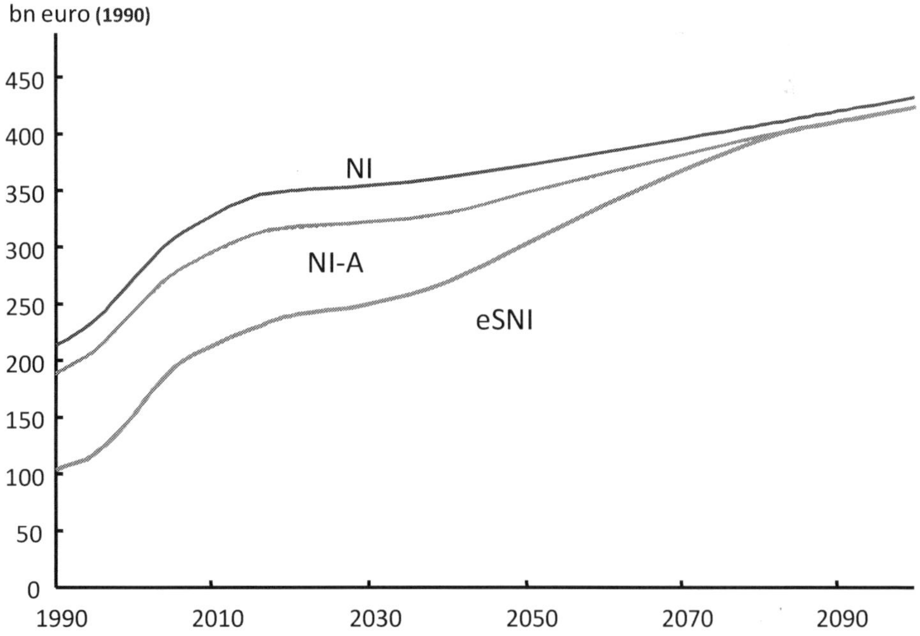

This hypothetical situation does not use a model and only draws some hypothetical lines from our imagination, to indicate what we expect to see *grosso modo* if we were to run a model. The horizontal axis contains years for which we hypothesise that there has been an estimate of eSNI, like **Figure 1**. The vertical axis gives hypothesised values for NI, NI-A and eSNI.

The base situation is similar to the Netherlands, with eSNI in 1990 chosen close to 100 billion euros, to emphasise that this uses hypothetical values. Chapter 7 on asymmetric bookkeeping discussed the difference A = NI – NI-A. For 1990 we hypothesise the values of NI at around 220 and NI-A at around 190, and thus A around 20 bn euros. We also hypothesise that this imaginary economy would reach environmental sustainability in 2080, when eSNI and NI-A are imagined to be measured and found to be equal.

For notation there are, with eΔ-A as the main variable of interest:

A = NI – NI-A
eΔ = NI – eSNI
eΔ-A = NI-A – eSNI = NI – A – eSNI = eΔ – A

These hypothetically drawn lines express our expectation that transition from NI to eSNI requires time because of adaptation processes in both consumption and production. The measurement in each year only allows production methods that are available in the year of measurement. NI in **Figure 7** shows a hypothetical rise over time also because of the transition measures. The production required for the transition measures raises not only NI but also NI-A and eSNI. We imagine that NI-A might be stagnant for some decades while eSNI rises.

When elimination measures have been applied then one might expect that the environment is restored, so that further elimination might no longer be needed, so that not only eSNI = NI-A but also NI would go down again. However, there are some reasons why both remain high and why there remains a relevant difference between NI and eSNI.

- It remains necessary to take measures for elimination, repair and compensation.
- Recovery of some vital functions may require hundreds or thousands of years, like the restoration of the carbon cycle with its impact on climate change, and the regeneration of ecosystems with their species.
- The standard of 1.5 degrees Celsius still allows a rise of the sea level and requires compensation measures for coming centuries for the raising of dikes. We allow only for compensation that keeps the vital functions intact.

10. *Calculation of eSNI*

10.1 *Abstract*

This Chapter gives an overview of the environmental issues chosen for the calculation of eSNI with the derivation of standards for the use in the model. First, data on the use of resources and emissions of matter and energy are determined, then the limits to this use are derived for safeguarding environmental sustainability, and finally the calculation of eSNI is explained that uses these standards in an applied general equilibrium model.

10.2 *Introduction*

The theory above has been applied for a calculation of environmentally sustainable national income of the Netherlands for the years 1990, 1995, 2000 and 2005, and for a rough indication for the year 2015. The results have been presented in **Figure 1** on page 22. It was clear from the beginning that the operation was more than a straightforward calculation. This chapter answers different questions: What data are needed, taken from where, and what problems are encountered both practically and theoretically? This work that started in 1986 can partly be compared to recent work by Rockström on planetary boundaries.

Environmental specialists do not present us directly with the standards that are required for the economic model. For example, they report that certain species will disappear under certain environmental conditions, like concentrations of chemicals or habitats. These reports must be translated into standards that the model can use. Two elements are required: the limiting values on both the state of the system and the use of the environmental functions. There is no general algorithm how this can be done. Each environmental function may need a unique transformation into a standard. Global environmental issues can be translated to local conditions for the Dutch economy. For practical reasons, some global issues have been treated as local ones. Specific Dutch issues have been looked at too.

Table 5. Environmental issues, included or not, Dutch situation 1990

	Included	*Not included*
1	acidification	erosion
2	climate change	extinction of species
3	dehydration, lowering of the ground water table	local nuisance by noise
4	depletion of the ozone layer	local nuisance by stench
5	eutrophication	oxygen deficiency in surface water
6	fine particles in air	solid waste
7	fossil fuel depletion	use of space
8	smog formation (photochemical)	
9	soil contamination.	
10	toxic substances in surface water	

10.3 *Practical choice of environmental issues*

In 1991 at the start of the eSNI-project, an inventory was made that identified 17 environmental issues for which Dutch economic activities contributed significantly to both global and regional / local unsustainability (Hueting, Bosch and De Boer 1992d). For reasons of budget and time 10 were included and 7 issues were excluded, see **Table 5**, although the extinction of species is a main determinant in the estimation of the standards for the included issues 1 – 5, 9 and 10.

10.4 *Overview of the calculation*

The calculation uses interdependent stages, as depicted in **Figure 8**, taken from Hueting & De Boer (2001b:63). Blocks represent models of (sets of) processes, lines represent (sets of) variables. The calculation is from left to right, unless arrows indicate otherwise. Crossover effects between environmental problem areas (themes) are not shown. The scheme has *state* (x) and *use* (u) variables. For the following discussion, variables with the same role in the process, such as types of use, are grouped into vectors. For example, remaining use u equals observed minus eliminated use, $u = u_o - u_E$.

The stages of the calculation are:

- The model on production, consumption and use of the environment requires the transformation of data from the System of National Accounts, the Environmental Accounts, the Environmental Statistics (all CBS) and the Emission Registration (MNP, PBL). Points of attention are: (i) The input-output table and many emission data, for instance, has to be aggregated into a smaller number of production sectors. (ii) If NNI is looked at then data on emissions and other use of the environment are to be supplemented or adapted in order to obtain their 'national' instead of 'domestic' levels – since the modelling exercise originally used NNI and not GDP. (iii) Data on the sustainable production levels of 'non-competitive imports' such as tapioca and raw coffee were hard to obtain or construct (Ensing, 1995). These imports were therefore treated as proportional to sustainable domestic production.
- Modelling of environmental processes is necessary for the identification and estimation of *standards* for the sustainable use of the environment, relevant to the selected environmental problems. Unsustainable effects of a kind of *use* of the environment generally are effects on the *state* of the environment. Insights in the relations between these causes and effects, possibly combined in a (preferably simple) quantitative model, are used to make estimates of the still sustainable levels of the considered types of use of the environment. If it appears possible to arrive at such sustainability standards for the influenced state variables (e.g. the average temperature of the earth's atmosphere). The simple mathematical model can be used to translate these standards for the state into standards for the concerned types of use of environmental functions. If this approach appears infeasible in the available project time, a rough estimate of the maximal sustainable use has to be made in order to enable the eSNI calculation. The thus derived standards for the use of environmental functions are generally constants. In those cases, this procedure does then not need to be repeated for each year for which eSNI is calculated.

Figure 8. Overview of the eSNI calculation

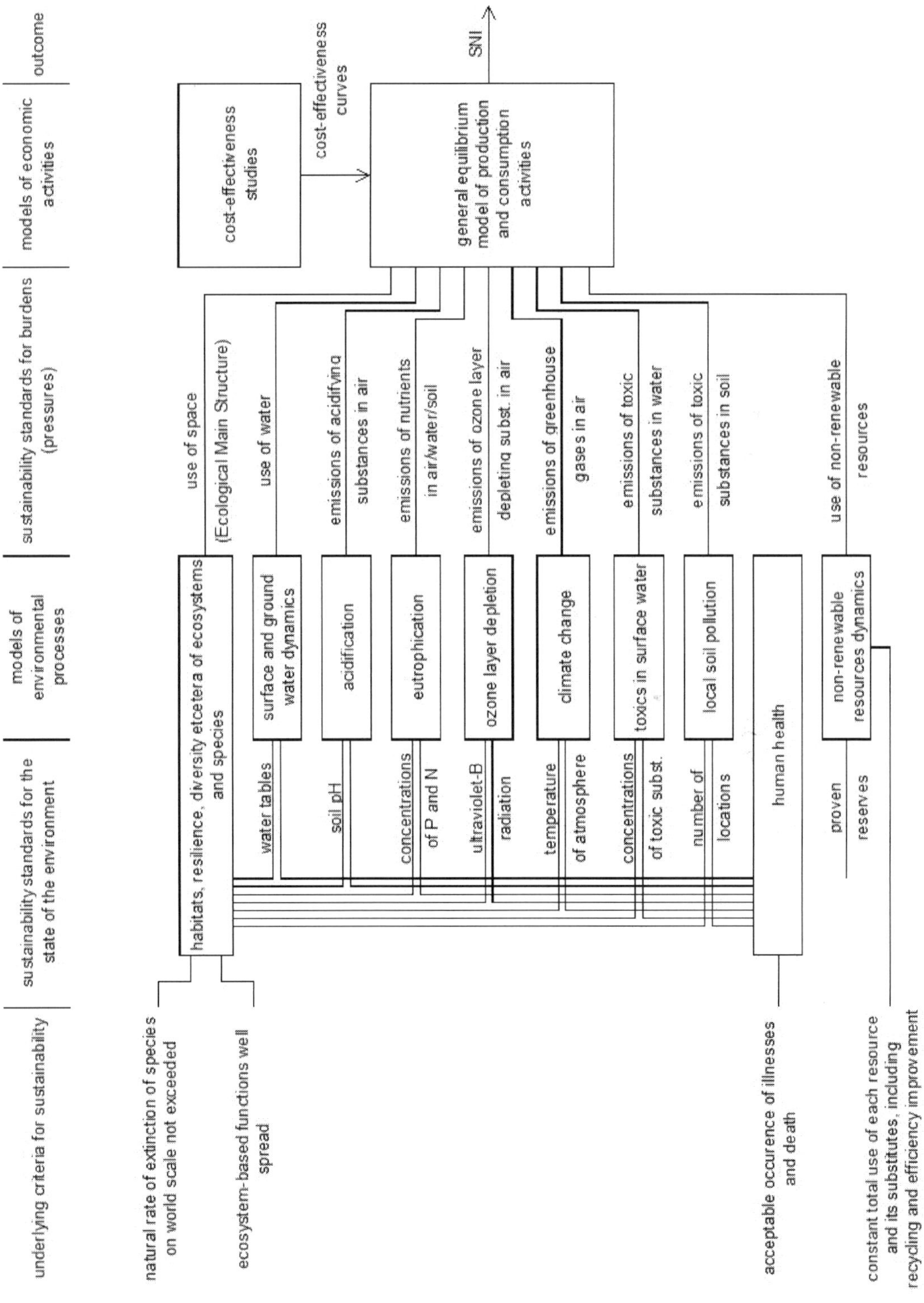

- Construction of *elimination cost-effectiveness curves*, however, *is* required for each distinguished *type of use* of the environment, for each reporting year, according to the method described in Section 9.6. The resulting elimination curve for a type of observed use of the environment u_o in a reporting year can be denoted as $E_u[u_E]$, since conventionally such data are expressed in terms of eliminated use u_E. This differs from the format $E[p]$ that has been used in **Figure 5** on page 79 that uses the availability or purity p of the environmental function. See the next Section for their relationship.
- Restoration of state x will be modelled via elimination of use u.
- The calculation of eSNI in the year under investigation generally concerns large changes in the processes of production and consumption. The eSNI of a country in a year is the NI of that country if its production and consumption processes were already adapted to use the environment sustainably, which generally cannot be realised in one year. This means that eSNI in a historical year is calculated as if the transition to environmentally sustainable production and consumption has taken place. If the required adaptations of the processes in the different sectors of production and consumption influence each other, the use of a dedicated static general equilibrium model is necessary, as has been done in the practical calculation of eSNI.
- If an aspect of this virtual transition to environmental sustainability is not fully understood, the relevant production, consumption and environmental processes could be simulated with a dynamic model during a sufficiently long period of time. This is done partially in the estimation of sustainability standards for climate change; see below. Another case for dynamic analysis concerns the conditions for environmentally sustainable development of production and consumption involving different ways of modelling preferences for environmentally sustainable production, see for instance Pethig (1994) and Pezzey (1994). Zeelenberg et al. (1997) found a theoretical elaboration and support of the theory of eSNI via this line of research.

10.5 *State and use, stock and flow*

Let us distinguish the following variables:

Y = NI = National Income in the System of National Accounts (SNA)
Y_{-A} = NI-A = National Income exclusive of asymmetrical bookkeeping
Y_{eS} = eSNI = environmentally Sustainable National Income
u = use of environmental functions (vector), u_o = observed, u_E = eliminated
u_{eS} = sustainability standards for the use of the environment (vector)
x = state variables of the environment (vector)
x_{eS} = sustainability standards for the state of the environment (vector)
$E_u[u_E]$ = elimination cost curves as functions of eliminated use (vector function)
p = availability or purity of the environmental function (vector)
$q = p + u$ = some constant, for the maximal or optimal level of the availability of the environmental function (for example 100%)
$E[p]$ = elimination cost curves, as function of availability (vector function)
m = measures (vector), that relate elimination to economic activities
m_P = measures for increasing or decreasing production (vector)
m_E = measures for the elimination of the use of the environment (vector)
n = (remaining) effects from nature

Figure 8 distinguishes state and use variables, or stocks and flows. Environmental functions are possible uses, and thus they are state variables (x), that are transferred to the next period or generation. They are related to remaining use $u = u_o - u_E$. The elimination cost curves $E_u[u_E]$ are expressed conventionally as dependent upon eliminated use instead of availability, since the data are commonly recorded in terms of use. **Figure 5** on page 79 shows the availability or purity p of the environmental function on the horizontal axis, and the elimination cost curve $E[p]$ on the vertical axis. This format with availability is relevant for the determination of standards, and to understand the underlying framework of demand and supply. The objective of this section is to show the consistency between these variables and figures.

The first link is that $p + u = q$, for some constant maximal or optimal level, for example q = 100% clean air. The value $p = q$ might be found by taking $u = 0$. In **Figure 5** q may be seen as taken at position M. In **Figure 5**, the natural availability of the function is JK, observed use u_o is KM, and if the elimination u_E is chosen to be KL, then the availability p becomes JL and the remaining use u is LM.

The second link is that there is a functional relationship between the former state and the new state, with an influence by the flow variables. In discrete time:

$x[t] = f[x[t\text{-}1], u[t], m[t]]$ (*) link between state variable and flow variables

In some cases a mass balance may be used to express this link in an accounting format. For scalar variables, and the same measurement unit for both stock and flow (except for the change in time [31]), we get the following, for example for x = the possibility to emit tons of CO_2 into the atmosphere.

$x[t] = x[t\text{-}1] - u[t] + n[t]$ mass balance for the *possibility* of emissions

$n[t] = n[t, x[t\text{-}1], u[t], m[t]]$ natural changes in the mass balance

Sustainability tends to require $x[t] \geq x[t\text{-}1]$, which implies the norm $u[t] \leq n[t]$.

With $p + u = q$, for some constant maximal or optimal level q, we can manipulate the mass balance:

$x[t] = x[t\text{-}1] - q + q - u[t] + n[t]$

We can substitute:

$p[t] = q - u[t]$ the availability of the environmental function

$v[t\text{-}1] = x[t\text{-}1] - q$ a predetermined value, as seen from t

Substitution gives:

[31] With state x at the end of the period and use u per period, then we must multiply $u\ \Delta t$ to get the same dimensions, even when we take Δt = 1 period. For convenience we drop this factor.

$x[t] = v[t\text{-}1] + p[t] + n[t]$ (**) link between state variable and flow variables

In a special case, $x[t\text{-}1] = q$ so that $v[t\text{-}1] = 0$. In that case the new value of the state variable would only consist of the purity created in the current period and the remaining changes caused by nature.

Overall, equations (*) and (**) show the link between the state or stock variable x and the use or flow variables p and u for the current period.

For the elimination cost functions there is, using $p_o + u_o = q$:

$$E_u[u_E] = E_u[u_o - u] = E_u[u_o - q + q - u] = E_u[-p_o + p] = E_u[p - p_o] \leftrightarrow E[p]$$

10.6 *Basic assumptions*

Hueting et al. (1992d) give a number of basic assumptions required for practical estimation of a country's eSNI. We mention the most important of these here; some have already been discussed.

- The transition to sustainable activities is made in every country in the world simultaneously and in the same way. This also prevents the transfer of burdening activities from one country to another.
- Sustainability standards for environmental pressures are set for the region in which they affect functions, i.e. national, regional or global. A given country's contribution to meeting a regional or global standard is equal to its contribution to regional or global pressure.
- Transition costs are not taken into account.
- The employment rate is kept constant
- Technology is kept constant.

10.7 *Deriving sustainability standards*

As discussed in Sections 9.6 and 9.9, assumptions regarding preferences for the availability of environmental functions allow for a one-way approach involving the application of standards. Similarly, assumed absolute preferences for sustained availability of functions can take the form of environmental sustainability standards for these functions. The demand curve of **Figure 5** is then replaced by a vertical line; see **Figure 6** on page 89 in Chapter 9.

Under such preferences for environmental sustainability, the optimal function levels are sustained for future generations and the green national income to be calculated is turned into the (maximally attainable, ad infinitum) sustainable national income. As it is difficult to estimate or even quantify these function levels, it is assumed that their existence is guaranteed by three practical conditions.

- The first is that *the extinction of biological species at the global level may not be accelerated by human influence*.
- The second condition is that *any changes in the state of the environment may have only a minor, acceptable impact on human health*. Health is generally described in the modern literature as a state of well-being extending beyond the mere absence of illness. Nonetheless, most 'maximum acceptable risk' levels in force for environmental state variables are construed with the aim of preventing illness. We identify the second condition with the latter goal.

- The third condition is that *when the effectiveness of a (vital) environmental function requires that the people using it are in direct physical interaction with particular elements or features, then those must be situated within reasonable travelling distance.* We take this distance as 200 km for large uninterrupted nature areas in general, but require additionally at least one smaller nature area located within cycling distance, say 10 km.

These conditions must be satisfied in the present and in the future. Each one imposes bounds on the acceptable variation in the state (quality) of the environment, however imprecise. From these limit values, *environmental sustainability standards* for the various forms of environmental pressure can be derived as discussed above, i.e. with the aid of environmental models, and subsequently environmental sustainable national income can be calculated by imposing these standards on the economic activity model, see Sections 9.9 and 10.13.

Generally, limits derived for different environmental problems (or themes) have to be tuned to each other in order to minimise combinatorial (synergetic) effects. They probably cannot be avoided completely and this is not necessary either, as long as environmental sustainability is (likely to be) warranted. Two kinds of combinatorial effects prevail.

The first effect is the way in which land use influences the admissible concentration levels. Whatever conditions to land use are put forward as a environmental sustainability standard, areas used for different purposes impose different bounds on the concentrations of various substances in air, local soil and local surface waters. If the processes determining the concentrations vary on roughly the same spatial scale as the adopted environmentally sustainable land use pattern, and the emissions locations may be changed on this scale, the nation-wide environmentally sustainable emission standards may be derived for less strict levels than would be found otherwise. This is the case for acidifying, eutrophicating, hazardous and some other substances in soil and surface waters. Hazardous substances, however, are treated in another way in this study. It is assumed that sustainability is warranted if the sustainable concentration limits of these substances are exceeded in only 10% of the soils or surface waters (on area basis) nation-wide. This assumption is not validated and may constitute a source of uncertainty.

Secondly, the concentration levels of different substances influence each other's effects on the health and survival of species, including humans. Concentrations of hazardous substances therefore have to comply with so-called negligible risk levels instead of the less strict but scientifically better underpinned maximum permissible levels, which are intended for single substances only (Crommentuin et al., 1997). Other interactions belonging to this category occurs between nitrogen and phosphorus nutrients limiting primary production on land or in water, and between the factors limiting ozone formation in the air, more specifically NOx and volatile organic compounds. These cases are discussed in the relevant sections of Appendix 21.

10.8 *Environmental standards are objective (intersubjective)*

We hold that environmental sustainability standards can be scientifically established. See Hueting et al. (1992) and Hueting and Reijnders (1998) for several examples and Bosch (1994), De Boer and Bosch (1995) and Dellink and Van der Woerd (1997) for a number of quantified standards. Thus environmental sustainability, defined as the situation in which vital environmental functions remain available ad infinitum, is an objective concept, to the extent that the natural sciences can be deemed objective (Hueting and Reijnders, 1998). As Costanza and Patten (1995) and Hueting and Reijnders (1998) have argued, in the context of the interaction between human activity (loosely referred to as 'the economy') and the environment, criteria for environmental sustainability are to be regarded as assumptions. Scientifically, therefore, it can only be established ex post whether the measures taken to fulfil these criteria, or standards, were indeed adequate.

As argued earlier, the availability of environmental functions depends on the quality, quantity and spatial aspects of the state of the environment (or (bio)physical surroundings), which is after all the vehicle or carrier of these functions. Environmental functions remain available for as long as this state remains intact. Environmental sustainability standards can thus relate to the qualitative, quantitative and spatial aspects of the biophysical surroundings, and environmental models are then used to translate these standards into standards for human activities: emission or withdrawal of substances, heat, species, etc. into or from the environment, for example, or land use, or use of raw materials such as crude oil or copper. State variables are related to pressure variables using environmental models. The elimination measures reduce the pressure variables to the permitted or environmentally sustainable level of environmental burdening. In doing so, a distinction is made between renewable and essentially non-renewable (i.e. very slowly forming) resources.

Environmental sustainability aims to maintain the functions of the environment provided by nature. As rightly pointed out by Goodland (1995), this definition of environmental sustainability goes beyond 'sustainable yield', a notion that is current in fishery and forestry circles. Environmental sustainability applies to aggregate natural resources, not just to a few species of fish or timber trees (Goodland, 1995). In the case of forestry, for instance, it includes biodiversity, ecosystem integrity, water source and water moderation values and contributions to geochemical cycles (including the carbon cycle) and climate. Apart from this, a level can be established above which a (plant or animal) species can be harvested sustainably (see below). Thus there is obviously a level, defined as a number of individuals of a species, below which the species is threatened with extinction; arriving below that level is unsustainable, remaining above that level is sustainable. Together with the condition that harvesting a species should not disrupt the ecosystem of which it forms a part (see Odum, 1971), this yields the environmental sustainability standard for the species.

10.9 *Natural regeneration*

In deriving environmental sustainability standards, we have taken as the basic point of departure the natural regeneration capacity of the environment: as long as this remains intact, environmental functions will remain available. The following examples illustrate how this quantity and the acceptable, i.e. environmentally sustainable burden can be derived. It can, for instance, be established that the rate of erosion of topsoil may not exceed the rate of formation of such soil due to weathering. Similar consumption standards can be derived for other natural resources. With respect to how environmental sustainability relates to species, then, the standard holds that the rate of human-induced extinction should not exceed the rate at which new species come into existence. This boils down to preserving all the species still alive today, for it is assumed that during the past several thousand years conditions have been such that, leaving aside drastic human intervention for the moment, the number of new species must certainly have at least equalled the number of species lost to extinction (Raup, 1986; Hawksworth, 1995). However, in contrast to the situation prior to human intervention, the rate at which natural species are becoming extinct is today at least a factor 10,000 higher than the rate at which new species are evolving (Raup, 1986). In the absence of drastic human intervention, the quantity and quality of renewable natural resources such as groundwater or biomass (including wood) generally show a substantial degree of constancy. In the absence of human intervention, environmental resources are thus characterised by a substantial degree of constancy or even increase.

10.10 *Allocation over countries*

If an environmental problem exceeds the national scale, the sustainability standard for the environmental pressure related to the problem is converted to a sustainability standard on national scale. Given the assumed absolute and general preference for environmental sustainability, the pressure reduction measures are distributed optimally among the countries involved in the environmental problem, if total costs are minimal, and thus if marginal abatement costs are equal in the countries involved. The cost effectiveness curves for the environmental problem are specific for a country, but are generally not known in each country. It is therefore assumed that the countries within the area affected by the environmental problem reduce their environmental pressure proportionally, that is, proportional to their contributions to the total environmental pressure. Because this approach is suboptimal, the standard for a country thus calculated might be too strict or too mild. Both the cost-effective solution as the approximation employed here will probably result in comparable emission reductions domestic and abroad. The influence of border crossing transport of substances through the environment on the state of the environment, and thereby on the environmental sustainability standard for the pressure, is therefore neglected. It is recommended to perform a sensitivity analysis on the importance of this assumption.

10.11 *Overview of the discussion in the Appendix*

The derivation of the standards is discussed in Appendix 21. **Table 6** summarises the standards found for all considered types of use of the environment in the Netherlands. In all calculations on eSNI reported here, these same standards have been used. The general documentation has been included in Verbruggen (ed) (2000), and in underlying reports by Bosch (1994) and De Boer (2003, 2004abc).

Table 6. Sustainability standards for the Netherlands used in this study compared to the involved environmental pressure in the year 1990

Environmental problem	*Standard*	*Use in 1990*	*Unit*
Acidification	10.0	38.4	billion Aeq/year
Climate change	53.3	251.0	billion kg CO_2-eq/year
Dehydration	100	100	% affected area recovered
Depletion of the ozone layer	0.6	10.4	million kg CFC11-eq/year
Eutrophication	128	312	million Eeq/year
Fine particles in air	20	44	million kg PM10/year
Fossil fuel depletion	1223	2265	PJ/year
Photochemical smog formation	240	440	million kg NMVOS/year
Soil contamination	100	100	% locations purified
Toxic substances in surface water	73.5	194.3	billion kg 1,4-DCB-eq/year

P = peta = 10^{15}, billion = 10^9, Aeq = acidification equivalent = 1 mole potential acid, as H^+, Eeq = eutrophication equivalent = 1 kg P = 0,1 kg N, PM10 = fraction of fine particles with diameter less than 10 µm, NMVOS = non-methane volatile organic substances, 1,4-DCB = 1,4-dichlorobenzene = aquatic ecotoxicity potential (AETP)

10.12 *Preventing double counting*

Emissions of fluoridised organics such as chlorofluorocarbons (CFC's) and fluorocarbons (HFC's) contribute to both climate change and depletion of the ozone layer. In the eSNI calculation, the emissions of these substances are therefore limited by sustainability standards for both effects. Double counting was prevented by correcting the emissions before doing the cost minimisation for the year 1990 (Verbruggen, 2000). For the years 1995, 2000 and 2005 this safeguarding approach was not discussed in the report anymore, because the emissions of these substances were almost, respectively fully, eliminated.

The emission of nitrogen dioxide (NO_2) in the atmosphere contributes, after precipitation, to both acidification and eutrophication of soils. This emission is limited by the two concerning standards. Partial double counting of the elimination costs was not prevented in this case. In 2005 the standard for eutrophication was reached, so the error of double counting occurred only in earlier years.

In the calculation of eSNI, IVM made sure that there was no double counting in the reduction of CO_2 emissions and the depletion of fossil fuels.

10.13 *Description of the eSNI model as used for the Netherlands*

The results for eSNI for the Netherlands as presented in Section 1.3 were obtained by the team at IVM. Gerlagh et al. (2000, 2002) and Dellink & Hofkes (2008) discuss the model that they developed. The modelling was an exercise in comparative statics, with an instantaneous imposition of environmental sustainability without looking into the dynamics of a possible transition path. For the standard economy, they took the tax incidence model that was originally developed by Keller (1980) and also used in the tax incidence study CBS Statistics Netherlands (1990). The Keller *TaxInc* model is an Applied General Equilibrium (AGE) model that employs nested Constant Elasticity of Substitution (CES) functions for both consumer utility and production functions. The IVM team extended this into the "SNI-AGE" model bij including substitution between pollution and abatement, as based on the abatement cost curves for the various environmental themes, and using a particular procedure to calibrate these new substitution elasticities. The model has 27 sectors and 9 abatement issues. The issue of depletion of non-renewable fossil fuels was excluded, see Verbruggen (ed) (2000: 157):

> "The technical and volume measures which are available to meet the fossil fuel sustainability standard are largely a duplication of those used to achieve the greenhouse effect sustainability standard i.e. the substitution of renewable for non-renewable energy sources and the reduction of activities which use fossil fuels. To include the cost of meeting both standards in the calculation of SNI would result in significant double counting. The extent to which these two sustainability standards overlap can be examined by comparing the initial estimates of the necessary reductions in fossil fuel use under each standard. The fossil fuel sustainability standard is estimated to require a reduction in fossil fuel use to 64% of its 1990 levels, whereas the greenhouse effect standard requires a reduction to a little less than 25% of 1990 levels. [ftnt] This suggests that including the fossil fuel sustainability standard in the model will not greatly alter the current results."

For this present book, there is no need to further look into the specifics of this model, and the reader is referred to the mentioned references.

Here it is relevant to recall the following observation by the IVM team. The *TaxInc* model was estimated with data that had variation over a limited range over the actual development of the economy. The model had been used for scenario analyses with a similar range, for example changes of a few percentages of national income. The eSNI exercise required changes even in the range of 50% of national income. Thus the behavioural equations were used far outside of the usual range for the uncertainty of the estimates. This increased uncertainty cannot be avoided because of the nature of the exercise, and it remains important to be aware of it.

For example, the elasticities adopted from the original Keller study had the particular effect in the eSNI calculation that the government sector shrunk while it would seem likely that an economy that gets closer to environmental sustainability would see a larger government sector in order to manage the additional regulations. It is advisable to better calibrate for such effects. Nevertheless, the modelling exercise provided much details about the various sectors of the economy and the implied shadow prices for their sectoral output, that are interesting by themselves, and that have not been restated in this present book.

Another comment is that the IVM team developed a scenario that did not implement sustainability, see Section 11.7 about the "Exclusively-NL scenario".

10.14 *Another key result of the calculation of eSNI for the Netherlands*

The outcomes of Verbruggen (ed) (2000) can also be characterised in a graph showing the decrease of income as the emission standards are approached step by step, see **Figure 9**. In the graph, the origin has "Business as Usual" (BaU).

Figure 9. Results per production factor

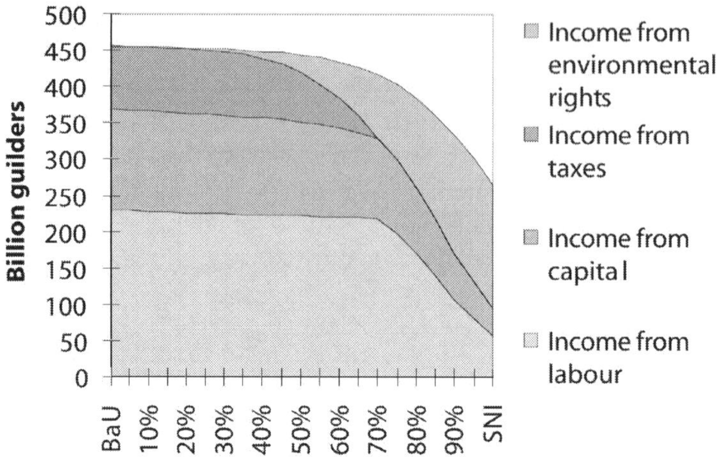

In the relatively flat segment, the technical emission reduction measures eliminate about 75% of the total non-sustainable use of the environment against about 10% of national income. The rest of the required emission reduction is achieved at major costs. All in all national income drops with 47% in this variant, and the correctly calculated eSNI is even 56% lower than the standard national income in 1990. The almost linear rightmost part indicates that direct shifts between production activities dominate here. The graph also gives some insight in the major components of national income and how they change towards sustainability.

10.15 *Some considerations for modelling in general*

The choice of the model depends upon various considerations. The IVM team used the Keller model because CBS had access to it. With more involvement by the Central Planning Bureau (CPB), the CPB might propose to use one of its own (larger) models and extend it with the feedbacks from the environment. For the World Bank, who might want to make models for more than 100 countries, it might be a consideration to impose some uniform structure rather than use the models that have been developed by the countries themselves.

In theory we need a reliable model of the relevant production, consumption and environmental processes. The model takes care of the interactions, the resulting volume and price changes and consequently maximises national income under environmental sustainability. The interactions in production and consumption are taken care of by production functions and utility or welfare functions (for consumption and environment), at least one function per activity and each function with multiple inputs. The uses of the environment, or the possibilities to do so, appear in both the production and the welfare functions. The model simulates the changes of stock and flow variables in the economy and the environment in their mutual dependence. In other words, the preferred model is dynamic. It has time dependent solutions, which form paths of the development of the state of production and environment. With such a rich model we could trace both welfare and the volume of national income as a measure of production and consumption. It appears to be important to have these two variables available in the modelling exercise because they provide information about the behaviour of the economy and the enviroment along the path. Hueting & De Boer (2001b) discuss a hypothetical path using such a dynamic model.

Generally, a sufficiently accurate integral economic-environmental model is so large and complex that a sustainable solution may not be found for all practical purposes. Therefore, we may suggest to approximate the environmentally sustainable path by using a set of models that co-operate in a sequential fashion, without the mutual feedback that would make the model collection generally valid. Importantly: the case of environmentally sustainable development allows this simplification without causing a large error. The economic activities of production and consumption are represented in one model, and additional models constructed for each of the various environmental problem areas. Ideally, information should then be transferred back and forth between the models in a process of iterative exchange. To avoid tedious iterations with the total model set, these interactions may be reduced to one-way information flows, i.e. to one-time operation of each model for a given period. This means that the overall optimum, i.e. the optimal path, can be calculated only approximately, as opposed to the case with the theoretical comprehensive model.

It seems feasible to achieve a reasonable approximation by assuming that the optimal function levels of the theoretical model can be formulated in words and/or roughly quantified. It may further be assumed that the levels of the state variables of the environment (quantities, qualities such as concentrations, space) corresponding to the assumed optimal function levels can be estimated, at least to within some range, on the basis of expert opinion or by using appropriate standards for the state of the environment. These standards are then entered as constraints in the model of each environmental problem, and standards for allowable environmental use or pressure (emissions and so on) are then derived by iteration. These pressure standards may be functions of time. However, in some cases these might be constant levels, independent of time. The standards are then entered as constraints in the economic model. In this step it is decided which technical measures, which direct production shifts and which levels of production shrinkage and population reduction are to be taken to arrive at the standards and, subsequently, what national income results from these actions at the time of interest, i.e. the year of investigation.

10.16 *For a future that has feedback by policy making*

The empirical results for eSNI for the Netherlands have been given for intervals of five years, see Section 1.3 for the proof of concept. The new proposal is that eSNI gets calculated annually, so that the distance eΔ = NI – eSNI and soon also eΔ-A can become part of the annual policy making process. A more frequent calculation will also affect the process of calculating eSNI, see **Figure 10**. The stages are characterised by boxes, connected by data flows, in a *block scheme*. The data flowing through the scheme are variables that depend on the year of calculation. The boxes drawn with solid sides represent the main steps of the calculation, while the box on policy making is drawn with dotted sides.

Figure 10. Block scheme with feedback per period

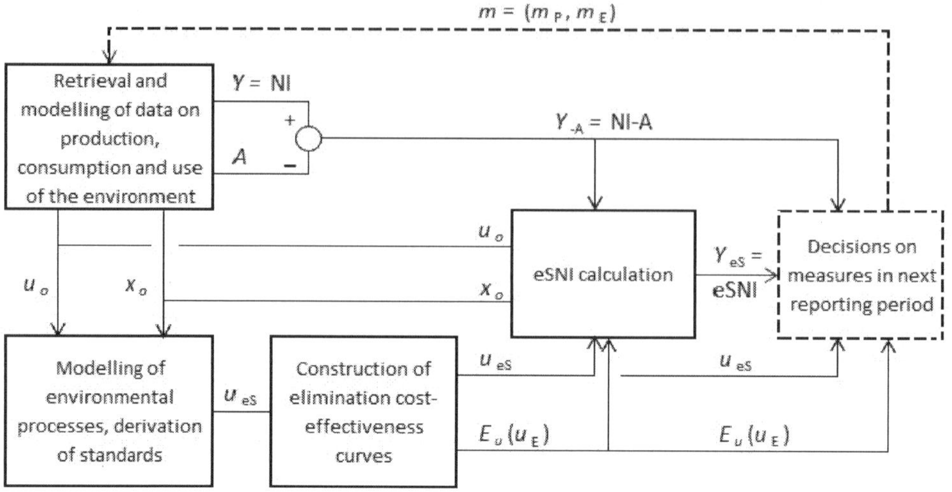

For each year of calculation, the elimination cost curves must be updated, for example because of shifting technology, exhaustion of measures, changes in the actual use of the environment. The elimination cost curves by definition sort the measures by cost-effectiveness. Policy makers might prefer another selection. For a statistical exercise there is no influence by policy making other than such decisions in the past. For a planning exercise, if policy making selects particular measures, potentially deviating from cost-effectiveness, then each period the elimination cost curves must be constructed anew also for this reason, also taking into account that measures can no longer be used when they are exhausted.

Part 4. Misunderstandings and comparisons

11. *Objections based upon misunderstandings*

11.1 *Abstract*

This chapter mainly refers to Hueting (2001d) "Rejoinders", and Colignatus (2008, 2009a, 2019c) "The Old Man and the eSNI".

11.2 *Other authors in Van Ierland et al. (2001)*

Hueting (2001d) has rejoinders to other authors in Van Ierland et al. (2001), the 1999 symposium book, namely Paul Ekins, Herman Daly, Richard Norgaard, Astrid Scholz, Sarah Fleisher Trainor, Wilfrid Beckerman, Kirk Hamilton, Giles Atkinson, Sylvie Faucheux, Martin O'Connor, David Pearce, Robert Goodland and Salah el Serafy. It is advised to read these rejoinders for better understanding of eSNI, e.g. for misunderstanding at the World Bank.

Herman Daly (2007), his selection of essays, also reprints his contribution to the Hueting symposium *"Roefie Hueting's perpendicular "demand curve" and the issue of objective value"*, yet he does not refer to Hueting's rejoinder to this article.

11.3 *The Old Man and the eSNI*

Colignatus (2008, 2009a, 2019c) "The Old Man and the eSNI" is an independent discussion also based upon interviews with Hueting. It provides an overview of the advances but also the misunderstandings and adversity. A key comment is, p32:

> "The fragmentation of knowledge may cause perverse effects. To understand the issue of eSNI requires 100% clarity on the subject, and, while many arrive at 90%, each researcher misses a different 10%, and each 10% may be sufficient for the issue to be rejected."

11.4 *Different research communities*

There are different research communities with different paradigms that play into misunderstandings, see Colignatus (2008, 2009a, 2019c).

- Since the 1970s there is a growing gap between the academia and the economists working within governance institutes like the statistical agencies and the planning bureaus. Before 1970 much of this work at governance institutes was in the R&D stage so that academics had a prime contribution, also resulting into Nobel Prizes for Frisch, Tinbergen, Kuznets, Hicks, Leontief, Myrdal, Meade and Stone who had been working on National Accounting and planning. Eventually the academia tended to regard this work as routine and switched to other frontiers. The Nobel Prize 2018 for William Nordhaus "for integrating climate change into long-run macroeconomic analysis" is a late recognition of work done since 1971, basically because the world only now is alerted to the problem by changing weather patterns, but also because Nordhaus has been a professor at the academia, which community is regarded as the guardian of science. While the scientific institutes of governance tend to check what happens at the academia, the academia do not tend to show an interest in return.

- The fields of economics and ecology are quite different, and for a long while policy making relied upon Ministries with those different flavours, often dominated by fellow economists who had no interest in the ecology. Policy makers are making amends only because people and voters can observe nowadays that weather conditions are worsening.
- The research community around the journal *Ecological Economics* is much influenced by thermodynamics by Nicholas Georgescu-Roegen and the application of entropy to economic issues. This approach would be relevant undoubtedly for the physics side of those issues, but would tend to miss out on neoclassical economics and the theory of economic welfare.
- Statisticians who focus on the past might have difficulty in understanding how environmental sustainability, that deals with the future, might be relevant for a statistical observation about the past.
- Accounting of national wealth started with William Petty (1623-1687) but only economic theory provided a frame of reference to understand what the figures mean. Statisticians who have forgotten about this economic framework and who restrict their work to tallying items and financial records would not quite know what they are actually doing in terms of theory, but take pride in the objectivity of their tallies.
- However, compare the analogy of financial products that might be too complex for policy makers and consumers, so that banks have stewardship. Such stewardship also holds for the ethics of science and statistics. A researcher cannot just present the outside world with a figure and leave it to the responsibility of others what they do with it. It is part and parcel of the scientific ethic that one clarifies what the figure represents, and that one tries to protect users from confusion. (For example, CBS (2018) provides explanations by the "Monitor Broad Welfare" but the national accounts still use the term "economic growth" for production growth, which is a wrong use of terms.)

11.5 *El Serafy on (over-) correction*

El Serafy (2013) supports Hueting's work on environmental functions but rejects eSNI. El Serafy has been a dear friend, and a kindred spirit in economics. In memory of El Serafy's involvement and judgement his message to Hueting from 2007 may be printed here. [32]

> "El Serafy to Hueting 2007-12-24:
>
> Merry Christmas, Roefie and Erna, and a very happy new year full of joy and good health to you both.
>
> Don't be discouraged Roefie. Not only are you the godfather of the whole topic, but actually its actual father, the one who directed attention to the 'new scarcity' while we were all slumbering. And your paper with Tinbergen had the felicitous section heading: "Society is Steering by the Wrong Compass", stressing the inadequacy of the traditionally estimated GNP and GDP. Unfortunately the younger generation are either shallow,

[32] http://www.sni-hueting.info/NL/Documentatie/2008-01-03-Brief-aan-Pronk-Wijffels-bekort.pdf

ignorant, or both. But the time will come when your invaluable contributions will be recalled.

The whole spurious initiative of 'genuine savings' has been demolished, among others, by my friend Eric Neumayer of the London School of Economics, and the World Bank in its ignorance has nothing better to offer [...] But the Bank has diminished in importance, and no better institution or group has come forward! Be patient Roefie, your record of contributions is safe and nobody can take it away.

With every good wish Roefie,
From Salah (and Susan)"

Hueting (1989b) and Tinbergen & Hueting (1991) – reproduced in Appendix 15 – used the expression "to correct NI". It would have been better to have said "to correct *the use of* NI". The term "correction" was borrowed from the tradition to continuously improve the relevance and accuracy of the System of National Accounts (SNA). However, these mentioned publications also compared NI and eSNI, and looked at their distance. Thus NI is not actually corrected itself but its *use* is corrected.

The calculation of eSNI does not involve a direct deduction of the decline of natural resource stocks from the conventional measures of national income – or any other correction of national income. The conventional measures (GDP, GNP and associated magnitudes) are calculated under the assumption that prices reflect collective preferences, and eSNI is calculated under the assumption of a collective preference for environmental sustainability, i.e. the present and future availability of vital environmental functions. The intention is to see whether the gap between eSNI and NI is increasing or not.

El Serafy (2001:190) correctly states:

"We should keep in mind that Hueting would leave the conventional estimates of income unaltered, but would produce alternative estimates intended to show the gap between these and the conventional numbers."

El Serafy (2013) quotes the publications on environmentally sustainable national income (eSNI) several times correctly and approvingly. His criticism on eSNI is mostly indirect and targeted at his definition of "strong" sustainability in general. On p164 he expresses criticism also directly at eSNI:

"To make matters worse some ardent environmentalists also joined the debate on the wrong side. They suspected ′weak sustainability′and preferred a stronger version. As I have argued previously the ′weak sustainability′ associated with the user-cost method is the appropriate level of sustainability that is compatible with national accounting. But its avowed 'weakness' branded it in the eyes of some adversaries as inferior to an ostensibly stronger sustainability. Some environmentalists seem to like the 'over-correction' that 'strong sustainability' would bring to the accounts, imagining that it must be better for environmental awareness than an accounting approach that would produce less pronounced adjustments. Using strong sustainability for greening the national accounts would deduct the *entire* decline in natural resource stocks from the conventional estimate of the flow accounts (GDP, GNP and associated magnitudes). Moreover, such adjustments to the net product if made would be entombed in extraneous 'satellite' accounts. It is interesting to note that in the green accounting literature supporters of this over-correction include Hueting (1989) (...)" [33]

Given El Serafy's earlier statement in 2001 that expressed his understanding that Hueting compares NI and eSNI, this statement that Hueting would "correct" and then also "over-correct" NI must partly be a victim of Hueting's choice of words around 1990. Neither does eSNI deduct the *entire* decline in natural resource stocks. However, on content there is quite some difference between eSNI and El Serafy's user-cost method, and this is discussed in Section 12.4.

However, other authors may indeed erroneously think that Hueting wants to *correct* NI, while the proper idea is to compare NI and eSNI, and look at the gap.

11.6 *Uncertainty, disputability and invalidity* [34]

There is a distinction between the error in measurement of a variable (its uncertainty) and the (in)validity of using it for a particular purpose, see **Figure 11.**

Looking at the range of uncertainty around eSNI (its box) is not irrelevant, see Van Tuinen (2009) on disputability generated by such uncertainty. Looking at the invalidity of NI with respect to environmental sustainability (the oval, also eΔ) is much more important.

Figure 11. Uncertainty and invalidity on NI and eSNI

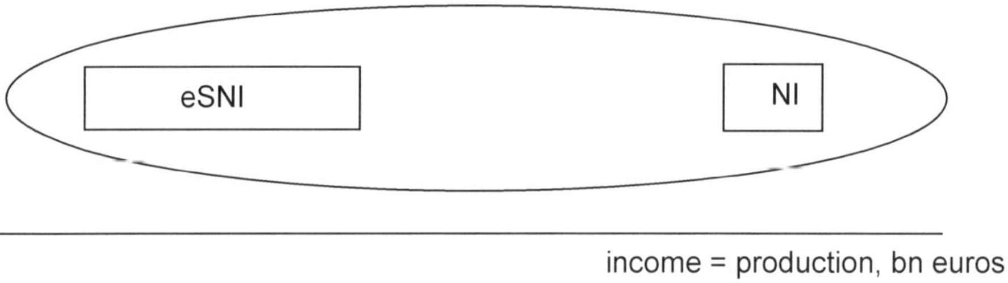

Legend:

NI and eSNI use the same raw data but account differently
NI = national income
eSNI = environmentally sustainable national income
boxes = *horizontal* ranges of error or uncertainty in measurement
boxes around NI and eSNI: technical issues around these definitions
oval, eΔ: (i) NI is invalidly called income if preferences are for environmental sustainability, (ii) eSNI is only part of income if preferences are not for environmental sustainability.

[33] Hueting (1989) is (1989b), the World Bank paper.

[34] Adapted from Colignatus (2019) and approved by the authors.

11.7 *The Exclusively-NL scenario*

The results in **Table 1** and **Figure 1** are outcomes of work done by IVM.

Environmental sustainability per definition pertains to the entire world. eSNI is mainly about global problems such as diversity and climate. Standards for the Netherlands are therefore derived from global standards. IVM made one study that properly imposed the standards on the world, including the Netherlands. However, IVM called this a "variant" and also made another "variant", for which it claimed that the standards applied to the whole world, but in which *world prices remained the same* while only the prices in the Netherlands changed. However, it is impossible to attain environmental sustainability without changing price ratios. Therefore this "variant" boils down to an "Exclusively the Netherlands scenario" (Exclusively-NL). In summary, IVM stated that it wanted to avoid a unilateral policy but still modelled it. This is a misconception and misrepresentation of the definition of eSNI, and generating a pseudo-eSNI. Hueting rejected this "scenario" from the start. Van Tuinen (CBS) called it "nonsense". [35]

This IVM confusion and misrepresentation was repeated uncritically by PBL in its report to the World Bank WAVES project, Oosterhuis et al. (2016).

Remarkably, in 2018 the IVM project leader Verbruggen (2018:89) contradicts his earlier explanation from 2000: [36]

> "Our calculations showed that one-third to one-quarter of standard national income must be sacrificed if the Netherlands would become sustainable by itself alone, and roughly half if the rest of the world were to produce sustainably too (Gerlagh et al. 2002; Dellink and Hofkes 2008)."

In 2000 the IVM team stated that both "variants" imposed sustainability standards so that both variants had world sustainability: the only distinction would be with respect to prices. In 2018 Verbruggen acknowledges that in one variant "the Netherlands would become sustainable *by itself alone*". The latter contradicts the first. Unfortunately, this remains a pure contradiction only. When queried in 2019 for the purpose of this present book, Verbruggen and none of the IVM team retracted the "variant" that contains the misconception. Thus they continue mispresenting eSNI as inaccurately defined and more uncertain than it is.

11.8 *Blindness to eΔ too*

Verbruggen (2018) states about his research findings on eSNI: [37]

> "But policymakers and politicians could not do anything with it. Too hypothetical, too far from reality. Nobody can imagine sustainable development with a halved income. "

---

[35] See Colignatus (2019c) or the last page of http://www.sni-hueting.info/NL/Documentatie/2005-05-31-Brief-JvdBergh-PrijsverhoudingBuitenland.pdf

[36] Dutch: "Onze berekeningen toonden aan dat van het gewone nationaal inkomen een derde tot een kwart moet worden opgeofferd, als Nederland alleen duurzaam wordt, en ruwweg de helft als de rest van de wereld ook duurzaam zou gaan produceren (Gerlagh et al.2002; Dellink en Hofkes 2008)."

[37] Dutch: "Maar beleidmakers en politici konden er niets mee. Te hypothetisch, te ver af van de werkelijkheid. Niemand kan zich een duurzame ontwikkeling voorstellen bij een gehalveerd inkomen."

The IVM team didn't properly explain that the focus is on eΔ = NI – eSNI and not on eSNI itself or the ratio eSNI / NI. The understanding about eSNI by Dutch members of parliament was not helped by the "explanation" given by the IVM team for the Exclusively-NL scenario, see former section. It remains curious that the research project wasn't put in the hands of Hueting but into the hands of a team who clearly didn't understand the intention of eSNI and could not explain it. The first calculation of eΔ for 1990 was only informative about the scale of the problem. Variants might have been considered, i.e. how eΔ depends upon policy measures, but the present research concerns statistics and not policy analysis. The true results came over time, so that the path of eΔ over time could be monitored, and related to its causes.

11.9 *Heertje 2006 and / or 2014*

We already referred to Heertje (2006) for his rejection of the notion of asymmetric bookkeeping. For the present purposes, it is useful to refer to the following quote (our translation) in Heertje (2014): [38]

> "In this context, reference is made to the work of Roefie Hueting, who has made a very deserving contribution to the field in question. He proposed correcting national income, regarded as a welfare indicator, for the sacrifices made for the purpose of limiting environmental damage. His proposal overlooks the insight that reducing the damage apparently has a positive welfare effect that comes from the accompanied earning of income. He also overlooks the fact that the reduction of damage also has negative external effects (Hueting, 1974)."

Heertje refers to Hueting (1974a, 1980) that does not yet contain eSNI. The statistical correction, which that book achieves, only concerns asymmetric bookkeeping, see Chapter 7 above. The statistical method for correcting asymmetry consists of shifting entries from one place to another. This only involves accounting (taking costs as *costs* indeed) and does not involve assumptions about behaviour from earning income and spending this on additional consumption. Thus Heertje mistakes mere accounting for a discussion about behaviour. However, for eSNI we concur with him that interactions and external effects must be included and internalised, as we have done by proposing to use an economic model, and as has been done by the IVM team. For eSNI this still remains a statistical method, leaves total NI unaffected, and only affects the decomposition of NI = eSNI + eΔ. For the term "correcting", see above section. Finally, again, we do not regard NI as a welfare indicator but as a factor that influences welfare.

---

[38] Dutch readers would look at this text in the 2014 ebook: "In dit verband wordt verwezen naar het werk van Roefie Hueting die zich op het onderhavige terrein zeer verdienstelijk heeft gemaakt. Hij heeft voorgesteld het nationaal inkomen als welvaartsindicator te corrigeren voor de offers die worden gebracht met het oog op het beperken van de milieuschade. Zijn voorstel miskent het inzicht dat het terugdringen van de schade blijkbaar een positief welvaartseffect heeft dat gepaard gaat met inkomensvorming. Verder ziet hij over het hoofd dat schadebeperking ook weer negatieve externe effecten heeft (Hueting, 1974)."

11.10 *Opschoor's Environmental (Utilisation) Space (Ecospace) 1987*

Opschoor (1987) adopted the term "environmental utilisation space", [39] referring to Siebert (1982), and translating what he regarded as a more theoretical notion into something for *practical policy making*. Currently Opschoor uses the term "ecospace". Mazijn (ed) (2000) looked at various authors who explicitly defined the term "environmental (utilisation) space". They diagnosed that those definitions basically have the same content. Mazijn cum suis quote the definition of "environmental space" by Opschoor 1995 in a Dutch article: "the possibilities that nature and the environment provide to society for present utilisation without restricting future options for usage". In English, Opschoor (1995) provides this definition, using the term "steady state" instead of "sustainability":

> "[Ecospace is:] The locus of all feasible combinations of environmental services that represent steady states in terms of levels of relevant environmental quality and stocks of renewable resources. It is a dynamic "utilisation possibilities frontier" comparable with the production possibilities frontier in standard welfare economics."

This notion of ecospace or environmental space 1987 thus focuses upon a single element in Hueting's definition of eSNI 1986b. For the term "functions", Opschoor (1995) refers to R.S. (Dolf) de Groot 1992 instead of Hueting 1974a (while De Groot refers to Hueting).

In **Figure 2** on page 28 (that uses comparative statics) the proper ecospace or environmental (utilisation) space is the rectangular area between the origin and point S, provided that one indeed adopts the given environmental standards for sustainability and the assumption on technology for eSNI. Other assumptions would generate other spaces. A steady state or sustainable space properly seen is *not* the Production Possibility Frontier (PPF) through point S, because the points on the PPF other than S are not environmentally sustainable. Thus the ecospace cannot be compared *directly* with the PPF in standard welfare economics.

For *practical policy making* only point S is relevant, and the other points of this ecospace (rectangular area) are suboptimal and too restrictive. In other words, when we are in a situation that is so inoptimal that the imposition of standards for vital environmental functions causes them to be binding, then it is dubious to suggest that the *practical* ecospace would be larger than this single point S. The relevant discussion would be about the derivation of the standards, that namely provide the empirical definition of environmental sustainability (steady state).

An environmental function comes with the notion of its limits (i.e. it is not suggested that the functions have no limits). In the early 1970s, Hueting (1974a, 1980) already referred to the purity or availability ("space") of the functions, and see there e.g. pages 14 and 144 for the search on (moral) limits and standards. In March 1986b Hueting presented the vertical demand curve, based upon the conditional hypothesis of preferences for environmental sustainability, and thus with the requirement to derive sustainability standards. Different assumptions create different environmental spaces (rectangles), provided that one can make sure that there are no restrictions to possibilities for future use.

---

[39] Dutch "milieugebruiksruimte". Dutch "ruimte" means space, area or volume.

It is instructive to consider the notion of "space" in general. An object that may take all possible positions and make all possible movements in *n* directions is situated in a *n*-dimensional space, and conversely. Semantically, *space* and *possibility of position and movement* are identical. Thus, semantically, the environmental functions (possible uses), when restricted to environmental sustainability, are identical to the environmental space. Thus we have only a different name for the same notion. The functions remain a more general concept since they also allow the description of unsustainable use.

Mazijn cum suis did not mention the identity of the notions. They noted the reference to Hueting (1974a, 1980), but they did not look at the semantics of the issue. Hueting did not write about a definition for the term "environmental space". Apparently for that reason, Mazijn cum suis did not consider environmental functions and their application to environmental sustainability as a possible definition: but semantically and analytically these approaches are identical.

At this moment of writing, it is still not clear to the present authors why Opschoor in 1987-2019 did not see the identical meaning of his term of "environmental space" and Hueting's definition of environmental functions with the inclusion since 1986 of the standards for environmental sustainability, and why there apparently has been so little effort on his part to discuss and refer to our research on eSNI. Since Opschoor is at the VU and the IVM team is at the VU, Opschoor was asked by De Boer, Hueting and Sigmond (2008), and again in January 2019 for the purpose of this book, to consider helping to resolve the issue of the Exclusively-NL scenario but has declined to do so.

11.11 *Assumption on preferences versus subjectivity (colloquium)*

At a colloquium in 2013 at the Dutch Ministry of Economic Affairs, at the occasion of the retirement of Roeland Bosch, Hans Opschoor stated (as recorded in the report, our translation):

> "He (Opschoor) understands that according to Hueting the valuation of the availability or the loss of environmental functions is impossible in most cases, but that monetarisation *is* possible under one or some assumptions of preferences. However, politicians and the public have different conceptions about sustainability. When you ask around you get different answers. He himself has the impression that many people find a rise in temperature of more than 2 degrees Celsius quite acceptable. This makes environmental sustainability a subjective concept." [40]

Hueting's answer at the colloquium was (our translation):

> "As stated many times before, you don't know whether or not there are preferences for the present and future availability of environmental functions, because you cannot measure them in most cases. However such a preference is rather probable, because of the following postulate that has not been challenged yet: (1) humans derive a part of the meaning of their existence from the company of others, (2) these others

[40] Translated from "Appendix 4. Kort verslag van het colloquium "Hoe meten we groene groei?" op 3 juni 2013 bij het Ministerie van Economische Zaken", see www.sni-hueting.info

include in any case their children and grandchildren, and (3) the prospect of a safer future is therefore a normal human need, and dimming of this prospect has a negative effect on welfare (Hueting 1987d). Environmentally sustainability is an objective concept and is defined as the condition that satisfies physical standards of sustainability. These standards are determined scientifically. When, for example, as in the sixties, fish are dying massively, then you don't ask politicians or the public what has to be done, but you ask this from a biologist or chemical engineer specialised in water management. When you are ill then you go to the medical doctor and not to a politician, do you? He refers to the articles that he wrote with Lucas Reijnders. [41]"

In that discussion, Bart de Boer and Henk van Tuinen recalled that also experts acknowledge margins of uncertainty in empirical estimates, also on standards for sustainability. Recognition of such margins is important. Yet eSNI would highlight the margin of uncertainty on economic welfare w.r.t. the standard measure of national income itself (though this is better seen as an issue of validity, see Section 11.6).

11.12 *Inside CBS Statistics Netherlands*

There is the book by De Vries et al. (ed) (1993) celebrating 50 years of National Accounts in the Netherlands. Hueting was head of the department of environmental statistics, was no staff member of the NA department, and was not requested to contribute to this book, while in 1991 the eSNI methodology had already been published as CBS Statistical Essays, M44. In his contribution to the CBS celebration book, Dr. Steven Keuning, then head of NA, wrote about eSNI. Hueting (2003b) mentions these points:

"(α) In his contribution to the CBS book "*The Value Added of National Accounting*", Steven Keuning first completely misrepresents eSNI. On this, he then bases six objections, all of which are wrong. But the most bizarre objection is: "This may lead to misleading policies: in the event of enormous damage which can be prevented or restored inexpensively, one is not encouraged to apply this measure precisely because it does little to improve 'green income'." In that one sentence Steven overlooks three essential properties of eSNI. (i) The measures are classified according to increasing costs per unit of environmental pressure avoided (see curve s in figure 3). (ii) Whether environmental damage is enormous is determined by the preferences (the curves d and d' in fig. 3). From this it follows (iii): the lower the costs, the higher (not the lower) eSNI, the smaller (not the greater) the distance to environmental sustainability and the greater (not the smaller) the incentive to take a measure. (By the way: family planning is one of the measures.) (β) On the authority of Steven's article "*The fiction of a green national income*" in Socialism and

[41] "Sustainability is an objective concept", *Ecological Economics,* 27(2) (1998b), 139-147, Dutch: "Duurzaamheid is een objectief begrip", *Economisch Statistische Berichten*, 4057 (1996), 425-427; "Uncertainty and sustainability", *Ecological Economics*, 29(1) (1999), 9-11, Dutch: "Duurzaamheid en preferenties", *Economisch Statistische Berichten*, 4062 (1996), 537-539.

> Democracy (9, 1996), Ferd Crone (PvdA) stated in the House of Commons on 23-10-96 that it is not possible to estimate an eSNI. When I spoke to Ferd about this, he said: "I find this such a pity. I thought that Steven also wrote on behalf of CBS and thus also on your behalf."

Hueting had these objections to this misrepresentation and course of events already at the time in 1993. Hueting (2003b)'s criticism of the misrepresentation by Keuning was also kept outside of the *liber amicorum* for Van Tuinen.

The report "The Old Man and the eSNI" shows both advance and adversity for the analysis of one of us. For CBS, it identifies misunderstandings at CBS with authors Henk van Tuinen, Steven Keuning, Mark de Haan, Frits Bos, Rutger Hoekstra, Jan-Pieter Smits, Sjoerd Schenau, Cor Graveland, Bram Edens, Maarten van Rossum, Frank Notten, Gerard Eding, and Tjark Tjin-A-Tsoi, and on occasion also Hueting and De Boer themselves.

11.13 *Retraction of a misconception in 2001 on statistics about reality* [42]

Authors may set up an argument that might seem convincing by verbal expression but we should be wary of the pitfalls of language.
De Haan, De Boer and Keuning (2001) state (our italics):

> "The manner of calculating green national incomes such as the eSNI was developed at IVM in collaboration with CBS Statistics Netherlands, on the basis of the work by Hueting [ftnt]. Statistics Netherlands takes the view that this has given a firm implementation to Hueting's ideas, but realizes at the same time that the outcomes are subject to large uncertainties because these are model calculations concerning a *situation that did not actually occur.* The main task of CBS is to *describe reality, as in the NAMEA system,* and, as an independent institute of knowledge, to provide clarification about the concepts, such as the limited value of actual national income as a welfare indicator and the possibilities and limitations of alternatives such as eSNI, and to support model simulations of the past and for the future." [43]

If current reality is not environmentally sustainable – *which above quote agrees with* – then the estimated distance eΔ-A = NI-A – eSNI accurately records, with some range of uncertainty, that it is *not,* and thus records an aspect of empirical reality – *which above quote does not agree with* (for NAMEA would give it).
The quote thus expresses an inconsistency.

---

[42] Adapted from Colignatus (2019) and approved by the authors.

[43] Dutch: "De berekeningswijze van groene nationale inkomens zoals het dni zijn bij het Instituut voor Milieuvraagstukken ontwikkeld in samenwerking met het CBS, op basis van het werk van Hueting [5]. Het CBS stelt zich op het standpunt dat daarmee een stevige uitwerking is gegeven van Hueting's gedachtegoed, maar realiseert zich tegelijk dat de uitkomsten met grote onzekerheden zijn behept omdat het hier gaat om modelberekeningen van een situatie die zich niet feitelijk heeft voorgedaan. Het CBS heeft vooral als taak om de werkelijkheid te beschrijven zoals in het NAMEA-systeem, om als onafhankelijk kennisinstituut tekst en uitleg te geven over de concepten, zoals over de beperkte waarde van het feitelijk nationaal inkomen als welvaartsindicator en de mogelijkheden en beperkingen van alternatieven zoals het dni, en om ondersteuning te bieden bij modelsimulaties over het verleden en voor de toekomst."

Remarkably, De Boer, who has been supporting Hueting in the implementation of eSNI, went along with this inconsistency in 2001. In this book, he withdraws this (participation in this article) as an error and oversight.

The discussion about sustainability requires a definition of sustainability. For environmental sustainability we can derive standards from the scientific literature. Those standards thus are statistical information too. We thus have the following identification of NI and eSNI:

- We can express NI as a weighted sum of the use of the environmental functions at current intensity, expressed in current market prices.
- We can express eSNI as a weighted sum of the standards, in shadow prices.

Current reality is environmentally unsustainable, measured by NI, but *how much unsustainable* is estimated by eΔ-A = NI-A – eSNI.

In above quote, De Haan, De Boer and Keuning (2001) claim with certainty that environmental sustainability did not occur. However, this is not really the point. The point is that we cannot know the *preferences* about this. The incomes NI and eSNI are true levels of income, conditional to assumptions on those preferences. NI is only income under the SNA assumption of "keeping capital intact" by adopting legal conventions on capital. This assumption has the ease of convention but is not reality per se. In reality, preferences might be quite different, and people might prefer to "keep natural resources intact". Thus, the quote above essentially misrepresents the argument, by hiding the uncertainty (in the preferences and their associated income level) and by presenting something as certain and factual (which is only one of the options).

11.14 *Focus on the SWF and "agrowth" with neglect of income* [44]

There is a wider movement in the world that wants to focus on welfare, which fits welfare economics. Some researchers in this movement seem to want to focus on welfare with a *deliberate neglect* of income. This however is not rational. The notion of income is important, and the distance eΔ = NI – eSNI relies upon two important applications of the notion of income. When a focus on welfare comes with a neglect of these incomes then the baby is thrown out with the bathwater.

Figure 2 in Section 1.10 is a reminder that the social welfare function (SWF) and the budget line (hyperplane) are related, e.g. under conditions that allow tangency. Some components in the budget line may have market prices and other ones may not be traded on the market and have shadow prices. While it makes sense to include the latter, this does not imply a neglect of the first. Given the close connection between SWF and the budget line in welfare economics, the idea to focus on the SWF with *deliberate neglect* of the budget line indicates that this suggestion does not derive from an understanding of welfare economics.

At VU and ICREA, Van den Bergh (2015) presents the "agrowth" approach, defined there on p6 as: *"Ignoring the GDP indicator means that we will be indifferent (neutral or "agnostic") about the desirability or undesirability of GDP growth."* However, there is a distinction between neutrality and indifference:

---

[44] Colignatus provided the draft for this Section which was approved by the authors. Colignatus (2019) Chapter 27 discusses that Van den Bergh in 1991-2019 referred to Hueting's work in incorrect manner and misrepresents it.

(i) Welfare economics is impartial or neutral w.r.t. GDP growth. There is no need for a new name like "agrowth" to express this impartiality or neutrality. It suffices to refer to welfare economics. (Then one must also explain about the connection between SWF and budget line. Van den Bergh apparently doesn't want to explain this connection because he wants to ignore income.)

(ii) Indifference is a position in utility and an expression of some preference. Such a position is no longer impartial or neutral. Calling for indifference is not economic science but social advocacy.

Related issues are:

(iii) Part of the problem with GDP growth is that it is often called "economic growth", which is an entirely different issue, see Section 1.11. It is better to *change this naming* (instead of suggesting to ignore something of which the name wrongly suggests that it would be desirable and cannot be ignored).

(iv) In other papers (see below), Van den Bergh has a tendency to present eSNI as an indicator of welfare (which it isn't) and then reject it because of its focus on the environment only and lack of inclusion of other aspects like happiness, income distribution and so on (while the actual analysis is on eΔ = NI – eSNI). Van den Bergh is a professor in environmental economics but blind to the *focus on the environment* in eΔ = NI – eSNI.

Van den Bergh (2005:504) states:

> "A correct economic welfare approach only regards changes as progress if they are accompanied by a sustainable use of the environment and nature. Hueting [1974a] realized this early on and his elaboration of a social welfare measure is based on precisely this insight." [45]

Issues are:

(1) It is false that "a correct economic welfare approach only regards changes as progress if they are accompanied by a sustainable use of the environment and nature." This is only a possible assumption. Hueting also mentioned an alternative assumption.

(2) Hueting (1974a) did not "realize" what Van den Bergh attributes to him.

(3) Hueting never presented a social welfare measure (or an "elaboration" of one). Hueting always explained that welfare differs from income, and that NI or eSNI may be only a factor that influences welfare.

(4) Hueting (1974a, 1980) presented NI-A and not eSNI. Hueting (1986b) presented eSNI. Both are measures of income and not of social welfare. The actual analysis results into a focus on eΔ and eΔ-A.

(5) Hueting since 1986 explains the relation between welfare and environmental sustainability by *conditionality* in the assumptions. He does not merely select one particular point of view (though at one moment he suggested that the Brundtland criterion could be seen as an expression of absolute preference).

---

[45] Dutch: "Een correcte economische welvaartsbenadering bestempelt veranderingen pas als vooruitgang, indien ze gepaard gaan met een duurzaam gebruik van milieu en natuur. Hueting (1974) heeft dit reeds vroeg ingezien en zijn uitwerking van een maatschappelijke welvaartsmaat is gebaseerd op precies dit inzicht."

In Pen et al. (2006), Van den Bergh states:

> "If GNP is replaced by GNP-corrections such as ISEW, GPI or Hueting's SNI, there is a risk that growth fetishism will focus on this sort of measures."

However, Hueting does not *replace* NI, and indicates that the distance between NI and eSNI is at issue. Van den Bergh also provides no evidence for such a risk of new growth fetishism. His reasoning is no other than the simplism that references to welfare must replace all references to income, and he suggests that this can be done consistently, while a welfare economist would have pointed to the connection between welfare and budget line (with the conditions for tangency, and to relevant techniques for the practice in statistics and econometrics – which are used within the analysis on NI, NI-A, eSNI, eΔ and eΔ-A).

Van den Bergh (2019:62) states correctly that GDP is production or income and no welfare and progress indicator. He then continues to discuss the deficiencies of GDP if it were to be treated as such an indicator of welfare. This argument has the structure of a counterfactual. He then mentions "alternative indicators", i.e. for persons who wrongly have taken GDP as an indicator of welfare. He then includes the "SNI by Hueting (1974)", but: (i) eSNI is not in the thesis of 1974, which Van den Bergh then likely did not read; and since 2007 Hueting uses "eSNI". (ii) eSNI is an indicator of income and not welfare. (iii) Van den Bergh doesn't use the format of a counterfactual here, and by implication he suggests that eSNI indeed has been proposed as an alternative indicator of welfare (which never was done so). (iv) He again overlooks that eSNI focuses on environmentally sustainable consumption and investment; and it is eΔ that focuses on the costs indeed.

Impartiality or neutrality with regard to outcomes about NI or eSNI would mean that one would provide the information, and not burk this information. Van den Bergh (2019:65) speaks of a "neutral or indifferent vision", that again allows for the role of the activist who influences preferences, and on p66 he wants less attention for NI, instead of better attention to both NI and eSNI and their distance.

Subsequently, Van den Bergh states that the rich countries have already reached a welfare ceiling, and he therefore expresses ex cathedra knowledge about the SWF, while welfare economics clarifies that one must provide good evidence for such a statement.

Van den Bergh (2017a) (in Nature Climate Change) claims to present a "review" of the literature but does not mention the work by Hueting or even Tinbergen & Hueting (1991). He speaks about "economic growth" as if it were a correct expression instead of a confusion. He creates an opposition between "economic growth" and "degrowth", which is basically a distortion, and then, instead of doing a *review,* changes the article into a presentation of "agrowth" as a third option, making the errors against welfare economics as discussed above.

PM. Dutch readers may benefit from the report about a discussion in 2005 between Hueting and Van den Bergh. [46]

[46] http://www.sni-hueting.info/NL/2005-Discussie-RH-JvdB.pdf

11.15 *The Dutch Monitor Broad Welfare 2019*

As stated in the Preface above, CBS Statistics Netherlands (2018), as editors of the Dutch "Monitor on Broad Welfare" (MBW) (actually a pleonasm), decided to refer to eSNI, which is the first official support of the measure, though CBS does not calculate it itself. At the presentation of this MBW in 2018, the minister of Economic Affairs already indicated that the MBW indicators – mostly taken from the recommendation of the Conference of European Statisticians (CES) – had to be integrated with the UN Sustainable Development Goals (SDGs). This has been achieved in 2019, but apparently with the effect that eSNI is no longer included in 2019.

The MBW is discussed better in this chapter on misunderstandings than in the following chapter on alternative indicators for the topic of eSNI. The MBW provides a set of various indicators, and thus it does not constitute a relevant indicator on the economy, production and the environment itself (which is the topic of next chapter).

We agree with the MBW that welfare is too complex to capture in one index, so that for *welfare* a set of indicators is required, that would support informed discussion in Parliament. One of these indicators would concern the *interaction of the economy, production and the environment.* For this, our proposal concerns eSNI and in particular the distances eΔ = NI – eSNI and eΔ-A = NI-A – eSNI. It is a remarkably common confusion that eSNI should be understood as an indicator of welfare itself, but it is definitely not (and the focus is on the distances anyway).

For the environment, the MBW contains some five indicators including the Living Planet Index, and the SDGs also contain some five indictors like action on climate change. These indicators are too meagre for a balanced judgement, and they do not provide standards that allow for an accurate definition of environmental sustainability. Thus, for the purpose of statistics and policy making on the environment, the MBW in its current form is inadequate.

It may be enlightening to draw attention to a circular process in scientific advice. Under Hueting's initiative in the 1970s, CBS Statistics Netherlands took a leading role in the development of environmental statistics and indicators. This also involved the development of eSNI. Afterwards, younger colleagues at CBS followed in his slipstream, but subsequently steered a course away from eSNI and towards MBW. The choice of the SDGs and the recommendations by the CES have been influenced by this leadership by CBS Statistics Netherlands. Presently, the MBW refers to the indicators as if they originate from the external consensus in the world, but in reality the younger colleagues at CBS had quite some influence on steering attention away from eSNI. They have done so with the confusion stated above.

12. *Comparisons with other environmental indicators*

12.1 *Abstract*

The discussion about NI itself started with the creation of NI. There are numerous comparisons of indicators for greening NI. A few are mentioned here. The use of satellite accounts only – as now happens in SNA and UN SEEA – has been discussed in Section 1.8.

12.2 *Table of comparions*

De Boer, Bosch & Hueting (2013) (Dutch) constructed **Table 7** with criteria and scores for the methods of eSNI, NI-A, Adjusted Net Savings (ANS) formerly known as Genuine Savings (GS), Ecological Footprint (EF) and ISEW. The negative scores for eSNI can be appreciated in a positive manner.

Table 7. Comparison of some key Green Indicators

		eSNI	NI-A	GS	EF	ISEW
1	Directly comparable with NI	+	+	-	-	-
2	Fundamental reliance upon physical norms	+	-	-	+	-
3	Norms hold for the entire world	+	-	-	+	-
4	Measures for improvement are explicit	+	+	+	-	-
5	Assignment of values where this is impossible	-	-	+	-	+
6a	Correcting current measurements of NI	-	+	+	+	+
6b	Use of a simulated path alongside NI	+	-	-	+	-
7	Explicit definition of what nature is	+	+	+	±	+
8	Other welfare factors than nature and NI	-	-	-	-	+

12.3 *NNI versus GDP*

When Hueting started thinking about this subject, economists used GNP as the main indicator for production. Over time, economists have switched to using GDP.

These gross measures include depreciation. The measurement of depreciation had and has some drawbacks. (1) For human-produced capital the assumptions on economic decay and its time horizon might be a rule of thumb rather than a true observation. (2) For not-human-made resources there is more likelihood that there is consumption that is counted incorrectly as income.

Hicksian income arises by keeping capital intact, thus El Serafy (2013:210) ftnt 1 states the common insight in national income accounting: "Strictly speaking national income is the NNP not GDP or GNP." This has the simple logic that (i) "national income" is not "domestic income", and (ii) "gross" cannot be "income" because one must subtract depreciation to keep income at its level. A more enlightened view though is that the National Accounts have a whole stable of notions of income with different flavours.

Hueting in 1986 chose to look at GNP minus depreciation = NNP = NNI. The calculations for eSNI have actually been calculations for eSNNI = eNNI. The results are in **Table 8** and **Figure 12.**

Table 8. Data for NNI and eSNNI, the Netherlands 1990-2015

	1990	1995	2000	2005	2010	2015	per year
NNI	344	379	441	495	530	538	1.8%
eSNNI	152	173	228	289		*334*	3.2%
Distance	192	206	213	206		*204*	0.2%
%	44%	46%	52%	58%		*62%*	1.4%
eFootprint	2.3	2.2	1.9	1.7		*1.6*	

Billion euro, prices 2010. Italics: rough estimate. eFootprint = 100 / %.
Source: Hueting and De Boer (2018, 2019)

Dutch net national income (NNI) rose from 344 in 1990 to 538 in 2015, or 1.8% per year on average. This includes a rise in population and thus is relatively low compared with the 1950-1970 period. In 1990, eSNNI was 44% of NNI, rather lower than the Tinbergen & Hueting (1991) rough estimate of 50%. However, eSNNI has been growing by 3.2% per year, and thus has been catching up with NNI to an estimated 62% in 2015. This growth was caused by a switch to the service industry, deliberate policies for environmental improvement, and the global financial crisis in 2007-2011.

Figure 12. NNI and eSNNI of the Netherlands 1990-2015, bn euro, prices 2010

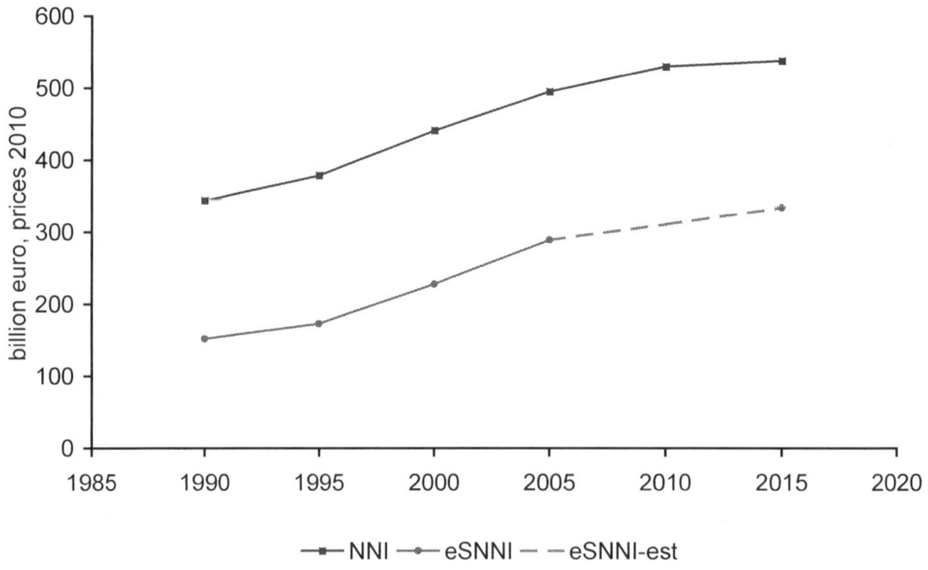

For this book, we want an easier link to the discussion about "Green GDP". We concur with El Serafy (2013:148) that it tends to be better to use a gross measure (except for the idea of actually "correcting" NI, since we think that comparison is better):

> "It is not by chance that the gross product, rather than the net product, is the preferred quantity for macroeconomic analysis. And it is often used as

a denominator for crucial macroeconomic ratios, with the nominator being money supply, exports, imports, external debt, debt service, savings, capital formation and so forth. As Hicks has suggested, the concept of net income is usually eschewed because it is always arbitrary. It relies on estimates of depreciation and inventory that are a mixed bag of historical costs and estimation based upon accounting conventions, tax laws and allowances, insurance company practices, as well as subjective valuation by economic agents who do the reckoning and who have a variety of expectations about the future (Hicks, 1969; see also Keynes, 1936) [ftnt]. From this perspective, if an income correction is to be made, it should apply to the gross product itself; and it is not enough to effect the adjustment at the net product level."

For the National Accounts, all measures like GNP, GDP, NNP and NDP are all measures for national income, in different flavours. Thus we can use the label "eSNI" as a label alongside "NI", and for actual measurement use a base that is best for both measurement and discussion.

Because of the way how depreciation D is calculated, we assume that it is not affected by the modelling exercise. The relevant relation then is that eΔ = GDP – eGDP = (GDP – D) – (eGDP – D) = NDP – eNDP. We also assume that eΔ calculated for NDP will be approximately equal to eΔ as calculated for NNI = NNP above. Thus we have eΔ = GDP – eGDP ≈ NNI – eSNNI. Using this result from **Table 8** we get eGDP = GDP – eΔ which gives **Table 9**.

Table 9. GDP and eSNI, the Netherlands 1990-2015, bn euro, prices 2010

	1990	1995	2000	2005	2010	2015	per year
GDP	405	454	562	600	639	666	2.0%
eGDP	213	248	349	394		*462*	3.1%
Distance	192	206	213	206		*204*	0.2%
%	53%	55%	62%	66%		*69%*	1.1%
eFootprint	1.9	1.8	1.6	1.5		*1.4*	

PM 1. Normalising GDP 1990 to 100 then gives **Table 1**.

PM 2. The estimates of eSNI are uncertain but it is unknown yet to which extent. The estimate of 2015 uses a rough manner without a model, see Hueting & De Boer (2018, 2019).

PM 3. Obviously this is a rough approximation only for the purpose of this book to link up to the commonly used indicator of GDP, using the available data for the Netherlands. Future modelling can e.g. test whether depreciation under environmental sustainability would be different in a relevant manner.

PM 4. An alternative assumption would be to presume that GNP, GDP, NNP, NDP and depreciation in the Dutch case are roughly proportional. This would give the alternative estimate: eGDP ≈ eSNNI / NNI * GDP. In that case, **Figure 1** and **Figure 12** would have the same shape and the estimate of eΔ is affected. There is currently no reason to assume this.

12.4 *El Serafy's user cost method*

El Serafy (2013) explains his *user-cost method* and its applicability on resource depleting, especially when the latter distorts standard GDP measurement in the current SNA, which highly applies to developing countries. In a nutshell, the method works as follows:

- Accountants can observe that a resource is being depleted over an expected time horizon, for example 20 years.
- The expected proceeds can be translated into a perpetuity at a selected rate of discount.
- The perpetuity would be proper income.
- The difference between current proceeds during the accounting year and this perpetuity are the user cost, i.e. the investments for maintaining the perpetuity.
- ("True") GDP* = GDP – user-cost.

From the point of view of environmental sustainability, it is a problem that El Serafy's method allows the complete depletion of the resource. The method does not take the ecological external effects into account that might be a reason to keep a part intact *physically*. While eSNI accounts for this, El Serafy calls this an "over"-correction, but this term only derives from his neglect of the issue of environmental sustainability.

This discussion clarifies that our focus is not only on "proper measurement of income" but also concerns environmental sustainability. While El Serafy wants to adapt GDP into GDP*, instead eSNI wants to maintain GDP as it is, since the gross expenditure flows in GDP contain the proceeds from the depletion of resources, which are actually costs for future generations.

The team at the World Bank was inspired by El Serafy's model to develop the *Genuine Savings* method, see El Serafy (2013:186) and below.

El Serafy and the authors of *Genuine Savings* were mostly at the World Bank. El Serafy points to this micro-economic 'net price method' as a rival approach (overlooking eSNI that is clearly not understood and even misrepresented there):

> "A rival method to the user cost, the 'net price method', has triumphed, having been backed in influential circles. Without a determined effort to extricate green accounting from its present stagnation, it will almost certainly not survive as a convincing tool for achieving what green accounting was meant for. (...) As I see it, a web of confusion and unhelpful contributions has shrouded this once promising tool (...) A *sine qua non* for such restoration would be a forceful and disinterested sponsorship by a leading institution with adequate resources and sustained determination."

12.5 *Adjusted Net Savings f.k.a. Genuine Savings*

In macro-economics it are the national investments that drive national savings. Economic agents may put money into the banks but when companies and government do not invest then there is no effect on production and income. The Keynesian $I = S$ equilibrium on the product market thus has I as the dog and S as the tail. The name of the *Genuine Savings* approach thus is somewhat peculiar.

Pearce, Hamilton and Atkinson (2001) give a succinct overview of the *Genuine Savings* method. The measure is in use at the World Bank and now is called *Adjusted Net Savings*. Hueting (2001d:365-371) is a rejoinder to Pearce et al.. The latter pages 370-371 give six conditions and the conclusion: "As long as these six conditions remain unsatisfied, the genuine savings method certainly cannot serve as an indicator for environmentally sustainable development." De Boer, Bosch & Hueting (2013:17-18) discuss GS / ANS in Dutch. Hueting (2013:96-98) returns to the issue more succinctly in English.

The World Bank report by Lange et al. (2018:31) states:

> "The wealth accounting approach provides two related sets of information: comprehensive wealth accounts (a stock measure in total and per capita values), and adjusted net (genuine) saving (a flow measure). Adjusted net saving (ANS) is measured as gross national saving minus depreciation of produced capital, depletion of subsoil assets and timber resources, the cost of air pollution damage to human health, plus a credit for education expenditures. The rule for interpreting ANS is simple: if ANS as a percentage of gross national income (GNI) is negative, the country is consuming more than it is saving, which will undermine long term sustainability; if ANS is positive, it is adding to wealth and future well-being."

We infer that the methodology of GS / ANS hasn't basically changed since 2001 so that the same objections hold.

At this point it is relevant to return to Pearce et al. (2001) and the Hueting (2001d:365-371) rejoinder. We may wonder why the World Bank since 1999 persists in the adoption of a clearly deficient measure. Perhaps colleagues at the World Bank have only read the Pearce et al. (2001) paper and have not read the rejoinder?

It is necessary to repeat that Pearce et al. (2001:216) misrepresent Hueting's approach:

> "Roefie's view has been that the governments represent a channel of 'revealed preference' so that the targets set by government act as shadow prices. But this presupposes a model of government rationality that is difficult to sustain. Indeed, it contains a contradiction. (...) If government was a perfect 'mirror' and conduit for those preferences we would have no more reason to use WTP as revealed by government target-setting than we have for measuring WTP directly from individual preferences. (...) But governments are well known for not acting in such a way, as the whole of public choice theory points out."

Hueting (2001d:365) files this protest:

> "As was the case with Herman Daly, their paper was completed after correspondence in which I clearly stated my position on (individual) preferences. Both Daly and Pearce et al. have ignored this information and in doing so they consciously misrepresent my views on preferences. In Herman's case, I strongly suspect that he was keen to provoke a

discussion on crucial issues (...). Although David et al. undoubtedly also had a reason, I cannot surmise what it might be.

It is painful to be criticised for advocating a method of (environmental) valuation that I have for 35 years attacked so vociferously in countless publications. In his contribution to the present volume Robert Goodland quotes as follows from one: "He criticized the official CBA of the construction of a polder in (...) an internationally important estuary. (...) Hueting's main objection was that the official CBA-assigned value of one hectare Waddensea estuary was set at the same value as one hectare marginal agricultural land (...) That was the value officially set for nature areas by the Netherlands Government. In his review of the official CBA, Hueting observed: 'This is not valuing at all, because it gives the Government the value which the same Government had already decided upon.' (...)" The quote is from 1978 and voices precisely the criticism formulated by David et al.: if the Government perfectly reflected subjects' individual preferences, quod non, valuation would be superfluous; economists providing such 'valuation' results make an easy living; it is circular reasoning."

The reader is referred to the summary of this book on page 9.

12.6 *MEW 1972, ISEW 1989, MBW 2018, GPI*

12.6.1 *Lack of awareness of what environmental sustainability means*

Nordhaus & Tobin (1972) "constructed a primitive and experimental "measure of economic welfare" (MEW), in which we attempt to allow for the more obvious discrepancies between GNP and economic welfare." In effect: "Our adjustments to GNP fall into three general categories: reclassification of GNP expenditures as consumption, investment, and intermediate; imputation for the services of consumer capital, for leisure, and for the product of household work; correction for some of the disamenities of urbanization." Herman Daly & Cobb (1989) presented the Index of Sustainable Economic Welfare (ISEW). CBS (2018) presented the MBW monitor of a broad concept of welfare. There is also a Wikipedia (no source but a portal) article on a Genuine Progress Indicator (GPI). [47]

Such issues are not our major concern, which is environmental sustainability. One cannot compensate ecological collapse with working part-time. eSNI would provide the best answer from welfare economics on the issue of ecological survival.

12.6.2 *Hueting (1974a, 1980) on Nordhaus & Tobin (1972)*

Hueting (1974a, 1980:183) footnote 40: "Nordhaus and Tobin [1972] state that they were not able to correct for encroachment upon the environment (p.49)". See also his continued discussion of the cost of commuting.

Nordhaus & Tobin (1972:49) still expressed a view about the size of the problem: "We have not been able to make this adjustment, but given the size of the other components of wealth, we do not believe it would be significant." In 1974

---

[47] https://en.wikipedia.org/wiki/Genuine_progress_indicator

Hueting skipped discussing this. The condition of environmental sustainability is highly significant.

There is also a clear conceptual difference between (i) economic planning with sustainable (in the meaning of *constant,* not only environmentally) consumption per capita, assuming a nonzero rate of technological progress, and (ii) the statistical measurement of environmental sustainability (safeguarding the environment) without risky assumptions on technological progress. Policy makers might assume so much technological progress that environmental concerns evaporate, yet statistics cautions us to stick to what can be observed.

12.6.3 *More on Nordhaus & Tobin (1972)*

Nordhaus and Tobin (1972:14) in section "Growth and natural resources" state:

> "Calculations like the foregoing are unlikely to satisfy critics who believe that economic growth per se piles up immense social costs ignored in even the most careful national income calculations. Faced with the finiteness of our earth and the exponential growth of economy and population, the environmentalist sees inevitable starvation. The specter of Malthus is haunting even the affluent society.
>
> There is a familiar ring to these criticisms. Ever since the industrial revolution pessimistic scientists and economists have warned that the possibilities of economic expansion are ultimately limited by the availability of natural resources and that society only makes the eventual future reckoning more painful by ignoring resource limitations now.
>
> In important part, this is a warning about population growth, which we consider below. Taking population developments as given, will natural resources become an increasingly severe drag on economic growth? We have not found evidence to support this fear. Indeed, the opposite appears to be more likely: Growth of output per capita will accelerate ever so slightly even as stocks of natural resources decline."

Such expectation depends upon different assumptions than apply to eSNI. In the calculations on the Netherlands, population growth is small, and such Malthusian scenario was not relevant. Subsequently:

> "These optimistic assumptions about technology stand in contrast to the tacit assumption of environmentalists that no substitutes are available for natural resources. Under this condition, it is easily seen that output will indeed stop growing or will decline. It thus appears that the substitutability (or technically, the elasticity of substitution) between the neoclassical factors, capital and labor, and natural resources is of crucial importance to future growth. This is an area needing extensive further research, but we have made two forays to see what the evidence is. (...)"

See above for how eSNI deals with (non-) renewable resources. Part of the optimism by Nordhaus and Tobin (1972) depends upon the market mechanism and the expectation that prices will rise when resources dwindle. They observe low prices and suggest that markets adequately incorporate future scarcity, yet above we have seen that markets can fail. They express caution though:

> "On the other hand, the warnings of the conservationists and scientists do underscore the importance of continuous monitoring of the national and world outlook for energy and other resources. Substitutability might disappear. Conceivably both the market and public agencies might be too complacent about the prospects for new and safe substitutes for fossil fuels. The opportunity and need for fruitful collaboration between economists and physical scientists has never been greater. (...) Possible abuse of public natural resources is a much more serious problem. (...) There are other serious consequences of treating as free things which are not really free. This practice gives the wrong signals for the directions of economic growth."

The idea behind eSNI is to use this caution for the construction of a statistical figure alongside standard NI. Subsequently:

> "The mistake of the antigrowth men is to blame economic growth per se for the misdirection of economic growth. The misdirection is due to a defect of the pricing system — a serious but by no means irreparable defect and one which would in any case be present in a stationary economy. Pollutants have multiplied much faster than the population or the economy during the last thirty years. Although general economic growth has intensified the problem, it seems to originate in particular technologies. The proper remedy is to correct the price system so as to discourage these technologies. Zero economic growth is a blunt instrument for cleaner air, prodigiously expensive and probably ineffectual."

We do not see ourselves as "antigrowth men". We neither blame "growth per se" for the misdirection of economic growth. Hueting as an economists supports the use of the market mechanism, and the use of taxes and subsidies to include externalities. Within economic theory, there is a case however to be "anti" the mistaking of production growth for welfare growth. Some production can be enhance welfare, other production can be counterproductive.

12.7 *Ecological Footprint*

The environmentally sustainability footprint eFootprint = NI / eSNI can be seen as an ecological footprint, as seen from welfare economics. **Table 1** shows values for the Netherlands. As said in Section 8.7 *The Ecological Footprint* (Wackernagel and Rees, 1996) translates to land rather than income. It is rather unavoidable that some regions are more densely populated and thus have such a large footprint. Even when the Netherlands would satisfy environmental sustainability NI-A = eSNI then the country would still tend to have a large "ecological footprint" in the original W&R 1996 method, merely since it is densely populated. We agree with Van den Bergh & Verbruggen (1999) that this is dubious. The W&R method cannot convince. It is remarkable that the notion still finds mention. The notion of a "footprint" is a wonderful way to express the environmental challenge for the world as a whole but may be less informative for a particular country. Also, calculation of eSNI is more involved than the original "ecological footprint" and thus may still be indicative of the challenges that a particular country faces. The current estimates for eSNI can be improved on the dimension of land space though. For governments it remains advisable to set up systems to monitor the environmental impact of the economy, and to integrate those data with NI to find eSNI.

Part 5. Epilogue

13. *Work not printed here*

13.1 *Abstract*

Work not printed here can be distinguished in (i) other work on the topic of this book, i.e. on environmental functions and the national accounts and the measurement of income and eSNI, (ii) general work on environmental economics and economic policy.

13.2 *Introduction*

This chapter mentions work that has been done but that is not printed in this book, so that the next chapter can focus on what still needs to be done. Readers of this book who miss some aspects are advised to first look into the work that has already been done in the past, for this work is rather voluminous, though with much overlap but also with continuous improvement, and there is a large chance that aspects have been discussed indeed.

It is useful to check http://www.sni-hueting.info including the lists of publications there in both English and Dutch, yet many publications are not on that website.

13.3 *Three myths*

Apart from modelling and measurement, Hueting also wrote in general about the transition to environmental sustainability. In these more general contributions, he of course benefitted from his perspective on modelling and measurement.

Advisable is Hueting (1996), "*Three persistent myths in the environmental debate*", that was also reprinted in Van Ierland et al. (2001:78-89).

13.4 *Combatting misleading information about economic growth*

Hueting (2011b), "*Five Ways to Combat Misleading Information about Economic Growth*", has a summary overview on eSNI. Let us summarise what those five ways are, and the reader is referred there for the details.

(1) Publish a series of NI-A alongside NI
(2) Publish a series of eSNI alongside NI and NI-A
(3) Refute the fallacy of essentially the political statement that production must grow to finance the safeguarding the environment
(4) Clarify why measures that support the environment do not conflict with employment, under logical conditions
(5) Show the wrongness of the statement that environmental conservation is unaffordable.

For the fifth misunderstanding we may quote:

> "A wide-spread fallacy about the environmental problem is: 'We would like to save the environment, but alas, it is too expensive'. However, the contrary holds true: all fundamental solutions for safeguarding the environment are clearly much cheaper than continuing the process that is threatening life on this planet."

13.5 *Relatively recent contributions to conferences*

In 1999 a conference on Hueting's work was held at the KNAW Royal Academy of Sciences in Amsterdam. The conference papers have been edited by Van Ierland et al (2001).

In 2001 the World Bank organised a seminar on this book, with the opening speech Hueting (2001e) and a report of the discussion by Hecht (2007). The panel was chaired by Joseph Stiglitz. (Included here are a report on that seminar, in Appendix 17, and a letter by Thea Sigmond to the Stiglitz, Sen & Fitoussi Commission in 2009, in Appendix 18.)

Hueting & De Boer (2001b) is the opening contribution to the Van Ierland et al. (2001) conference book. Parts have also found their way into this present book. Not transferred are an extensive discussion of weak and strong preferences for environmental sustainability and the (transition) time paths for those.

Hueting (2007a) is a presentation for an OECD conference in Istanbul. Van Tuinen was also at this conference and Van Tuinen (2009) expressed support for further research on eSNI.

Hueting (2010ab) are contributions for the De-Growth conferences.

Hueting (2011c) is for the EU Beyond-GDP project – partly reworked for the *Five Ways*.

13.6 *Calculations by IVM*

Verbruggen (ed) (2000) and Verbruggen et al. (2001) and Dellink & Hofkes (2008) have already been referred to. The reader is alerted to their references. Relevant are also Gerlagh et al. (2002), Hofkes et al. (2002), Hofkes et al. (2004) and Kuik (2006).

13.7 *Work in Dutch*

De Boer, Bosch & Hueting (2013), for Dutch readers, is the colloquium at the Dutch Ministry of Economic Affairs.

The Dutch section of http://www.sni-hueting.info contains articles and also discussions with Dutch researchers on this topic. There are remarkable many ways for not understanding eSNI even when one has been trained as economist.

14. *Work to be done*

14.1 *Abstract*

Given the age of the authors, we only indicate what others might want to look at.

14.2 *Some references*

It is fairly obvious that national statistical agencies are continuously improving the quality and scope of their measurements. This will also happen when eSNI would be included into the System of National Accounts (SNA).

At this point, it suffices for us to mention some references:

(1) Hueting (2007b) is a summary for the *Beyond GDP* project by the EU, now called *GDP and Beyond*. The statement on the future is:

> "Plans are elaborated in notes for (1) model improvements, (2) the set up of, among other things, defining the measures and estimating their costs to arrive at sustainable use of soil that prevents erosion, one of the serious problems in developing countries and (3) eSNI estimates in other countries e.g. Germany and some developing countries. Representatives of The World Bank and the OECD have insisted on this. Although the Dutch Parliament has asked for funding this and the Dutch government has promised to do so, subsidies have not been granted. [[48]] The theory and elaboration of eSNI has received international scientific recognition. It is the eldest and most complete environmental indicator as follows from e.g. the four points mentioned in the Section 'Need'. It provides information not given by any other indicator. However, because of lack of funding further development of eSNI is hardly possible. Hopefully the European Union will help to change this situation."

(2) Colignatus (2012) *Work in Progress* is included as Appendix 19 and contains some suggestions for further improvements.

(3) Currently, the environment is recorded in satellite accounts to the SNA. El Serafy (2014) invites economists to get more involved with the National Accounts. We can only support that invitation.

14.3 *Awareness about the information that is provided*

We have not seen other authors who adopt the same approach. Thus this book presents an approach that is unique. The work done here hasn't been done before. The approach is quite logical and not really difficult to explain or to understand in its outcomes. It concerns an issue that we all talk about. It also concerns something that needs to be done to provide for proper information, which is required everywhere. Thus it would be advantageous to increase the awareness about this approach.

---

[48] It may also be that these have been mislaid at RIVM / MNP / PBL.

14.4 *Improved education about the meaning of eSNI*

It will be important to improve the education about the meaning of eSNI. It still appears to be a subject that causes misunderstanding, and henceforth it will be fruitful to develop clarifications that make for easier understanding. A crucial insight is that the current generation may be stealing from its children and future generations. Who produces something and destroys it, like a painter who destroys a self-made painting, cannot be said to be stealing. However, for the not-human-made physical surroundings, that we received from the past, we cannot hold that we made them ourselves. It is a fair notion that we want to pass on this benefit to later generations. If we impair the vital functions of the not-human-made physical surroundings we are actually stealing from our children and grandchildren. It are such insights that would contribute to a better education on the meaning of eSNI and the distance between NI and eSNI.

Appendices

15. *GNP and market prices: Wrong signals for sustainable economic success that mask environmental destruction*

Jan Tinbergen and Roefie Hueting 1991 [49]

15.1 *Abstract*

Jan Tinbergen (1903-1994), who helped develop the system of national accounts in the 1930s, expresses support for Hueting's 1986b concept of environmentally sustainable national income. [50] The authors reason that its level is around 50% of standard national income. They advise negative growth of population and production, and that the North makes room so that the South can still grow in per capita income, reducing the income gap between rich and poor countries from 10:1 to 4:1.

15.2 *Society is steering by the wrong compass*

The market is rightly considered a mechanism that generates manufactured goods and services according to consumer preference. This mechanism allows culture and technology to put into practice inventions enriching human life. It works efficiently and stimulates productivity increase, which is the motor raising the quantity, quality and diversity of manufactured goods thus becoming available to consumers.

An effective measure of the level of production and its changes from year to year – national income – was devised in the 1930s (Tinbergen, quoted in Hueting, 1980a). People working on this research were well aware that national income would not form a complete indicator of economic success (welfare). But given a fair distribution of income and perfect competition it no longer matters what is produced, only how much of it is produced. Consequently at that time great value was attached to the compilation of a series of figures on the total production of goods and services. In the 1930s, external effects, like environmental deterioration, did not yet play an important role.

This situation has changed drastically. Over the last forty-five years, the period in which, based on the above reasoning, growth of national income has been given the highest priority in economic policy, the following picture emerges. The production of manufactured goods and services has increased unprecedentedly, but has been accompanied by an unprecedented destruction of the most

[49] Published in 1991 in R. Goodland, H. Daly, S. El Serafy and B. von Droste zu Hulshoff (eds.), Environmentally Sustainable Economic Development: Building on Brundtland, Ch 4: 51-57. United Nations Educational, Scientific and Cultural Organization, Paris, 1991. Also published in: R. Goodland et al. (eds.), Population, Technology and Lifestyle: The Transition to Sustainability, Ch. 4: 52-62. Island Press, The International Bank for Reconstruction and Development and UNESCO, Washington, D.C., 1992. Also published in: Environmentally Sustainable Economic Development: Building on Brundtland. R. Goodland et al. (eds.), Environment Working Paper 46, The World Bank, Washington, D.C.

[50] This application of national accounting is to be distinguished from the relevance and appreciation of this analysis for environmental economics itself, see footnote 82 on page 211.

fundamental, scarce and consequently economic good at human disposal, namely the environment. This process has already caused much human suffering. Much of what are called natural disasters, such as erosion, flooding and desertification, is caused by mismanagement of the environment. This process threatens the living conditions of generations to come. Furthermore, part of the growth of national income consists of production increases in arms, alcohol, tobacco and drugs. Few people consider this progress. Part of GNP growth is double counting. [51] Thus, in the System of National Accounts (SNA) environmental losses are not written off as costs, but expenditure for their partial recuperation or compensation is written up as final consumption. The same holds true for expenditure on victims of traffic accidents and diseases caused by consumption, such as smoking.

Increase in production is distributed very unequally. In rich countries, people are led to consume more because of seductive billion-dollar advertising campaigns. But 20 per cent of the population in poor countries are deprived of basic needs, such as adequate food, shelter, potable water, taps and toilets. Economic research has shown that once basic needs have been met, relative income has a greater impact on welfare than absolute income. Finally, production increase has not prevented persistence of high unemployment world-wide and considerable child labour.

The market works well, but not all factors contributing to human welfare are captured by it. Consequently, market prices and economic indicators based on them, such as national income and cost-benefit analyses, send misleading signals to society and therefore must be corrected. The factor for which correction is most urgently needed is the environment.

15.3 *The relationship between growth and environmental destruction*

Environmental degradation is a consequence of production and its growth. The burden on the environment is determined by the number of people, the amount of activity per person and the nature of that activity. These three factors are all reflected in the level of national income. The increase and decrease of the first two burdening factors – population and per capita activity – parallel the increase and decrease of production levels. For the third factor (the nature of our activities) it roughly holds that the more burdensome for the environment our activities are, the higher their contribution is to national income, and vice versa. Thus driving a car contributes more to GNP than riding a bicycle. This emerges from an analysis of the Netherlands national accounts. The sectoral composition of the Netherlands accounts does not differ appreciably from that of the United Kingdom, nor probably from that of most other Northern countries. What follows is therefore by and large valid for industrialized countries.

Production growth results largely from increase in productivity, in which the loss of scarce environmental goods has not been taken into account. Increase in labour volume plays a minor role. A quarter to one third of the activities making up national income (notably state consumption) do not contribute to its growth, because increase in productivity is difficult to measure. Other activities result only in slight improvements in productivity. Average annual growth must therefore be achieved by much higher growth among the remaining activities. Some 30 per

---

[51] This book uses the term "asymmetric bookkeeping", see Chapter 7.

cent of activities generate about 70 per cent of growth. Unfortunately, these are precisely the activities which, by their use of space, soil and resources or by their pollution in production or consumption, harm the environment most. These are notably the oil, petrochemical and metal industries, agriculture, public utilities, road building, transport and mining.

Measures to save the environment will have the following effects on growth rates and on production levels. To maintain current life-styles as much as possible, all available technical measures should be applied to the fullest extent affordable. Such measures include end-of-pipe treatment, process-integrated changes, recycling, increasing energy efficiency, terracing agricultural slopes, and sustainably managing forests. Because they require extra input of labour, these measures reduce labour productivity and therefore raise product prices, which in turn checks growth of national income (corrected for double counting). The check of growth can be alleviated by the absorption of unemployed workers, up to the point where full employment has been attained.

Saving the environment without causing a rise in prices and subsequent check of production growth is only possible if a technology is invented that is sufficiently clean, reduces the use of space sufficiently, leaves the soil intact, does not deplete energy and resources (i.e. energy derived from the sun and recycling), and is cheaper (or at least not more expensive) than current technology. This is hardly imaginable for our whole range of current activities. But when such technologies become available, the above mentioned effects will be avoided.

Applying technical measures cannot completely avoid a change in our consumption pattern, because price rises resulting from the measures inevitably cause a shift toward more environmentally benign activities, such as bicycling and using public transport. Technical measures often do not really solve the problem, either because the growth of the activity overrides the effect of the measure, or because of the persistent and cumulative character of the burden. In this case, the measure only retards the rate of deterioration. Thus, to stop the Netherlands' contribution to acidification of forests and lakes, apart from applying all available technical means, the people in the Netherlands must reduce the number of car-kilometres and farm livestock by about 50 per cent (Fransen, 1987). For some problems no technical measures are available: for instance the loss of habitat of plant and animal species as a result of the use of space, and the formation of cirrus clouds that contribute to the greenhouse effect (CO_2 accumulation may be partly solvable). In these cases, in addition to the technical measures, a direct shift in behaviour patterns must ensue, forced by do's and don'ts, rules, incentives and taxes.

A direct shift in production and consumption patterns will also check GNP growth as follows from the analysis of national accounts (the environmentally most burdensome activities contribute most to GNP growth). Moreover, in terms of national accounts, environmentally benign activities represent a smaller volume. Thus a bicycle-kilometre represents a smaller volume than a car-kilometre; a sweater a smaller volume than a hot room; an extra blanket a smaller volume than heating the whole house; beans a smaller volume than meat; and a holiday by train, a smaller volume than holiday flights. This is mainly because the exhaustion of environment and resources is not charged to national income as costs. If it were, the differences would become much smaller or nil.

From the above, it follows that saving the environment will certainly check production growth and probably lead to lower levels of national income. This outcome can hardly surprise. Many have known for a long time that population growth and rising production and consumption levels cannot be sustained forever in a finite world. The outcome of the above analysis should arouse optimism rather than pessimism, because environmentally benign activities are remarkably cheap. Thus, a bicycle is much cheaper than a car, a blanket is cheaper than central heating, and rearing two children is cheaper than bringing up ten. This means that saving our planet is indeed possible.

Our fervent goal – to arrive at environmental sustainability, as advocated by the Brundtland Report (WCED, 1987), and by politicians and institutions around the world – can indeed be fulfilled, though only under limiting conditions. In particular, population growth should be avoided as soon as possible. Moreover, activities with little or no material throughput can increase practically forever. As we have seen, this will not result in great increases in national income. Decision-makers should not become upset by this. Changes in national income levels by no means indicate the economic success of their policies because they conceal the destruction of our life support systems, as long as [the uses of] the figures are not corrected for environmental losses. [52]

15.4 *Correction of national income based on sustainable use of the environment*

Attempts to correct [the use of] national income for environmental losses started in the early 1970s with the following train of thought (Hueting, 1980a). The environment is interpreted as the not-human-made physical surroundings of humanity, on which it is completely dependent (from breathing to producing). Within the environment, a number of possible uses can be distinguished. These are called environmental functions. When the use of a function by an activity is at the expense of the use of another (or the same) function by another activity, or threatens to be so in the future, loss of function occurs. Environmental functions then have become scarce goods, because the use of a function implies, wholly or partly, the sacrifice of another. This fully meets the definition of scarcity that demarcates the economic discipline. This approach links ecology and economics, and places environment centrally in economic theory.

Because national income is recorded in market prices, shadow prices have to be estimated for functions (and their losses) that are directly comparable with prices of manufactured marketed goods. For this purpose, supply and demand curves for functions have to be constructed. It appeared possible to construct supply curves, consisting of the costs of measures eliminating the burden on the environment, arranged by increasing costs per unit burden avoided. But in most cases no complete demand curves can be found. This is because the possibilities for

[52] In 1990 the expression 'to correct NI' was used, borrowing this term from the tradition to always improve the relevance and accuracy of the National Accounts. This article however already compares the standard measure Y = NI and Y' = eSNI. It is more accurate to say that when NI is still used, it is not corrected, but compared with eSNI.

preferences for environmental functions to be manifested via market behaviour are very limited. Other methods, such as willingness to pay or to accept, do not yield complete demand curves, certainly for functions on which current and future life depends. Standard setting was also considered, but the questions of what standards were to be set and by whom could not be answered at that time.

This situation has now changed. Especially after the 1987 Brundtland Report, politicians and organizations worldwide declared themselves in favour of sustainable use of the environment. This preference, voiced by society, opens up the possibility of basing a calculation on standards for the sustainable use of environmental functions instead of (unknown) individual preferences.

Therefore, the following procedure is proposed for correcting [the use of] GNP for environmental losses (Hueting 1986b, 1989b). First define physical standards for environmental functions, based on their sustainable use. These standards replace the (unknown) demand curves. Then formulate measures to meet these standards. Finally, estimate the money involved in implementing the measures. The reduction of national income (Y) by the amounts found gives a first approximation of the activity level which, in line with the standards applied, is sustainable. Needless to say a correction for double counting, mentioned above, must also be made. If the sustainable level is Y', the difference between Y and Y' indicates, in money terms, how far society has drifted away from its desired goal of sustainable use of the environment.

The standards can be related to environmental functions. Thus it is possible to formulate the way in which a forest should be managed in order to attain a sustainable use of its functions. Sustainability then means that all present and future uses remain available. For renewable resources such as forests, water, soil and air, as long as their regenerative capacity remains intact, then the functions remain intact (for example, the function 'supplier of wood' of forests, the function 'drinking water' of water, the function 'soil for raising crops' of soil and the function 'air for physiological functioning' of air). This means that emissions of substances that accumulate in the environment, such as PCBs, heavy metals, nitrates and carbon dioxide, may not exceed the natural assimilative capacity of the environment, and that erosion rates may not exceed natural soil regeneration. As for non-renewable resources, such as oil and copper, 'regeneration' takes the form of research and bringing into practice flow resources such as energy derived from the sun (wind, tidal collectors, photo-voltaic cells), recycling of materials and developing their substitutes.

The measures to meet standards include: reforestation, building terraces, draining roads, maintaining landscape buffers, selective use of pesticides and fertilizers, building treatment plants, material recycling, introducing flow energy, altering industrial processes, using more public transport and bicycles, and use of space that leaves sufficient room for the survival of plant and animal species.

The method is applicable for cost-benefit analyses of projects with long term environmental effects. The method seems to be the only way to confront national income with the losses of environmental functions in monetary terms. The physical data required for comparison with standards come down to basic environmental statistics, which have to be collected in any GNP and market prices case if a government is to get a grip on the state of the environment. The formulation of measures to meet standards and estimates of the expenditure involved are indispensable for policy decisions.

In other words, the work for supplementing national income figures might be laborious, but it has to be done in any case if we wish to practise a deliberate policy with respect to the environment. We therefore strongly urge decision-makers to stimulate this kind of research in their countries. The Philippines and Sweden already are interested in following the lead of the Netherlands.

15.5 *Our debt to future generations*

A rough order of magnitude of the debt to future generations the world has been accumulating during the last few decades, and how it is to be paid off, is estimated below. We base this on the use of energy and corresponding CO_2 emissions.

One aspect of sustainability could be that the annual consumption of fuels such as coal, oil and natural gas, expressed as a percentage of known reserves, is equal to the rate of efficiency growth in the use of energy, while keeping the level of production constant (Tinbergen, 1990). Tinbergen found that a figure for this efficiency growth close to reality is 1.67 per cent. By this behaviour, it would be theoretically possible to use a finite stock for an infinite period of time. However, it is not certain whether this will be feasible, because it would mean that the production and consumption of today's package of goods has to be generated with an ever smaller amount of energy. Thus after 315 years, today's package must be generated with 0.5 per cent of today's energy use. 315 years is a short period in relation to the speed of natural processes in question when addressing environmental sustainability. Therefore, if we also want to avoid the hazards of nuclear energy, development of new technologies such as flow energy (derived from the sun) is less risky.

To avoid greenhouse risks, global CO_2 emissions are estimated to have to be reduced by 75 to 80 per cent. In the period 1950-1988, CO_2 emissions, energy use and GDP ran parallel. Around 1950 both world GDP and energy use amounted to 25 per cent of the 1988 level. This means that, other things being equal, the GDP level must be reduced by 75 per cent. Assuming that a CO_2 reduction of 25 per cent is possible at low cost, and considering that a number of environmental effects are not eliminated by reduced energy use, we conclude that to pay off global environmental debt we would have to halve the level of global activities. This demonstrates the urgency of allocating all available resources, such as know-how and capital, towards the development of new technologies (such as flow energy and recycling), instead of towards increasing production, while halting and then reversing population growth. The last thing the world can afford is to wage war, such as that in the Gulf.

The outlook of such changes in technology seems to be promising. For example, Potma (1990) shows that techniques like splitting water molecules by solar energy in deserts and transporting the resulting hydrogen fuels, can provide the world with sufficient clean energy at twice current energy prices. Desertic developing countries thus have a major export potential. This would allow a sustainable use of the environment while regaining current production levels in 50 to 100 years. This is because sufficient clean energy would become available for both eliminating some environmental effects other than the greenhouse effect and compensating for the necessary decrease in production where no solutions are available with additional production of another kind. Moreover, room would be created for raising per capita production levels in the South by a factor of 2.5. This would reduce the income gap between rich and poor countries from 10:1 to 4:1, with the condition of no further throughput growth in rich countries.

The uncertainties are, of course, far too great to attach great value to the outcome of this scenario. But the above clearly demonstrates that continuing prevailing growth paths is blocking our chances of survival, for which possibilities still remain.

15.6 *Conclusion*

In order to achieve sustainable use of the environment, we conclude that the highest priority should be accorded to devising and implementing economic policies that: (a) accelerate development of new technologies, such as flow energy and recycling; (b) permit no further production growth in rich countries; (c) stabilize the global population as soon as possible; (d) improve international income distribution.

15.7 *References*

Fransen, J.T.P. 1987. *Zure Regen: Een Nieuw Beleid*. Utrecht, Natuur en Milieu Foundation. 27 pp.

Hueting, R. (1974a, 1980). *New Scarcity and Economic Growth*. New York, Oxford University Press. 269 pp.

-. 1986b. A Note on the Construction of an Environmental Indicator in Monetary Terms as a Supplement to National Income with the Aid of Basic Environmental Statistics. Jakarta, Ministry of Population and Environment. 10 pp. (Mimeo, available from the author.)

-. 1989b. Correcting National Income for Environmental Losses: Towards a Practical Solution. In: Y. Ahmad, S. El Serafy and E. Lutz (eds.), Environmental Accounting for Sustainable Development, pp. 32-9, Washington, D.C., World Bank. 100 pp.

Potma, T. G. 1990. Interrelationships Between Environment, Energy and Economy (A paper for the Dutch National Energy Authority). Delft, Center for Energy Conservation and Clean Technology (nowadays CE Delft). 17 pp. (Unpublished MS.)

Tinbergen, J. 1990. Le Incognite del Terzo Millenio. Dimensione Energia (Rome), Vol. 38, January/February, pp. 36-41.

-. 1990. How to Leave Enough Natural Resources for Future Generations. NRC Handelsblad, p. 8, 22 June. (In Dutch.)

-. 1991. Personal communication, and quoted in Hueting, R. 1980a, pp. 153 and 157.

WCED, 1987. Our Common Future. (The Brundtland Report). Oxford, World Commission on Environment and Development/Oxford University Press. 383 pp.

16. *Roefie Hueting: Defining a statistical figure with a model*

Thomas Colignatus 2001 [53]

16.1 *Abstract*

Roefie Hueting (born in 1929) put environmental economics right on the map in Holland in 1974, with his thesis *"New scarcity and economic growth"* (Hueting (1974a, 1980)) written under promotor Jan Pen. In a sense he did so even for the world map, but the English translation had to wait till 1980 and then there were also publications by others. [54] Hueting was head of the environmental department at CBS Statistics Netherlands since 1969, and he saw to it from the start that the environment did not remain a theoretical exercise but was described statistically and made accessible for policy making. The high quality of the Dutch environmental statistics is world famous amongst statisticians. Subsequently, in the late 1980s, Hueting enriched economic science with the concept of environmentally sustainable national income (eSNI). With Hueting we thus find theory and measurement linked and closely tuned.

16.2 *National accounts*

To understand Hueting's work, we have to go back to the foundations of economic theory. The concept of 'national income' is founded in the theory of economic welfare. [55] The concepts of general welfare and the national accounts have been developed in the period 1930-1960 by Tinbergen, Hicks, Kuznets, Samuelson, Bergson, Meade and Stone. Attention is focused on the development of general welfare, while the importance of the production of goods and services is derived from this. For example, when more chairs are produced, then material production rises. However, welfare does not necessarily increase since there may be no need for more chairs.

While the main focus of interest is the measurement of general welfare, this becomes frustrated since the welfare function cannot be observed directly. It is for this reason that income is used as an approximation, as this can be derived mathematically from the tangent plane to the utility function. If one assumes that the market is optimal, then observed market prices can be used to deflate this income. This is, in a nutshell, the economic theory that forms the foundation for statistical practice.

In the period since 1960 the theory itself seems to move more to the background, and for many the national product becomes the yardstick for economic success. That was the situation when Hueting started to consider the issue of the environment.

---

[53] Originally published in Dutch, as Thomas Cool, "Roefie Hueting en het DNI", Economisch Statistische Berichten 24-8-2001, p652- 653.

[54] R. Hueting, "New scarcity and economic growth", North-Holland, Amsterdam 1980. Dutch title: "Nieuwe schaarste en economische groei".

[55] Addendum 2019: Historically, the National Accounts derived from practical purposes for government policy and the interpretation in welfare economics was in parallel and always critical.

16.3 *Environmental functions*

Hueting's first contribution to economic science is the concept of 'environmental function'. A component such as water has different functions or applications, such as drinking, fishing or use in industrial processing. In this, a function is defined in relation to human needs. As one of few economists, Hueting delves in ecology, chemistry and physics, clarifies the various functions of the ecology, and subsequently identifies their economic meaning. Where environmental functions in the past were abundant and consequently did not have a price, nowadays they are scarce and do have a price. In the common calculation of national income, this increase in price is taken as an increase in value that causes a higher income. Here Hueting called attention to a major misunderstanding: these higher prices actually mean an increase in cost, so that real welfare decreases. Take for example an environmental disaster or the introduction of catalysts on cars. In these cases labour and tools are used to repair the damage. Hueting calls it asymmetric, when on the one hand these costs are entered into the accounts and cause an increase in national income, while on the other hand the environmental damage is not subtracted. This asymmetry still is current statistical practice.

16.4 *Demand and supply*

By scarcity, environmental functions get a price. But do they get the right price? Is the assumption of market optimality satisfied? As a first step to answering this question Hueting tries to specify the functions of demand and supply. His analysis has gone through a development here. In his thesis he was able to determine a supply function for environmental functions based upon elimination costs of pollution and such. For a demand function, however, he had to refer to decisions by the government and 'social forces'. He made a sharp distinction between consumer preferences and what turns up of those in government decisions, but he did not have a solution for the tension between the two.

When governments all over the world, in the wake of the Brundtland report of 1987, decided to adopt 'sustainable development', Hueting concluded that this actually implied a 'vertical demand curve'. [56] Seen from one perspective he only follows the governments, seen from another perspective he provides an economic foundation to the notion of 'sustainability'. [57] Hueting pointed out that sustainability actually means that the freedom of future generations to use environmental functions becomes the centre of focus – where the concept of freedom is wider than the concept of income, just like Amartya Sen recently did. [58]

16.5 *Two questions*

Hueting answers two questions with this analysis. First, one might think that initial statistical errors would disappear when environmental functions become scarcer and the prices rise, and when the environment thus becomes a cost factor and is integrated into the economic system. According to Hueting the statistical

---

[56] This book Figure 6 on page 89.

[57] Addendum 2019: The theoretical emphasis is on the other perspective. (i) The definition of eSNI is a conceptual notion independent from what governments actually say or do. (ii) The Brundtland "sustainable development" still is not "environmentally sustainable" yet.

[58] A. Sen (1999), "Development as freedom", Knopf, New York

error does not disappear all by itself. As the example of the car catalyst shows, there is still a problem with statistical accounting. Secondly, one might think that the error should disappear in a democracy in which expenditure should be close to the social optimum. However, when governments on the one hand state a choice for sustainability, but on the other hand don't implement this in practice, and when they hence do not apply the prices that are required for sustainability, then the appeal to 'democracy' is also an appeal to inconsistency. Inconsistency does not provide a basis for statistical measurement. Hueting refers to the 'prisoners' dilemma' and other arguments of government failure by which the consumer preferences are 'blocked' and cannot be expressed in market prices. With respect to the two questions just mentioned, it therefore is a misunderstanding, according to Hueting, to think 'that the information is all right'.

A correct statistical description requires another figure alongside traditional national income, namely the distance to [environmentally] sustainable national income. In Hueting's view, both numbers are fictitious, since he considers it impossible to know the true preferences. Publication of both figures seems to him the best solution for meeting the need for information. That need for information is clear from the discussion in society.

16.6 *Revolution in statistics*

Concerning the calculation of the distance of NI to eSNI, Hueting actually performs a small revolution in statistics. He namely uses a model as an integral part of observation, and in this model the hypotheses [59] with respect to the future play a key role. Many people regard statistics as only the observation and recording of phenomena in the past. For Hueting, however, theory leads to the insight that the use of a model cannot always be avoided. [60] [61]

Recently, the eSNI according to Hueting's methodology has been calculated for Holland. [62] A discussion is in Verbruggen (ed) (2000). This calculation was carried out for 1990, which underlines that Hueting, as a statistician, is interested in the past, namely 1990, and not 2010. The model contains a development path to the future, [63] with valuations by the generation of 1990 of the positions of future generations. It is striking that in this way hypotheses and preferences concerning the future are used to estimate a figure for the past. The approach as such is consistent, though.

---

[59] Addendum 2019: The original had "expectations" but "hypotheses" is relevantly clearer.

[60] Addendum 2019: Hueting actually prefers to avoid a model as much as possible. A model adds to discussion of model content though with possibly little addition to accuracy. The Hueting e.a. (1992d) methodology avoids models in the same manner.

[61] Addendum 2019: The revolution is actually larger than the use of a model per se. The basic revolution is that dealing with the risk on the environment requires conditionality for NI and eSNI.

[62] H. Verbruggen (ed) (2000), "Final report on calculations of a sustainable national income according to Hueting's methodology", Instituut voor Milieuvraagstukken, Vrije Universiteit Amsterdam, report O-00/10. A discussion in Dutch is in H. Verbruggen, R. Gerlagh, M.W. Hofkes en R.B. Dellink (2001), "Duurzaam rekenen", ESB dossier "Vernieuwende statistieken", March 15.

[63] Addendum 2019: This is an awkward formulation. In the current implementation, sustainability is imposed instantaneously without a transition path, and perhaps a transition might be better.

The calculation shows that Dutch eSNI is less than half Dutch NI, which would mean that the Dutch generation of 1990 lived in too grand a style and passed on too many costs onto future generations. These figures are likely to appeal more to one's imagination when more data points can be compared, with a monitoring of the distance between NI and eSNI. Calculation of eSNI appears not all that expensive, for it is a calculation at a high aggregate level, that uses data that have already been collected for other purposes. Therefore, regular calculation appears to be possible in practice.

16.7 *Conclusion*

Hueting has the position of the statistician who sees it as his task to provide correct information. He is not only the theorist who goes back to Tinbergen and Hicks and he is not only the practitioner who introduces the required improvements in his field, but he is also the unwavering scientist who sticks to his role as supplier of information. [64]

[64] A longer version of this paper is available as "The seminal contribution of Roefie Hueting to economic science: Theory and measurement of Sustainable National Income", see http://thomascool.eu/Papers/Environment/HuetingsContribution.html. [Included in Colignatus (2009b, 2015, 2019).] See also the 'Hueting Congres' book by E. van Ierland, J. van der Straaten en H. Vollebergh (eds) (2001), "Economic growth and valuation of the environment: a debate", E. Elgar, to appear by the end of September 2001.

17. *Report on the World Bank seminar on economic growth and valuation of the environment. A debate on Sustainable National Income. Held at the embassy of the Netherlands, 1 October 2001, Washington DC*

Foundation for research on Sustainable National Income (FSNI)
Third edition, 2007 [65]

This report was prepared by dr. Joy E. Hecht [66]

17.1 *Invitation & programme*

You are cordially invited to participate in the World Bank seminar:

"Economic Growth and Valuation of the Environment"

Chaired by H.E. Minister Jan Pronk

at The Royal Netherlands Embassy, Washington DC [67]
on Monday, the First of October 2001, 14 - 17 hrs, reception to follow

Dr. Joseph Stiglitz will lead a panel to discuss the book dedicated to the work of dr. Roefie Hueting

Prof.dr. Ekko van Ierland will outline the new book *"Economic Growth and Valuation of the Environment: a Debate"*. Dr. Hueting will present the scientific basis for calculating "sustainable national income". Ir. Bart de Boer will discuss the economic model used, and the quantified results for the Netherlands. The book includes the views of leading environmental economists, such as David Pearce, Wilfred Beckerman and Herman Daly, on the subject. The concept of sustainable national income is essential to thinking about national welfare. It could have a major impact on the political discussion about environment, economy and sustainable development. These issues are relevant in the run-up to the 2002 Earth Summit. Because of the risk of demonstrations the seminar will be held in the Dutch Embassy. Minister Pronk will hand the first copy of the book to Mr. Wolfensohn, President of the World Bank Group. There will be ample opportunity to participate in the discussions.

Programme

- Opening speech by Jan Pronk, Minister of Environment for the Netherlands.
- Presentation by dr. Ekko van Ierland, Professor of Environmental Economics, Wageningen University

---

[65] Foundation for research of sustainable national income (FSNI) (2001), http://www.sni-hueting.info/EN/Others/2001-10-01-Seminar-at-Worldbank-3rd-imprint.pdf
[66] Consultant on environmental and information systems, Arlington, Virginia, USA
[67] The seminar was relocated from the World Bank to the Dutch Embassy because the center of Washington DC was closed off because of 9/11.

- Presentation by dr. Roefie Hueting, retired from Statistics Netherlands.
- Presentation by ir. Bart de Boer, Statistics Netherlands.
- Comments by the Discussants dr. Joseph Stiglitz, Professor of Economics at Columbia University and former Chief economist at the World Bank and dr. Ian Johnson, Vice President of the World Bank.
- Discussion with members of the audience, presided by Minister Pronk.

17.2 *Opening Speech by minister Jan Pronk*

Jan Pronk, Minister of Environment for the Netherlands opened the meeting at 2:15 pm.

MINISTER PRONK: Roefie Hueting, who has been at the piano here on the stage, is well known in the Netherlands for his seminal work on environmental economics and sustainable national income, as well as for being the founder of the Downtown Jazz Band. The book that we are introducing today, *Economic Growth and Valuation of the Environment,* is a debate on the concept of sustainable national income. Dr. Hueting and I have been colleagues since the 1960s. I began as a lecturer on national income accounting, while dr. Hueting was in the Central Bureau of Statistics with an interest in greening the accounts. Our careers have evolved in tandem, Dr. Hueting's in economics and accounting, and my own in politics.

The World Bank, to whom we are presenting the book today, has organized today's seminar. Both their interest in organizing this seminar and their willingness to receive the book signify their commitment to sustainable national income. While this meeting is being held at the Netherlands Embassy, it is a World Bank event. We owe thanks to Robert Goodland for the Bank's support of the book itself and of this seminar. A copy of the book will be handed to President Wolfensohn tomorrow. Unfortunately he has been unable to join us today. I am pleased to introduce in his place dr. Ian Johnson, Vice President of the World Bank, who is involved with mainstreaming concerns about environment and sustainability at the World Bank. The book is being presented to the Bank because as an institution it is making an intellectual contribution both within this field and in the larger context of development and globalization.

Minister Pronk presented a copy of the book to dr. Johnson.

DR. JOHNSON: Minister Pronk has been a key figure in bringing together concerns about environment and development. I hope that Minister Pronk will accomplish as much at Rio+10 as at the recent Climate Change meetings, which he Chaired. The major issue for Rio+10 is how to make the debate real. This is a question of measurement and of the use of valuation. The new book sets out the debate well.

17.3 *Presentation by Ekko van Ierland*

Your excellency, ambassador, ladies and gentlemen: Our environment, our climate and the world's biodiversity continue to be at risk as a result of unbalanced economic growth and rapidly expanding economic activity, world wide. The book *'Economic growth and valuation of the environment'* deals exactly with these issues, in particular with the question of how to measure income, how to value the environment and how to calculate sustainable national income.

The content of the book, which is centred around the work of Roefie Hueting, is important because we need a thorough understanding of what economic growth is and how it affects the environment. That understanding is a prerequisite for formulating policies to reduce poverty and to protect the environment. The analysis in the book clearly defines the implications of the vague and often confusing concept of sustainability, by explicitly defining sustainability standards.

17.3.1 *Content of the book and the debate*

The book focusses on three topics:

1. The shortcomings of the present system of national accounts, which can be considered a misleading compass for environmental and macro-economic policies.
2. The characteristics of the concept of sustainable national income as defined by Hueting, in particular on the divergence between standard national income and sustainable national income as calculated by Hueting and his co-researchers.
3. The question of how transition towards the path of sustainable growth is to be made!

The standard system of national accounts is well-defined and serves many purposes as clearly explained in the chapter by Salah El Serafy. However, it shows very serious shortcomings in dealing with the environment: it neglects externalities; it does not reflect the overexploration of common property resources and it fails to register the overexploitation of the environment. If we think in terms of man-made capital, human capital and ecological capital (as sketched by Paul Ekins in chapter 3 of the book) it becomes clear that the traditional system of national accounts measures what we are producing, but it fails to consider what we are sacrificing in order to produce these goods and services. In this respect the term 'steering by the wrong compass' as introduced by Roefie Hueting is relevant.

Hueting states: "These losses are not entered in the system of national accounts, nor in the majority of cost-benefit analysis. Over and against the unentered costs stand the revenues (more produced goods) which are entered". Although economists like Pigou, Mishan, Hennipman and Tinbergen paid attention to these problems, we are still struggling with solving the most important questions. Because preferences for environmental goods can be measured only very partially from market behaviour, Hueting concludes that assumptions on preferences have to be made, as a practical solution for an unsolvable problem. Thus sustainable national income is based on the assumption of strong preferences for sustainability and standard national income on the assumption of weak preferences for sustainability.

For measuring these costs Hueting specifies sustainability standards indicating sustainable levels of emissions and resource use. Next he uses a general equilibrium model to calculate the maximum level ofnational income that can be reached, while meeting these sustainable standards.

The book contains a full debate on whether this approach is theoretically justified and useful, and also what its limitations are. The well known British environmental economist David Pearce and his co-authors compare the method with measurement of environmental values for example by means of the contingent valuation approach.

I consider both approaches (which are clearly different in their principles) both useful to provide information on how we value environmental attributes. One measure may be in inches, the other in centimetres; they measure different aspects but as long as it is made explicit how the yardstick is defined we obtain clear information. Herman Daly clearly pinpoints the shortcomings of the present system of national accounts: "Consequently, what we currently call national income is decidedly unsustainable, necessitating the awkward pleonasm 'sustainable national income' for the connected figure, in order to convey the original meaning of income".

Daly then in a very rich and well elaborated chapter, discusses the problem of identifying sustainability standards and claims, as contrasted with Hueting, that these standards can be considered as 'objective values', based on sustainability of natural processes.

No need to say that the debate on the objectivity of these values is far from completed, and so is the debate on what economic or ecological targets (in greek: telos) should be.

Dick Norgaard (the president of the Ecological Economics Association) and his co-authors challenge in this context the utilisation approach in economics, for instance on the basis of the dilemma of the aggregation of individual values and the fact that values are socially constructed in education and social interaction. They claim that economists have systematically overlooked the limitations of methodological individualism and utilitarianism. It is time to reconsider the actual processes in which people express and act out their values and to develop a policy framework that allows for multiple, co-evolving values, referring to the co-evolution of our society and the ecological processes.

My personal opinion is that it is essential for our understanding of what our economic position is to have information on the level of sustainable national income, despite some of the unresolved methodological issues in its calculations.

By calculating sustainable national income we at least get clearly presented that there is a tremendous gap between standard national income, and the level of income that could be sustained without overexploiting the natural environment. More importantly it identifies some key areas for environmental policy, like climate change, acidification and toxic compounds.

17.3.2 *The results of the sustainable national income calculations*

The calculations are made by a research group of the Vrije Universiteit in Amsterdam, led by professor Harmen Verbruggen, in close co operation with Hueting and Bart de Boer from Statistics Netherlands. They calculated SNI on the basis of sustainability standards in a CGE model. The model comprises basically three options to meet these standards:

1. by means of end of pipe technologies (like catalytic converters);
2. by substitution: use more clean products in stead of polluting ones;
3. and by changing our life styles and reducing economic activity in certain sectors.

In the calculations these restrictions are introduced by means of tradable permits: the stricter the sustainability standard for each aspect of environmental policy, the higher will be the shadow price of the environment and the stronger are the incentives to reduce pollution, both for producers and consumers: Externalities are now internalized!

The calculations provide very interesting results of which I would like to highlight two:

1. SNI for the Netherlands is about 50% of traditional national income, which is indeed a tremendous distance;
2. More promising, the calculations show that a long trajectory of the path towards sustainability can be made at relatively low costs: up to 70% to 80% of the road to sustainability can be reached at cost of about 10% of standard national income.

But, please be aware, these results apply to a highly industrialized, densely populated country with a production structure that includes highly intensive agriculture, energy-intensive petro-chemical industries and high traffic density. In addition to these interesting results, the application of the method proposed by Hueting clearly revealed the need for further improvement and extension of the analysis, in particular to include the pressure on the use of land and space and the related impact on biodiversity. Another aspect is the availability of new technologies in the future, including sustainable energy and better options for reuse and recycling.

17.3.3 *The implications for future research and policy*

Now we have confirmed some serious shortcomings of national income accounting and as we know that we are on an unsustainable path of economic growth the question arises how to make the transition towards sustainable economic growth.

It is evident that in decision making we need to use a correct compass. We need in all decisions an analysis of what is sacrificed and destroyed, and we should compensate for these losses where possible.

- In CB analysis we should continue to include externalities and impacts on the public good characteristics of the environment.
- We should use resources efficiently, where for instance the same tasks and services can be performed with only 25 % of energy used before.
- Develop clean and sustainable technologies and anticipate on their introduction, and make these widely available.
- Eliminate persistent toxic chemical compounds and dispersation of heavy metals into the environment, for example the use of mercury in gold mining.
- Reduce emissions of greenhouse gases and other transboundary pollutants.

In particular for climate change and losses of biodiversity we need to focus on avoiding irreversible changes and reducing the risk of catastrophic events (even if it is considered a risk with small probability; because the effects can be extremely large and unprecedented in history).

In order to solve the global environmental problems we need strong public institutions, strong governments, based on democratic principles to express society's preferences for environmental quality. To make correct decisions we need insight in sustainable national income and the relevant factors that determine its level.

17.3.4 *Conclusion*

I do not hesitate to conclude that the publications of Roefie Hueting, and the debate with the colleagues – sometimes 'opponents', but they are essential in the debate – have contributed to understanding environmental and ecological economics. His work is well documented and found its way to new generations of economists and politicians and to international institutions that may contribute to protecting the environment.

Finally, I would like to thank all who contributed to the completion of the book and the organisation of today's seminar, Robert Goodland in particular.

The book is the result of our common concern to fight poverty and to reduce the risk of ecological disaster. It now is a challenge for the international institutions including the World Bank and UNEP to gain national and international support for sustainable policies on climate change, protection of biodiversity and elimination of harmful and toxic compounds.

17.4 *Presentation by Roefie Hueting*

I must confess that I am just a salesman, selling environmental information and jazz music. I wish to draw your attention to the fact that the book may be purchased here with a large discount, and I encourage members of the audience to do so. Copies of my speech are available on the seats. I apologize for it being dull, but I feel this is an efficient way to present the information. To leave room for discussion later on, my introduction will be brief. This brevity will certainly provoke questions, but I hope these will be addressed in the second part of the seminar.

In the theoretical basis for the calculation of sustainable national income, the environment is defined as the not-human-made physical surroundings, or elements thereof, on which humanity is entirely dependent in all its doings, whether these be producing, consuming, breathing or recreating.

(... see the body of this book ... [68])

Any price rise in real terms means a decline in the volume of national income and therefore a check on production growth. For a given technology, product costs will rise progressively as the yield (or: effect) of environmental measures is increased. Technological progress leads to higher yields, of course. As production increases further, however, so too must the yield of the measures in order to maintain the same state of the environment, while the fact of progressively rising

---

[68] This presentation overlaps with the contents of this present book. The text can still be found in http://www.sni-hueting.info/EN/Others/2001-10-01-Seminar-at-Worldbank-3rd-imprint.pdf

costs with rising yield remains unaltered. There is thus a 'race' between environmental technology and production growth, the outcome of which cannot be predicted.

17.5 *Presentation by Bart de Boer*

The subject of this presentation is the way in which the sustainable national income (SNI) is actually computed; it also shows the main results. The explanation cannot do without a brief overview of how the calculation should be done in theory, however.

(... see the body of this book ... [69])

17.6 *Comments by the discussants Joseph Stiglitz and Ian Johnson*

DR. STIGLITZ: I think this kind of work is very important. In my remarks, I will explain why this is so important, but why at the same time it is very difficult to implement. First, let me make a few prefatory remarks. Two underlying premises of this work are taken as a given today; first, that we must focus on long-term sustainable growth and second, that we must take intergenerational equity concerns seriously.

Why are accounting frameworks like that being presented here so important? This is not measurement for its own sake; such frameworks have an enormous impact on how we think about policy decisions. There is a view that, if we can't measure something, it doesn't exist. While that is not true, nevertheless things that are not measured often don't get the weight they deserve when policy decisions are made.

This issue is therefore part of the economics and politics of information. Accounting frameworks are one way to bring information to bear on decision-making. Policy-makers at the national and international levels must have accounting frameworks to help guide their thinking. The fact that these frameworks are imperfect, while true, does not mean we should not develop them.

Let me give some examples of where our standard accounting frameworks fall short. To begin, GDP is not a measure of welfare; it is a measure of economic activity. Recent events illustrate the difference clearly. While some people think war will raise the level of economic activity, it clearly does not increase welfare. When people do not recognize this, they say defense expenditures are good for the economy. They are not – they are a waste of resources, except to the extent that they allow us to enjoy safety and security.

Many developing country economies depend heavily on the exploitation of natural resources. The use of those resources increases the GDP. However this is frequently no more than the conversion of assets from one form to another; the economy may not be growing in any sustainable way. This makes it important to distinguish development based on natural resources from other forms of development, such as that based on human capital.

A third point relates to innovations, such as energy conservation. A technological innovation that leads to a reduction in demand for and therefore to a reduction of

[69] This presentation overlaps with the contents of this present book. The text can still be found in http://www.sni-hueting.info/EN/Others/2001-10-01-Seminar-at-Worldbank-3rd-imprint.pdf

production of oil, might reduce GDP, whereas in fact the standard of living might have gone up (depending on price ratio's and consumption pattern). Thus a decision-maker focusing on GDP will not focus on innovations in conservation, because they might reduce rather than increase the target variable.

My fourth example relates to a set of policy decisions frequently made by macro policy decision-makers. Suppose there is a global crisis and we raise interest rates. We are interested in the implications of raising those interest rates. Such increases may lead to less food production, causing riots and the destruction of social capital, which will in turn reduce growth in the future. Higher interest rates may also lead to increased forest harvests, while the capital tied up in the forests may better be diverted to other assets whose value grows faster. Health problems will also erode human capital. None of these impacts is captured when we focus on a single variable like GDP; a broader system of accounting is needed in order to capture them.

How would we go about developing better accounting schemes that are more congruent with measures of welfare? Let me first make two preliminary observations. First, it is important to recognize that accounting frameworks are a language we use to communicate with each other. They are imperfect. However, they can still convey important information, especially in comparisons across countries. It is, therefore, important to develop new frameworks that include the environment even if they are imperfect. This is a feature of modern science; we must recognize that there is uncertainty in everything we do. We must be aware of the varying degrees of imperfection in all our measures, but those imperfections do not constitute an argument against building and using them. All accounting systems have a lot of arbitrariness; we must live with that.

Let me give you a different example that illustrates these points. This is from the area of corporate or GAP accounting (generally accepted practices). Many people think corporate accounts follow hard and fast rules. However, one of the recent trends in many countries is that executives are paid with stock options. This amounts to taking resources from other shareholders and giving them to the management of the firm. It is important for ordinary shareholders to know the value of outstanding stock options in order to know the value of their own stock. There has recently been some discussion of how to include these stock options in the GAP methods. Firms in Silicon Valley, which make great use of such options, were strongly opposed to including them, because it would have greatly hurt them if the value of outstanding stock options were known. The argument they gave for their opposition was that we don't know how to measure the value of stock options accurately. The shareholders responded that the firms could at least estimate a minimum value, but the firms didn't want any information to be made public at all.

We must consider three key issues regarding valuation:

- what items we should include in the accounting frameworks,
- how we should quantify them, and
- how we should value them.

What we should include: There is some consensus on including environmental and resource impacts in the accounts. Most of us also think we should, if possible, include impacts on social capital.

How to quantify them: Quantifying environmental impacts is not nearly as difficult as quantifying social impacts. There is still considerable controversy over how to measure even natural resource impacts, however. For example, consider resource depletion. The accounts include all impacts on reserves, netting depletion against new discoveries. This is inappropriate, since the discovery of new reserves does not actually mean new reserves have been created (because the reserves were present already).

How to value impacts: The economic answer to this is "the shadow price." However, how do we calculate shadow prices? Are they close to prices in current markets? If you think the economy is close to the optimal path, then shadow prices are close to market prices, and there is no problem. This concern arises in particular when we think about the role of time, i.e. valuation of future impacts. If we use market interest rates to discount future impacts, then impacts a century or more in the future have very little value today. In response to this, some suggest that we should not discount at all, or we should use very low discount rates. The shadow prices we place on emissions in the future would then be high, and the net value of income much lower. The choice of shadow prices reflects an array of judgments, and will be the subject of much controversy.

Despite all of these debates, the basic goal of attempting to assess our sustainable national income is nevertheless essential.

My final question, which I will not answer but will leave for subsequent discussion, concerns the growing sense around the world that we will only be able to sustain a focus on environment if we are able to develop these accounting frameworks. How do we get both developed and less developed countries to use them? How about if the IMF, when it announces GDP numbers, also announced a set of parallel numbers showing "true GDP"?

DR.JOHNSON: I would like to pick up on a number of issues in the presentations, particularly regarding the implementation of SNI. First, this book is part of a continuing intellectual journey, which needs to be a public policy journey as well as an intellectual one. In what ways will these results make a difference for the choices we make at the level of society?

The debate over measurement of sustainable development has two components. One concerns items that are not captured in the marketplace; externalities and non-marketed goods and services. The other problem is that we are all guilty of gross myopia, both political and economic. Politicians think on a two to four year horizon, whereas economists use ten-percent discount rates that give no importance even to impacts ten years hence, much less on future generations. In the case of climate change, this is particularly important, and the use of a zero discount rate may be appropriate. These two problems are the key elements of our battle for sustainability, and have become even more apparent as we have moved further towards free market economies. This movement does not allow for a new round of creative public policy.

My second general point relates to measurement – the idea that "we are what we measure." At the sectoral level, information has become a powerhouse; for example, in my own country – England – emissions data have become very important in marketing automobiles. At the micro level, that kind of information may be a powerful incentive for using measurement and indicators, because of the pressure they put on public policy. However we have been less successful at the macro level in putting that kind of pressure on public policy makers to use better information.

The next point is absolutely vital; that is the issue of natural capital. In most countries of the world, it is valued at zero. Were we private accountants, we would have long since been fired for not thinking about the depreciation of natural capital. When we see the convergence of the economic costs of such depletion with the financial costs, we will get wake-up calls. This is particularly clear in the water resource business. This is going to lead to discontinuous cost curves in many countries, as they are forced to suddenly jump to new technologies due to lack of supply. Historically, policy-makers have refused to think in terms of water pricing that reflects real scarcity, but with the increased role of the market, costs formerly thought of as hypothetical are beginning to affect economic growth in the short to medium term.

Strategies for measuring the depletion and repletion of human capital will be equally important. Sustainability is not just about the environment; it is about society as well. These issues will rise rapidly up the public policy agenda. While environmental issues are more easily measured, we should not give up on measuring social capital as well.

We must think about global sustainability as well. The world is becoming so interdependent that we must think about how we capture this in national data. How do we internalize global impacts of our activities in a national accounting system? We could use trade, but this is insufficient. This concern has some ways to go before it will be resolved.

A final concern is that of equity among countries. The inequality among countries must be addressed, although doing so will increase global consumption. This is one reason why it is particularly important to start measuring what is happening in developing countries. The North must take the lead here; if they don't do so, developing countries never will. Dr. Stiglitz suggested that the IMF do this. However, until such time as the South sees the North developing, publishing, and using such data, they will not begin doing so themselves. The work of the Netherlands is particularly interesting from this perspective. How do the results in the Netherlands play out with the public and with policy-makers? This will be particularly important for seeing how this will evolve in the future.

Let us not make the search of the perfect indicator become the enemy of the good. We can do a lot with what we have, and we must not get sidetracked in the intellectual journey.

MINISTER PRONK: I propose that we combine the panel and audience in order to save time, and resume after a short coffee break.

17.7 *Discussion*

MINISTER PRONK: We would like to focus on two issues: first, the methodology, and second the broader issues. Both discussants have referred to particular measurements. They have said that while there are problems with measurement, it is possible to overcome them. How are Hueting and de Boer overcoming these problems?

DR. HUETING: It is impossible to measure the value of environmental functions, because you need both a supply and a demand curve. The former reflects opportunity cost of restoring and maintaining environmental functions which can be estimated. The latter reflects preferences for those functions. Those preferences can be obtained only partially through revealed preference techniques, e.g. compensation costs, expenditure on restoration. Therefore in most cases it is not possible to value environmental functions. We offer as a practical alternative to make assumptions about preferences and see what are the opportunity costs that match these preferences. One assumption is that people prefer sustainability; based on this we can estimate the opportunity cost of that particular preference set. Of course, if we knew that that was the "real" preference set, we would no longer have any need of policy-makers. It follows from this that both standard and sustainable national income are based on assumptions about preferences.

MINISTER PRONK: Let me confirm. You are saying that it is not possible to value environmental functions. Instead we make assumptions regarding preferences, and then use scientific analysis to derive scientifically derived standards, which are ceilings for the level of activity (e.g. emissions). Given that, my question to Dr. El Serafy is whether it is possible to make such calculations, leading to standards, for a country such as India or an African country? Could you measure SNI in a developing country?

DR. SALAH EL SERAFY: My friend Roefie is more interested in showing the gap between conventional and this "welfare-oriented" concept of income. I am an imposter in this group because I am not an environmentalist. I am an economist concerned about the false numbers used by economists, and the fantastic models they build using them. Countries sell their natural assets and call that growth, but this is not growth. Professor Stiglitz did not touch upon the fact that conventional GDP is wrong because it does not capture that loss in natural assets. I am disappointed in his treatment of the subject when he was at the World Bank. I agree entirely with Roefie because his contribution is to tell us that we must not read welfare from these numbers.

MINISTER PRONK: Dr. Stiglitz, you are being attacked by an imposter.

DR. STIGLITZ: The whole point of my remark was to say that the sale of natural resources does not lead to a good measure of welfare.

MINISTER PRONK: I would like Dr. El Serafy to answer the question I posed to him, whether it is possible to calculate SNI in the developing world?

DR. EL SERAFY: Of course it is. We can't afford to have different systems for rich and poor countries; we must have one standard system. If it can be done for the Netherlands, it can be done anywhere.

MINISTER PRONK: Does the lack of data in developing countries make this less feasible?

DR. EL SERAFY: Yes, but we haven't attempted to generate these data in countries like Mali.

MINISTER PRONK: Let me address a question to Dr. Herman Daly. Roefie considers himself a positivist, whereas Daly says in his chapter in the book that he thinks on normative lines. Could you explain this?

DR. DALY: I very much support Roefie's methodology and think it correct. As he has emphasized, you must make an assumption about preferences. He assumes a preference for sustainability. This is not a revealed preference, it is assumed. In my contribution to the book, I wanted to add further support for the vertical demand curve that results from this assumption. I wanted to see factual or normative arguments for it. Roefie is more of a positivist, in that he prefers to simply think of it in these analytical terms, whereas I argue that if you want this to be more than simply a set of interesting numbers, you must determine which assumptions about preferences are most normatively correct. This takes you out of the economic framework in which one person's preferences are as good as another; you need some meta-preference system to decide which are best.

MINISTER PRONK: Your question is which preferences are normatively most correct. I think, in my terminology, that this is all based on preference for strong sustainability. You (Bart de Boer) translated this into three boundary conditions presented in your talk – no further acceleration of extinctions, no impacts on health, and environmental functions available to people worldwide. Dr. Daly, do you consider these sufficient?

DR. DALY: Those are normative. They reflect deeply held values that we must analyze. The idea behind sustainability is that we must extend our system of justice.

MINISTER PRONK: Yes, but are they sufficient to ensure sustainability?

DR. DALY: I'm not really sure, but they are sufficient for the time being.

MINISTER PRONK: Could Bart and Roefie please explain why they chose these? Why were there no assumptions about the availability of natural resources?

IR. DE BOER: An assumption concerning natural resources should be added in, that was simply an omission. However the biodiversity constraint is more important. It was developed based on an intuition that this was closely linked to the functions of the environment on a global scale. The constraint related to health stems from a belief that the world will not be sustainable if we are all ill.

MINISTER PRONK: In this methodology the SNI is also to be based on assumptions about standards that impact international as well as domestic relations. Is that reasonable, to include an ecological footprint thinking in a sustainable national income analysis?

DR. STIGLITZ: First, a different point. Zero is not a sustainable level of extinctions, since they occur all the time. So assuming that what you meant was to minimize rather than eliminate extinctions, the question is at what resource cost we wish to do this.

MINISTER PRONK: The SNI does not say no extinction, it says no acceleration of extinctions.

DR. STIGLITZ: Okay. We must include global effects in any welfare SNI measure. With a globally integrated world, we must talk about impacts on the global atmosphere.

MINISTER PRONK: The results were for the Netherlands, SNI about 55% lower than conventional NI in 1990. Would the gap be equivalent for countries such as India or the US?

DR. JOHNSON: We must begin by looking at the damage functions for depletion. The impact is probably much greater in a country like India than for this country. Then we must look at what price we are paying for that depletion – it is probably much higher in India. For this reason, their real savings rates would be much lower than what would be otherwise estimated. However, I'd like to turn this around, and focus on the "so what" debate. At what point does this analysis tell you that you may need to look at policy options? At what point do these measures introduce uncertainty about your policies? That's what we should be looking at in developing countries.

MINISTER PRONK: I would still like an intuitive answer to my question.

DR. EL SERAFY: Here's a non-intuitive response. Developing countries derive their prosperity from resources that are being depleted, much more so than do wealthy countries. This would make the gap larger there than in the Netherlands.

MINISTER PRONK: In other words, the difference between SNI and conventional national income would be greater in the developing world?

DR. EL SERAFY: Yes.

DR. HUETING: If the future will be worse in the developing world than in the Netherlands, then their SNI would be less than 50% of conventional income. From my experience in the Sahel, we see the deserts advancing because of excess pressure on the resource base.

MINISTER PRONK: According to the SNI methodology, the intuitive answer is that the gap would be larger in a poor country than in a wealthier one. How about a richer country?

DR. STIGLITZ: Let me raise an aspect that I find troubling. One element in calculating sustainability relates to the rate of technical progress. If innovation is very fast and you can conserve resources and extend their lifespan, then the level of sustainable income is higher. If the US had a higher rate of technological progress, its SNI might be higher than for other countries.

MINISTER PRONK: Ian Johnson, you said that you are very much in favor of such efforts, at both sectoral and macro level. Could the Bank, on the basis of such an approach, make an effort to make these SNI calculations in countries where it is very active? Would this be helpful for country policy-making by the Bank?

DR. JOHNSON: Yes. We have worked for a number of years, including the work of Salah El Serafy and Kirk Hamilton, making estimates of real savings, which focus on depletion of resources. This points out that if you are living off of your natural capital and not investing for the long term, you are living off your capital. This is very imperfect, of course. We are concerned not only about how you deplete your capital, but also about how you invest it, since if you are reinvesting in human capital, you may do more for future development in the long run than the harm you cause by depleting your natural resources. We must think more about the circumstances under which this makes a difference. To get that debate going, you must see developed countries taking the lead. Until there is global equity in the ability and willingness to measure, you will not make headway. If the North is not measured by the same standards as the developing world, we will not make progress.

DR. STIGLITZ: There is another reason why this is important – because many inferences about economic policy and the impacts of international capital flows are contingent on our assessment of what economic output is. If we only capture some capital investments but not others, our interpretations will be incorrect.

MINISTER PRONK: That means all measures must be comparable, and we must use the same methods in all countries. But how many different green national incomes are there? Is this method – the Hueting one – worth repeating in other countries? Is it possible? Is it too costly? Would it be useful for international policy functions, or would we prefer a less elaborate methodology?

DR. JOHNSON: The search for the perfect indicator is rapidly becoming the enemy of the good. Instead, I would like to see agreements at Rio+10 that countries will measure welfare and income (or GDP) in a different way. Countries must agree that this is a public policy issue for which all of them must be held accountable across the board. There is enough information to be able to make plausible information available across all countries. The conventional accounts are imperfect in many other ways as well, but we move forward anyway; the same could happen here.

MINISTER PRONK: Why doesn't the Bank offer to make these SNI calculations for some other countries, and not only developing countries? Would that not be useful?

DR. STIGLITZ: Some standardization is worthwhile. However, regarding this methodology, we do not yet have a sense of how robust the results are. To what extent would different assumptions about technology or preferences lead to markedly different results? This method tries to be parsimonious with regard to preferences and technology. If there is support for this, then calculating it for other countries will be useful. As economists, we think more in terms of what the shadow prices are. A translation of this into assessment of how different methods would lead to different shadow prices would be useful.

DR. JOHNSON: The United States is not one of our clients at the Bank. In terms of the precise approach, I am not sufficiently informed to make a judgment as to whether it would be useful. At the end of the day there are not huge differences of methodology among the different approaches – we all agree on the need to handle depletion of natural capital differently.

DR. DALY: I'm interested in moving from concepts of measurement to their implications for policy decisions. If, for example, to measure sustainable GNP we hypothesize these environmental limits, the next step would be to institutionalize the limits, so we actually generate something that is sustainable. That would imply the implementation of these vertical demand curves. How might we do that?

Through existing cap-and-trade systems for pollutant emissions? I was intrigued by the example of the impacts of interest rate increases.

MINISTER PRONK: Are there people here who think better policies could be defended if there were a better information base? For instance, would the SNI measurement make a difference?

JOHN FITZGERALD (USAID): USAID has noted development of these measures with favor, because we expect to be able to use them to assess what we do and what the Bank does and proposes to do. We would like to see them applied to individual loans, to see whether "the micro meets the macro."

MINISTER PRONK: As a policy maker, I understand that micro-level analysis and action are not sufficient. I wonder, however, whether I am greatly helped by such a macro national figure. I think sectoral figures would be more useful. Must it be either micro or macro, or is there something in between that is more useful for policy-makers?

IR. DE BOER: The calculation also gives insights into sectoral effects on production and environmental burden. These effects and the measures causing them can be integrated into national economic and environmental planning.

DR. STIGLITZ: I can offer one concrete example of how macro-level figures have influenced policy – the opposition in the US to taking action on global warming was based on estimates of the impacts on GDP.

HANS VEROLME (British Embassy): One example is the proposal to elevate EPA to a cabinet level organization. Opposition to this has been fueled by the economic cost of regulation, and by an estimate that 90% of regulatory costs in the United States were caused by environmental regulation. With a measure like that of Hueting, this figure might be cut in half.

MINISTER PRONK: Could Mr. Fitzgerald comment on that?

JOHN FITZGERALD: He might be right, but that is an academic question if we have not done the calculations.

CHRIS HERMAN (USEPA): I would support the point made by Hans Verolme, though I haven't seen the figures. This points to another issue, which is the increasing use of cost-benefit analysis in regulatory rule making. This starts from the opposite perspective, by establishing a fixed value for human life and then authorizing all environmental policies that cost less than the value of the lives that would be lost otherwise. If you have underestimated the value of a life, you will end up with results that are not sustainable, because you will not invest enough to sustain human life. Have the panelists reflected on the disconnect between the implications of this use of cost benefit analysis at the micro level and the national analytical framework you raise here?

MINISTER PRONK: Could Dr. Hueting comment on this, and also on whether the assumptions here also apply to cost benefit analysis?

DR. HUETING: This is a cost benefit analysis, because we compare the costs with the benefits. On the cost side are the opportunity costs of attaining a specified standard. The benefits are the decrease of the demand curve, or the damage done. As far as they cannot be measured because of blockages, then the benefits are simply fulfilling the assumed preferences.

CHRIS HERMAN: I understand that you are making fixed assumptions about a set of values or standards, and are proceeding from there. If, as occurs in cost benefit analysis in the US, you work in the opposite direction by assuming a fixed value for human life (as a proxy for environmental benefit) and let that be the drive of your decision—making, then you will end up with a different result.

MINISTER PRONK: Please continue this discussion later, as it is too technical.

KRISTALINA GEORGIEVA (World Bank): You asked whether we need to move towards a system of national accounts that includes environmental assets and impacts as well as social assets. Clearly we do, and more discussions are needed. You also asked whether we can apply this methodology to developing countries. Here I am less optimistic, because of the data requirements. These data simply are not available. I would move forward by asking for this to be applied to more OECD countries first. We should work on it in the developing world, but it will be better to begin in the OECD countries. I would also like to raise a third point. Why does this framework not include anything on population growth? National income per capita will make a great deal of difference in how we interpret the results.

IR. DE BOER: Regarding data requirements, the search for the data required to get a general picture of the use of (or pressure on) the environment is going on in developing countries, whether or not we calculate SNI. Once the data are available, calculating SNI is worth the additional cost.

DR. HUETING: The standards for specific countries are derived from global standards, so the first step for every country has been made. Regarding population, we are working on a geological time scale, so the time frame within which population is an issue – a few hundred years – is only a split second. If population growth continues, then no technology will be sufficient to attain sustainability. If technical measures entailing direct shifts from burdening to benign activities are insufficient to achieve sustainability, we assume population will drop in order to arrive at a sustainable development path. Therefore policy-makers must include a population policy to manage that drop.

DR. STIGLITZ: GDP numbers are very imperfect. There was an enormous discussion on this when the SNA was being developed. Now this is not even taught in graduate schools, we simply assume that these are meaningful measures. I conclude, therefore, that as we develop environmental frameworks, there will be a lot of discussion, but we will end up with standards that will allow for a reasonable degree of comparability. They will be imperfect, but they will be used anyway. Moreover, GDP numbers in developing countries are much worse than those in developed countries. Accounting frameworks in developing countries are better now than they were thirty or forty years ago. Low quality of data is not an argument for not doing the work at all.

DR. JOHNSON: We are closer to the truth with poor data than we would be with no data. The 55% gap in the Netherlands will not lead to immediate policy conclusions, but it will stimulate debate and lead to more detailed analysis of the

18. *For the Commission on the Measurement of Economic Performance and Social Progress (Stiglitz, Sen, Fitoussi)*

Thea Sigmond 2009 [71]

To: the Commission on the Measurement of Economic Performance and Social Progress [72] [73]
Subject: draft summary of the report on indicators dated June 2, 2009
From: [T.S. , address, email], The Netherlands
With assistance from Ir. Bart de Boer [address, email]

Date: 5 July 2009

Dear members of the Commission,

Thank you for giving me the opportunity to comment on the above-mentioned report as an interested citizen. After having read your report with great interest my first reaction is surprise that the forty years of pioneering work of Dr. Roefie Hueting on the environmentally sustainable national income (eSNI) is not mentioned.

In the mid sixties he started publishing articles about the relationship between growth and the environment. In 1969, on recommendation of Tinbergen, Hueting founded the department of environmental statistics at Statistics Netherlands. In 1974 Hueting obtained a Ph.D. in economics (cum laude) on the study 'New scarcity and economic growth: more welfare through less production?'. Between 1965 and 2009 he published over 150 articles, half of which in English. Between 1983 and 1989 Hueting was a writing member of the UNEP-World Bank Working Group on Environmental Accounting. In 1999 an international symposium was held in the Academy of Sciences in Amsterdam dedicated to his work. The articles of the participants (Daly, Pearce, Beckerman and others) have been bundled in the *Festschrift* 'Economic growth and valuation of the environment: a debate' [1]. The first copy was offered by Minister of Environment Jan Pronk to the president of the World Bank at a symposium dedicated to the eSNI in Washington D.C. Dr. Joseph Stiglitz was one of the discussants with positive comments on the eSNI [2].

Below I give a short summary of the eSNI theory quoting from articles on eSNI, because it offers solutions to a number of objections raised in your report against the discussed indicators. I am aware that some of the points mentioned are also in your report. However, this is done for the sake of consistency and clarity.

[71] http://www.sni-hueting.info/EN/Others/2009-07-05-Letter-to-Stiglitz-Commission.pdf
[72] https://www.insee.fr/en/information/2662494
[73] https://www.oecd.org/statistics/measuring-economic-social-progress/

Hueting [3] posits the following. All economic activity is aimed at the satisfaction of wants, in other words at welfare, defined as the satisfaction of wants derived from our dealings with scarce means. Welfare is, besides on production, dependent on quite a few other factors. Consequently the term 'economic growth' can mean nothing other than increase in welfare, defined as the satisfaction of wants derived from our dealings with scarce goods. Welfare is not a quantity that can be measured directly 'from outside'; it is a category of individual experience. For this reason the statistician focuses in practice on charting trends in factors that *can* be measured and that can plausibly be argued to influence welfare. Some important welfare-influencing factors are: the package of goods and services produced; scarce environmental functions; time, i.e. leisure time; the distribution of scarce goods, i.e. income distribution; the conditions under which scarce goods are acquired, i.e. labour conditions; employment *casu quo* unemployment.

These factors often conflict with one another. For scarce goods it holds by definition, however, that more of one is less of another, for a good is scarce when something else has to be sacrificed in order to obtain it (sacrificed alternative, opportunity cost). Nowadays environmental functions (see below) have become scarce goods. All other things remaining equal (including the technological state of the art), more production therefore means less environment and vice versa. When (1) in a small or broad margin, preference is given to the environment over production, so when people are willing to sacrifice part of the production to obtain a safer environment, and (2) a government imposes controls on production processes and consumption habits that lead to a smaller volume of goods and services produced, then there will be an increase in the overall satisfaction of wants obtained by means of scarce goods. *A decrease in production will then lead to greater welfare.*

In the theoretical basis for the calculation of sustainable national income, the environment is defined as the non-human-made physical surroundings, or elements thereof, on which humanity entirely depends, whether producing, consuming, breathing or recreating.

In our physical surroundings, a great number of possible uses can be distinguished, which are essential for production, consumption, breathing, et cetera, thus for human existence. These are called environmental functions, or in short: functions; see Hueting [3, 4, 5]. As long as the use of a function does not hamper the use of an other or the same function (by overuse), so as long as environmental functions are not scarce, an insufficiency of labour (that is: hands and brains, intellect or technology that increases traditional productivity) is the sole factor limiting production growth, as measured in standard NI. As soon as one use is at the expense of another, though, or threatens to be so in the future, a second limiting factor is introduced. The emergence of competition between functions marks a juncture at which functions start to fall short of meeting existing wants. Competing functions are by definition scarce and consequently economic goods. Indeed they are the most fundamental economic goods at the disposal of humanity. In the situation of severe competition between functions, which prevails today, labour not only reduces scarcity, thus causing a positive effect on our satisfaction of wants (welfare); but it also increases scarcity, thus causing a negative effect on welfare. The same holds for consumption. In the SEEA manual of the UN Statistical Office is written: "Much of the initiative to look at an alternative path for the economy rather than a different measure of the economy came from the work of Hueting in the late 1960's and the early 1970's. He introduced the concept of environmental function referred to throughout this manual, explaining how pressure on functions leads to scarcity or competition for these functions (...) [6].

The availability of functions, or, in terms of the System of National Accounts (SNA), their volume, decreases from 'infinite' (abundant with respect to existing wants) to finite, that is falling short with respect to existing wants. As a result, the shadow price of environmental functions rises, and with it their value, defined as price times quantity, from zero to an ever-higher positive value. *This rise in value reflects a rise in costs*. To determine the extent of the loss of function, in order to estimate the environmentally sustainable national income (eSNI) (see below), we must know the value of the function. Since environmental functions are collective goods that are not traded on the market, supply and demand curves have to be constructed. Because, according to standard economic theory, determination of value is impossible without data on *both* preferences (demand) *and* opportunity costs (supply).

The estimated costs of measures necessary to restore functions, that rise progressively per unit of function restored, can be seen as a supply curve. We call this the cost-effectiveness curve or the elimination cost curve, because it refers to measures that eliminate the pressure on the environment. Except in the case of irreparable damage, this curve can always be constructed. The most severe environmental problems such as climate change and biodiversity occur at a global scale. In those instances first the global burden is established, then the contribution of a country to the global burden is determined and finally the costs of eliminating this contribution are estimated.

Preferences for environmental functions (demand), on the contrary, can only partially be determined, since these can be expressed only partially via the market, while willingness to pay techniques cannot yield reliable data precisely for vital functions; see Hueting [8]. Therefore, it is not possible to construct a complete demand curve. Expenditure on compensation for loss of function and restoration of physical damage resulting from loss of function, however, constitute revealed preferences for the availability of functions, so that some impression of these preferences can be obtained. One example is the additional measures for the production of drinking water as a result of the loss of the function 'drinking water' because of pollution (overuse of the function 'water as dumping ground for waste'). Another example is the restoration of damage caused by flooding due to excessively cutting forests etc. (overuse of the function 'provider of wood' etc.) that consequently are losing their function 'regulation of the water flow'.

Because individual preferences can be measured only partially, shadow prices for environmental functions, which are determined by the intersection of the first derivatives of the constructed curves for demand and supply (see Figure 1 page 5), cannot be determined. Consequently, these shadow prices – and the value of environmental functions – remain unknown. This means that the *correct prices for the human-made goods* that are produced and consumed at the expense of environmental functions remain *equally unknowable*.

However, to provide the necessary information, *assumptions* can be made about the relative preferences for environmental functions and produced goods. *One* of the possible assumptions is that the economic agents, individuals and institutions, have a dominant preference for an environmentally sustainable development. This assumption is legitimate since governments and institutions all over the world have stated support for environmental sustainability. The national income connected to this path is eSNI. *Another* possible assumption is that the economy is currently on an optimal path that is described by the changes in standard NI. So *both eSNI and standard NI are fictitious* in the context of what is at issue in economic theory and statistics, namely to provide indicators of the effect of our actions on our welfare.

When assuming dominant preferences for sustainability, the unknown demand curves must be replaced by physical standards for sustainable use of the physical environment. The standards are scientifically determined and in this sense objective. They must, of course, be distinguished clearly from the subjective preferences for whether or not they should be attained. Examples are: the man-made rate of extinction of species should not exceed the rate at which new species come into being, for safeguarding the many functions of ecosystems; the emission of greenhouse gases has to be reduced by 70 to 80 % in order to let life support systems restore the climate; the rate of erosion of topsoil may not exceed the rate of formation of such soil due to weathering, for safeguarding the function: 'soil for raising crops'.

From an economic perspective, sustainability standards approximate demand curves that are vertical in the relevant area of a diagram that has the availability of functions measured in physical units on the *x*-axis and the demand for functions and their opportunity costs (the factor costs involved in attaining a certain degree of their availability) on the *y*-axis. The shadow prices for environmental functions – and their value - based upon the assumed preferences for sustainability then follows from the intersection of the vertical line and the marginal cost-effectiveness curve. In this manner the distance to sustainability, denoted in physical units on the *x*-axis, is translated into monetary units. See Figure 1 page 5, which shows the relationship between economy and ecology. Of course, bridging the gap requires a transition period.

For a correct approximation of eSNI (see below), such calculations have been done with the aid of a general equilibrium model, which also generates the shadow prices for produced goods in a sustainable economy. From this, the level of sustainable national income follows. The model is used to trace the consequences of (1) the reactions to the change in price ratios (environment burdening activities become relatively more expensive, whereas environmentally benign activities become relatively cheaper) and (2) direct shifts to environmentally less burdening activities.

Environmental sustainability is defined as the situation in which vital environmental functions are safeguarded for future generations. So the issue at stake is that the *possibilities* to use them remain available. Environmental sustainability can only be attained with drastic changes in the price ratios between environment burdening and environmental benign products in all countries of the world [9]. So eSNI evidently does not work with current market prices.

Environmentally sustainable national income (eSNI) is defined as the maximal attainable production level by which vital environmental functions remain available for future generations, based on the technology available at the time; see Hueting and De Boer [9]. The OECD has accepted this definition [10].The difference between NI and eSNI indicates the volume of production that is produced and consumed unsustainably. Thus eSNI provides information about the distance between the current and a sustainable situation. In combination with standard national income, the time series of NI and eSNI indicate whether we are approaching environmental sustainability or drifting farther away from it. Because of the precautionary principle, future technological progress is not anticipated in the calculation of eSNI. When constructing a time series of eSNIs, technological progress is measured after the event on the basis of the development of the distance between eSNI and standard NI over the course of time. If the distance has decreased it can be estimated which part of the decrease has been caused by progress in environmental technology and which part by direct change to environmentally benign production and consumption (e.g. more biking).

A first rough estimate of eSNI for the world in 1991 by Tinbergen and Hueting [11] arrives at about fifty percent of the production level of the world: the world income. The Institute of Environmental Studies estimate for The Netherlands in 2001 also arrived at about fifty percent of the production level or national income of The Netherlands [12]. Estimates for the years 1990, 1995 and 2000 show that in the period 1990 - 2000 the distance between NI and eSNI increased by 10% or 13 billion euros [13].

According to standard economic theory, producing is adding value. National income (NI) equals the sum of the values added. So NI measures - the fluctuations in the level of -production. It does so according to its definition and according to the intention of the founders of its concept to get an indicator for one of the factors influencing welfare - and a tool for quite a few other purposes. See Tinbergen and Hueting [11]. (Nobelist Jan Tinbergen was one of the founders of the concept of NI and its quantification).

This value is added to the non-human-made physical surroundings. Consequently, environmental functions remain outside the measurement of standard NI. This is logical and easy to understand, because water, air, soil, plant and animal species and the life support systems of our planet are not produced by humans. So losses of functions, caused by production and consumption, are correctly *not* entered as costs. However, expenditures on measures for their restoration and compensation *are* entered as value added. This is asymmetric. These expenditures should be entered as intermediate, as they are costs. By entering these expenditures as final instead of intermediate, the growth of production is overestimated, thus obscuring what is happening with both environment and production.

I think the above text shows that the eSNI offers the following remedies for some objections to indicators discussed in your report.

1) The problem of leaving out the international nature of sustainability (paragraph 166, the fourth full paragraph on my page 2 and the fifth full paragraph on page 3).

2) The problems with respect to the stocks of the non-human made physical surroundings (if you wish natural capital) as well as the problems with respect to weak and strong sustainability are solved by using the concept of environmental functions. Then the only thing that matters is that the possible uses of our physical surroundings remain intact for future generations. This can be accomplished by technical measures, direct shifts to environmentally benign activities, developing alternatives for non-renewables (see the method developed by Tinbergen, Hueting and Bosch [9]) and population policy.
3) The eSNI is an environmental sustainability indicator which is directly and completely comparable with the National Income, that is an indicator for the level of production, because it uses the procedures of the system of national accounts (SNA). This solves the problem of confusion of having two GDP indicators (your paragraph 180). They should be used together to observe the development of the distance between the current production level GDP and an environmentally sustainable production level eSNI.
4) The ANS is based on current market prices (your paragraph 164), while the eSNI uses prices including the cost for attaining sustainability standards.

I do hope that the information given above convinces you that the eSNI theory should be included in your report.

With kind regards,

[T.S.]

(Reproduction of **Figure 6** above)

[1] E.C. van Ierland, J. van der Straaten and H.R.J. Vollebergh (eds), *Economic growth and valuation of the environment, A debate*, 2001, Edward Elgar, Cheltenham, UK – Northhampton, MA, USA.
[2] Foundation for research of sustainable national income, 2001, Report on the World Bank seminar on economic growth and valuation of the environment, A debate on sustainable national income, Delft.
[3] Hueting R. New Scarcity and Economic Growth: More Welfare through Less Production? Amsterdam: North Holland Publishing Company, 1980. Original Dutch edition published by Agon Elsevier, Amsterdam, 1974.
[4] Hueting R. Functions of Nature: Should Nature Be Quantified? London, World Wildlife Fund, 1969.
[5] Hueting R. The Economic Functions of the Environment. In: Ekins P, Max Neef M, editors. Real Life Economics: Understanding Wealth Creation. London, Routledge, pp. 61–69,1992.
[6] Integrated Environmental and Economic Accounting 2003 (SEEA 2003)
[7] Easterlin RA. Does Economic Growth improve the Human Lot? Mim. paper, University of Pennsylvania, 1972.
[8] Hueting R. The Economic Functions of the Environment. In: Ekins P, Max Neef M, editors. Real Life Economics: Understanding Wealth Creation. London, Routledge, pp. 61–69,1992.

[9] Hueting R, De Boer B. Environmental Valuation and Sustainable National Income According to Hueting. In: Van Ierland E. C. *et al.*, editors. Economic Growth and Valuation of the Environment: A Debate, pp. 17–77. Edward Elgar, London, 2001.
[10] http://stats.oecd.org/glossary/detail.asp?ID=6587
[11] Tinbergen J, Hueting R. GNP and Market Prices: Wrong Signals for Sustainable Economic Success that Mask Environmental Destruction. In: Goodland R, Daly H, El Serafy S, Von Droste B, editors. Environmentally Sustainable Economic Development: Building on Brundtland. United Nations Educational, Scientific and Cultural Organization, Paris, 1991. Also published in: Goodland R *et al.*, editors. Population, Technology and Lifestyle, The Transition to Sustainability. Island Press, The International Bank for Reconstruction and Development and UNESCO, Washington, D.C., 1992. Also published in: Goodland R *et al.*, editors. Environmentally Sustainable Economic Development: Building on Brundtland. Environment Working Paper No 46, The World Bank, Washington, D.C., 1991.
[12] Verbruggen H., Dellink RB, Gerlach R, Hofkes MW, Jansen HMA. Alternative Calculations of a Sustainable National Income for the Netherlands According to Hueting. In: Van Ierland EC *et al.*, editors. Economic Growth and Valuation of the Environment: A Debate. Pp. 275–312, London, Edward Elgar, 2001.
[13] Milieu- en Natuurplanbureau. Milieubalans 2006, p. 21, 2006.

19. *Environmentally sustainable national income: Work in progress*

Thomas Colignatus 2012 [74]

19.1 *Abstract*

The calculation of environmentally sustainable national income is not only relatively easy, it is also the best measure compared with other comparable alternative indices. The index deserves more attention because it is a useful scientific tool to provide society with essential information to decide upon future strategies of economic policy.

19.2 *Introduction*

Hueting (2011) proposes a change of method at the national statistical bureau's and the agencies for the evaluation and forecasting of economic policy. First, the figure of "national income" (NI) can be adapted for asymmetric bookkeeping. Secondly, we can create the figure of "environmentally sustainable national income" (eSNI). The gap between NI-ex-asyms and eSNI indicates whether the world becomes grayer or greener. Colignatus (2009a) discusses Hueting's intellectual path. Some selected comments put Hueting's paper in more perspective.

19.3 *A relatively cheap correction*

A new reader might think that the calculation of eSNI is expensive. The cost of modelling and collection of all these ecological data might seem prohibitive. However, the relevant data are collected already for normal policy making. Governments already need to keep track of clean air and water, and so on. The eSNI calculation is only a relatively small modelling exercise at the top of the pyramid of the integration of statistical indicators. At Statistics Netherlands the costs were only 0.25 percent of its budget. Such a cost can be quite acceptable for such an important indicator.

The power of Hueting's analysis is that it is embedded both in the tradition of economic theory and established procedures on economic statistics. The world has a huge machine of statistics, see e.g. the Statistical Commission of the United Nations. Hueting's contribution to the environmental statistics base of the System of Environmental Economic Accounts of the United Nations (UN SEEA) is already well accepted. This machine only requires a small nudge to start producing the figure for eSNI too.

[74] Published as Thomas Colignatus, "Environmentally sustainable national income: Work in progress", Ökologisches Wirtschaften, 2012, no 2, p12-13

19.4 *The need for some focus*

This small nudge doesn't yet come about because of a mere lack of focus by all actors involved. The prime problem is that people don't study Hueting's work. Perhaps some of his scientific statements trigger the wrong reactions or push the wrong buttons. But the statements are grounded in economic theory and statistical practice, and there is no other way than use those precise words. Readers concerned about economics and the environment are advised to study Hueting's work to resolve their misgivings.

19.5 *Distracting temptations*

One problem is that statisticians observe the present while sustainability refers to the future. If Hueting had worked at a forecasting bureau he would have developed an analysis on the future, and the statistical component would have been a corollary. Now Hueting worked at Statistics Netherlands and developed the proper statistical approach, namely eSNI depends upon assumptions on preferences of present people about the future. Now the future is a corollary. The difference is immaterial. But it may take an additional round of explanation.

Hueting's analysis has long fallen into a gap between economists who neglected the environment and environmentalists who disliked economics. Now that the world can actually observe how the climate is changing, there is more attention for environmental economics. Still, there are all kinds of indicators, like the Footprint, Genuine Progress, etcetera, that destroy focus. Statisticians aren't front page people and may not be 'seen' by professors at the academia who want to have their publications. The front page statistician by exception is Bjørn Lomborg but he does not refer to Hueting's work. [75]

Recently there is a lot of attention for happiness, but ecological survival is a prerequisite that then apparently is neglected. Authors on happiness could be advised to focus on getting eSNI accepted first amongst economists, statisticians, policy makers and the general public, who currently are quite misled by using only NI.

One group of researchers proposes to abolish NI altogether but it would seem that this kind of academic discussion is better done while NI and eSNI are smoothly running in the background. Governments needed a figure like NI since they needed more overview to manage our ever complexer societies. NI has been hugely beneficial. But the new scarcity of the ecology requires an adaptation in this method, so simple is the issue.

19.6 *How to do science*

Hueting's work can be understood in the tradition of Leibniz with the spirit 'Let us sit down and look at the formula's' (no quote). NI is well-developed but still work in progress and the latter also holds for eSNI. The work and results are scientifically warranted because of this attitude. Who reads Hueting's work notes that he personally cares about the environment but also how he focuses on what is scientifically warranted. The role of the scientist is to provide information, and it is up to democratic society to decide. If society doesn't have the proper information

---

[75] Addendum 2019: A discussion of Lomborg's approach is in Colignatus (2009, 2015).

however it can only guess at its policy and instruments. Thus the scientific ethic of creating the required information is essential.

Over the last decades, the Anglo-Saxon method of the debating society has grown in prominence. In a world of uncertainty, let the best debater win, is the idea. A recent book by Stephen Schneider is "Science as a contact sport". My suggestion is to be openminded. Debating can be enlightening but Leibniz better has the last word. I am regularly amazed how often people did not sit down and study the formulas, Colignatus (2009a). The story of Global Warming is not only about a world economy spinning out of control but also about scientific mores. Let us learn from these decades.

19.7 *Work in progress*

As said, NI and eSNI are work in progress. Some critical points for the modelling in eSNI are:

(1) eSNI doesn't include yet the competing use of space, e.g. for plants and wild life, nor the costs for the development and use of alternative resources.
(2) The physical norms for sustainability are based upon judgement [76] and thus are open to criticism, uncertainty and scientific progress.
(3) The estimates of price and income elasticities in demand and supply functions rely on current conditions. Those will change in a process towards sustainability, but yet unknown how.
(4) eSNI uses comparative statics. A dynamic model would give a transition path from one state to the other, with an influence of policy-instruments on the speed of adjustment.
(5) An eSNI for one country assumes that all countries adopt sustainability, otherwise there will only be a relocation of the burden on the environment. In practice policies will differ with different effects on eSNI. A pilot for e.g. Germany and Holland would show how large the effects could be.

19.8 *References*

Colignatus is the name in science of Thomas Cool, econometrician in Scheveningen, Holland.

Colignatus, Th (2008, 2009a), "The Old Man and the SNI. A review of advance and adversity in Hueting's research in sustainable national income (SNI), economic growth and the new scarcity from the environment", http://mpra.ub.uni-muenchen.de/12690. An edited version is available in p27-60 in Colignatus, Th (2009b, 2015), "The Tinbergen & Hueting Approach in the Economics of Ecological Survival", https://mpra.ub.uni-muenchen.de/63904/

Hueting, R (2011), "The future of the Environmentally sustainable national income", Ökologisches Wirtschaften 2011, no 4, p 30-35

[76] Addendum 2019: The norms are derived from the scientific literature, and the literature may contain judgements on scientific grounds.

20. *Frequently Asked Questions on Hueting's eSNI concept*

Peter Stauvermann 2007 [77]

20.1 *General critics*

20.1.1 *Question 1a – Statics versus dynamics*

The concept of strong sustainability does not fit to the real world, because the real world – especially nature – is not in a static equilibrium, at best in an dynamic one. We do not know for example whether climate change is more induced by human behaviour or by the evolution of the Earth, because the change of climate does not necessarily depend on additional CO_2 emissions caused by production.

20.1.2 *Answer 1a.1*

With respect to the first part of this question the following *answer* can be given. In the article *Sustainability is an objective concept* by Roefie Hueting and Lucas Reijnders in Ecological Economics 27 (1998b) is stated, on page 140, left column, that vital environmental functions have to stay available in a *dynamic* equilibrium. This is described on p. 139 as an equilibrium between activities by humans (especially production and consumption) and their natural resources. We most probably agree (1) that the Earth since its origin, around five billion years ago, has been changing continuously and *drastically* and that this process will continue on a geological timescale and (2) that humans since their origin, roughly hundred to two hundred thousand years ago, have been constantly busy, in particular with adding value to the non-human-made physical surroundings: producing. Hueting and Reijnders therefore state in the article that in these dynamic processes the vital possible uses of those surroundings have to stay available on penalty of a collapse of the production to far below a sustainable level now (because this is already happening in some places, see: Hueting and Reijnders, *Broad sustainability contra sustainability: the proper construction of sustainability indicators*, in Ecological Economics 50, 2004a) and in the future (precautionary principle for the sake of generations to come).

20.1.3 *Answer 1a.2*

With respect to the second part of this question the remark can be made that according to climatologists the plausibility that climate change is caused by human activities is much greater than that is not caused by man. Furthermore: the precautionary principle is underlying the concept of environmental sustainability, which in turn is underlying eSNI.

20.1.4 *Question 1b – Direction of evolution*

The concept of strong sustainability contradicts the concept of evolution, but we do not know in which direction the evolution will evolve the Earth.

[77] May 2007, edited, http://www.sni-hueting.info/EN/2007-05-Stauvermann-FAQ.pdf

20.1.5 *Answer 1b.1*

The eSNI is not based on strong sustainability per se. In Hueting and De Boer, *Environmental valuation and eSNI according to Hueting*, in *Economic Growth and Valuation of the Environment, a Debate*, E. van Ierland et al. (eds), Edward Elgar, Cheltenham, 2001, the following remarks are made about strong and weak sustainability.

QUOTE

The figures thus found can be no more than rough estimates, of course.

In the context of non-renewable natural resources, though, this is an approach that does justice to the principle of sustainability, which is the point of departure of our estimates. Our approach would be comparable with that of Solow (1974), Hartwick (1977, 1978) and others, if the latter were to exclude unfeasible substitution of renewable resources by other resources and by capital (see below), that is if they were to abandon their faith in the extreme areas of formal production functions.

When using the concept of environmental function, the only thing that matters in the context of sustainability is that vital functions remain available. What does the conservation of vital functions imply for the distinction between renewable and non-renewable resources and for the distinction between strong and weak sustainability?

As for renewable resources, functions remain available as long as their regenerative capacity remains intact. Regeneration in relation to current use of 'non-renewable' resources such as crude oil and copper that are formed by slow geological processes is close to zero. 'Regeneration' then takes the form of efficiency improvement, recycling and, in the final instance, developing substitutes. The possibilities for this are hopeful (Reijnders, 1996; Brown et al., 1998). So, economically speaking, there seems to be no essential difference between the two types of resource: sustainability is attained if their functions remain available.

Advocates of 'weak sustainability' take the line that all elements of the environment can ultimately be substituted by man-made alternatives, implying that restoration of lost elements can be postponed in anticipation of cheaper substitutes provided by future technologies. However, the life support systems [78] of our planet, on which a number of vital functions depend, are not substitutable at all (Lovelock, 1979; Roberts, 1988; Reijnders, 1996).[79] Consequently, there can be no such thing as 'weak sustainability' for the functions of these systems.

---

[78] Life support systems are understood as the processes that maintain the conditions necessary for life on Earth. This comes down to maintaining equilibria within narrow margins. The processes may be of a biological or physico-chemical nature, or a combination thereof. Examples of biological processes include the carbon and nutrient cycles, involving the extraction of such substances as carbon dioxide, water and minerals from the abiotic environment during biomass creation, and the return of these substances to the abiotic environment during biomass decomposition. Examples of physico-chemical processes include the water cycle and regulation of the thickness of the stratospheric ozone layer. As the examples show, there is interaction between the processes, with the possibility of equilibrium being disturbed. The water cycle, for example, may be disturbed by large-scale deforestation.

[79] The same holds for most of the functions of natural ecosystems, especially in the long term (see, for example, the remark on the function of 'gene pool' in Section 4 of R. Hueting and B. de Boer (2001b), *Environmental valuation and sustainable national income according to Hueting* in:

Advocates of 'strong sustainability' hold it to be impossible for humanity to substitute many of the elements of the natural environment. In its strictest form, however, this implies that stocks of non-renewable resources should remain fully intact, an unrealistic aim, as already discussed. Consequently, strong sustainability for non-renewable resources seems to be impossible.

In conclusion, there seems to be only one kind of sustainability, whereby non-renewable resources must gradually be substituted by other elements of our physical surroundings in order to guarantee the availability of functions, and substitution of a large class of renewable resources is impossible, particularly life support systems, including ecosystems.

UNQUOTE

20.1.6 *Answer 1b.2*

As for the uncertainty about direction the evolution will evolve the Earth, this question boils down to the question "Can the term at which vital functions have to remain available objectively be determined?" The *answer* is: yes, this is possible, but only with great uncertainties. First of all, to clarify the problem: if, as a result of reaching sustainability standards, possible uses have been made available and unthreatened, and they have to remain so in the future, then these sustainability standards have to be respected in the future from generation to generation, over and over again for generations to come (this is the basic assumption of eSNI: predominant preferences for maintaining environmental functions which are for humans; of course the resulting reallocation sacrifice for maintaining the standards can decrease by improved technology). So the point is whether the length of the period during which sustainability standards have to be maintained can be objectively determined.

Partly this period is restricted by the term of life of the object in question: Homo Sapiens. The geological history learns that the family of species to which humans belong (the primates) are characterized by a term of life per species in the order of 100,000s to around one million years. The longest term of life of a mammal is in the order of tens of millions of years. There isn't a single reason to suppose that humans as a species will persevere on Earth for five billion years, when the sun comes to its end. Long before mammals will have disappeared from the Earth (in particular because of a too high temperature). When humans disappear so does the concept of sustainability.

For another part the period is limited by Earth's geophysical processes. Further to the above remarks on maintaining vital functions in the dynamic processes of the Earth and human activities (the definition of environmental sustainability), the following statement is made in the afore mentioned article by Hueting and De Boer, Edward Elgar book p. 59 under 6.6 (in connection with previous pages). In order to prevent a collapse of production, vital functions have to stay available in the future on a therefore required level. In theory the future is infinite, but in practice we limit this to the time span "in which the influence of geophysical processes on the environment is unlikely to exceed human influence, say several

---

Economic growth and valuation of the environment, A debate, E.C. van Ierland, J. van der Straaten, H. Vollebergh (eds), Edward Elgar, Cheltenham, UK – Northhampton, MA, USA, pp. 27-33.

millennia or longer". Besides geophysical processes also biogeochemical processes have to be considered. That period is, put succinctly, equal to now up to the moment upon which the effect of environmental pressure on functions is neutralised c.q. overruled by geophysical or biogeophysical processes. This time span can by rough estimate be objectively determined by natural scientists. For example it has been estimated that in about 40,000 years there will be a new Ice Age. Generations to come have to take measures to eliminate the effect of extra greenhouse gases on functions to keep them available only up to the turning point. Thereafter, then living humans can decide to survive in the cold. (The necessary measures then are obviously not costs but value added, because the cold is not caused by humans.)

So it is stated that environmental sustainability cannot be determined for ever (a difficult concept just as infinite) and that when the sun is burned-up the concept of environmental sustainability doesn't exist anymore because humans then, and probably earlier, don't exist any longer.

Herewith environmental sustainability is determined as remaining available of vital environmental functions, a situation that can be objectively determined (while the preferences for whether or not wanting to reach this situation are subjective).

20.2 *Specific critics*

20.2.1 *Question 2a – Technological change*

It is assumed that the technological change is zero while calculating the eSNI of a specific year. It could be that an important invention could be made to reduce the abatement costs to protect of the environment is much cheaper in the future. Then it would be efficient to restore environmental damages in the future in stead of today.

20.2.2 *Answer 2a*

The eSNI is not a policy for how to restore functions as efficient as possible, but an instrument that provides information about the question whether society is drifting further away from environmental sustainability or approaching environmental sustainability, formulated as the situation in which vital possible uses of human's physical surroundings remain available for future generations with the technology in the year of investigation. In the first case (drifting away) the gap between eSNI and standard NI becomes greater, in the second case (approaching) this gap becomes smaller. Thus, to give an example, in the Netherlands this gap has increased by about 10 billion euro in the period 1990-2000. If, as has been included in question 2a, in some year *x* in the future an important invention is made that reduces the abatement costs, then this helps to reduce the distance between eSNI and NI (the gap) in that year *x* and consequently helps to bring society closer to environmental sustainability in year *x*.

20.2.3 *Question 2b – Time frame*

Additionally, to what extent are eSNI's of different years comparable?

20.2.4 *Answer 2b*

eSNI's of different years are compatible in the same way as standard NI's of different years, because they are estimated according to the same rules, and therefore eSNI's and NI's in the same year are compatible too. However, the uncertainty of the eSNI estimates is of course much greater than the uncertainty of the NI estimates.

20.2.5 *Question 2c – Zero cost of extinct species*

Assume the following: A specific species has died out, that means that this species cannot be protected anymore, which would decrease ceteris paribus the costs of protecting the environment and consequently lead to a higher value of eSNI. This would be a paradox.

20.2.6 *Answer 2c*

[Updated 2019] Biodiversity is one of the areas that are not yet covered fully in the calculation of Dutch eSNI. This is a good question. When there are subsidies for including biodiversity then this issue should be addressed. Hueting has often published that no elimination costs can be computed for irreversible, unrepairable losses, so his *'demand and supply of functions'* method fails in these cases. No measures can be formulated to bring species back on Earth, so no (direct) costs can be computed. The sustainability standard and question would concern species that have a crucial rule in a vital environmental function. The relevant costs then concern protection indeed. If it was *assumed* that the species was crucial, but after extinction it doesn't appear to be so, then this would lead to an higher value of eSNI in the subsequent period indeed. If a crucial species becomes extinct then both eSNI and NI eventually collapse, with some reaction time. However, in the current calculation method the collapse would be instantaneous.

20.3 *Practical problems*

20.3.1 *Question 3a – Shape of abatement cost curves*

Do we really know the shape of the abatement cost curves?

20.3.2 *Answer 3a*

Yes, by and large we do. Elimination cost curves (elimination is defined as eliminating the burdening of functions at the source, see *New Scarcity*) are constructed by arranging the five kind of elimination measures (technical, alternatives, direct shifts, reduction of activities and reduction of population- as ultimum remedium) by increasing annual costs per unit of function(s) regained (expressed as a physical parameter, e.g. 1000 tons CO_2). So you get a number of dots in the diagram with money on the *y*-axis and the function in physical units on the *x*-axis and then draw a line between the dots which is the elimination cost curve using the technology in the year of investigation.

20.3.3 *Question 3b – Cans or bottles*

How should the following problem be handled: Assuming we could only choose between cans and bottles for Coke, what is then preferable? On the one hand it would be possible to reduce the consumption of bauxite to produce cans, on the other hand we would increase the quantity of water to clean bottles and it much less energy consuming to transport one litre Coke in a can than in a bottle. How shall this problem or trade-off be solved?

20.3.4 *Answer 3b*

Referring to *answers 1b.2 and 2a*, the following remarks can be made. The purpose of eSNI is to estimate a burdening of vital functions that can be sustained from generation to generation in such a way that these functions remain over and over again available for the next generation (see *answer 1b.2*). So as for the non-renewable bauxite, water and fossil energy carriers we deal with the costs of recycling and with the costs of developing and bringing into practice alternatives. For how to deal with non-renewables see the solution given by Tinbergen-Hueting-Bosch, mentioned at pages 67 (at the bottom), 68 and 69 in *Economic Growth etc. etc.,* Edward Elgar, Cheltenham UK, 2001. The costs of the measures resulting from this solution will increase the prices of bauxite, water and energy. Depending on the relative rises in prices of these non-renewables the prices of cans and bottles will be affected and depending of the relative rises in the prices of cans and bottles the choice between cans and bottles will be made. As you will understand, the above is a primitive and incomplete description of what is happening in the model, in which more factors play a roll. Again, the question shows that the colleague who asked the question has a wrong idea about what eSNI is: it is not a policy tool for special cases but a macro approach for giving information about a sustainable production level that can be attained by a sustainable burdening of the possible uses of the non-human-made physical surroundings, as an indispensable supplement to the standard NI. However, the new price relationships in the estimated environmentally sustainable situation will give some indication of what can be expected if society is approaching this goal.

20.3.5 *Question 3c – eSNI requires too many assumptions*

Too many assumptions are needed to calculate an eSNI, especially on the behaviour of foreign countries, consumer behavior, production functions etc.

20.3.6 *Answer 3c*

It is quite usual to have this number and types of assumptions in economic modelling. As for foreign countries, without the assumption that other countries proceed simultaneously to environmental sustainability according to the definition given, you get a result that is complete nonsense, because then ‘pollution’ is exported; this assumption is self-evident, logical and inescapable. As for consumer behaviour, empirical long term demand elasticities for changes in prices are available to start off, but elasticities for great changes are uncertain indeed. But one has to realize that they are dictated by the requirement that a sustainable production level must be attained; so they *must* be estimated even if they are uncertain. The same holds true for production functions. In conclusion, uncertainties are inescapable. However, the greatest uncertainty by far is to make no estimate of eSNI’s. eSNI’s cannot be replaced by any other approach, including the ecological footprint or the natural step.

21. *Deriving sustainability standards*

21.1 *Abstract*

This Appendix elaborates upon De Boer in Verbruggen (ed) (2000) and supports Section 10.7. The selection of topics reflects the Dutch situation around 1990.

21.2 *Acidification*

A number of air pollutants contribute to the formation of acids that threaten vulnerable ecosystems ("acid rain"). The most important acidifying substances emitted by human activities are sulphur dioxide (SO_2), nitrogen oxides (NO and NO_2) and ammonia (NH_3). Their reaction products are acids (H_2SO_3, H_2SO_4, HNO_2 and HNO_3) and aerosols that may be converted into acids. These substances cause chemical and biological changes in terrestrial and aquatic ecosystems that are not strongly buffered.

Soil chemistry has changed in many affected nature areas. One of the effects is the increased leaching of aluminium to ground water. Poorly buffered ground and surface water is most vulnerable to acidification. Very soft water is therefore no longer found in the Netherlands. Many 'soft' lakes in Sweden have been severely acidified in the past decades, mainly due to emissions in Western Europe. It is also evident that species have disappeared from acidified ecosystems.

Several plants and trees suffer from damage to roots or leaves in acidified areas. The decline in the health of forest in central Europe in the 1990s has been attributed to acidification. Limits to the acidity of soils have therefore been set that must prevent that the uptake of nutrients by plants is severely obstructed by damage to the roots, or that the soil is leached out (De Vries, 1993 and 1995).

Isolated, oligotrophic and poorly buffered aquatic ecosystems are very vulnerable to acidification. Many moors and lakes previously falling under this description have changed in chemical and biological composition. Several species specific for oligotrophic, soft water have disappeared; in Sweden several lakes have completely died-off. Acidity limit values designed to protect the most vulnerable aquatic species were reviewed and assessed for Dutch surface waters by, among others, De Vries (1993 and 1995).

The critical acidity levels for prevailing Dutch types of terrestrial and aquatic ecosystems were converted into critical depositions (or loads) by the use of chemical steady state models. De Vries (1993, 1995) shows that the critical depositions of nitrogen compounds in coniferous and deciduous woods on well drained sandy grounds for the limitation of acidification are 1.6 to 1.8 times less strict than the corresponding critical nitrogen depositions for the limitation of eutrophication. For surface waters, the critical nitrogen loads for acidification are 2.4 times stricter than the critical nitrogen loads for eutrophication. The critical loads for surface waters probably have a small influence on the total admissible emission. The national standard for acidifying emission in air is therefore chosen 1.5 to 1.7 times less strict than the national standard for the nitrogen emission in air for the prevention of eutrophication, as reported by De Boer (2004a). Expressed in moles of potentially available acid (H^+), called acidification equivalents (Aeq), the sustainability standard for the national emission of acidifying substances in air is 10 (6...15) billion Aeq/year. The emission of acidifying substances in air in the year 1990 is 38.4 billion Aeq/year, respectively (CBS, 1999). The required emission reduction is therefore 28.4 (23...32) billion Aeq/year.

The estimate for the sustainability standard has to be improved in due time. The goal for the year 2010 issued in the second National Environment Policy Plan for the Netherlands is stricter: 4.3...8.6 billion Aeq/year (VROM, 1994). For a new calculation of eSNI it would be relevant to investigate the background of these more stringent targets and consider adaptation of the sustainability standards for eSNI.

21.3 *Climate change*

Some gases in the earth's atmosphere, especially water vapour (H_2O), carbon dioxide (CO_2), methane (CH_4) and nitrous oxide (N_2O), absorb short wave radiation of the sun such as light and emit the captured energy in the form of longer wave heat radiation, thus maintaining temperatures of the atmosphere which are essential for life as we know it: without these so-called greenhouse gases, the atmosphere's average temperature would be some 20 degrees Celsius lower than it is now (Houghton et al., 1990 and 1992). H_2O is the most important greenhouse gas.

Humanity's economic activities since the start of the industrial revolution have led to increasing emissions of CO_2, CH_4, N_2O, and synthetic greenhouse gases such as chlorofluorocarbons or freons (CFCs), bromochlorofluorocarbons or halons and similar fluoridised organic compounds, and thus to increased concentrations of these substances in the atmosphere. Moreover, mankind 'harvests' the planet's forests on a large and growing scale, thereby diminishing their important function as a 'sink' for carbon dioxide, beside posing other threats to environmental sustainability.

Following these processes with retardation, the atmosphere's mean temperature at ground level has risen more than a half degree Celsius from the pre-industrial level. Scientific evidence is growing that the temperature rise must be attributed, at least for a substantial part, to the increased abundance of these gases in the atmosphere. Several other changes in the global climate, such as the increased occurrence and intensity of storms and heavy gales, are expected to be related to the temperature rise.

If no measures will be taken in the near future to reduce the emissions of greenhouse gases, an increase of the globally averaged temperature of the atmosphere by several degrees Celsius and consecutive other serious climate changes are likely to occur in the next century (Houghton et al., 1992). Important consequences will probably be the movement of moderate and sub-boreal climate zones towards the poles and of lower mountainous climate to higher mountainous regions. This in turn will lead to partial melting of tundra permafrost and polar ice shields, the latter resulting in a rise of the sea level. Melting permafrost may release methane rather quickly, thus accelerating the global warming process. Thus, boreal, alpine, lowland and corral reef species may become extinct because their habitats change or disappear. These and some other not yet expected effects of the enhanced greenhouse effect will lead to losses of environmental functions.

Assuming that functions remain available at the least self-supporting levels as long as no species become extinct globally due to man's actions, the temperature should not increase more than 1.0 to 2.0°C at ground level (Sprengers et al., 1994 and Vellinga and Swart, 1991, respectively) at a rate not exceeding 0.01°C per year (Jäger, 1988, RIVM, 1993 and Rotmans, 1990). The results reported here are based on assumed sustainability limits of 1.5°C for the ultimate increase of the average temperature of the atmosphere of 0.01°C per year for the rate of change of this temperature on the long run. See De Boer (2003) for a review of the arguments considering the choice of these standards.

Converting these limits into corresponding sustainability standards for global emissions of greenhouse gases and deforestation poses some problems. It requires quantitative knowledge of the involved processes in the atmosphere, in the oceans and on land, and their dynamic properties. The large time scales of many of these processes make it difficult to find constant relations between the temperature limit values and the required global levels of emissions of greenhouses and deforestation.

A reasonably reliable approach for the estimation of emission standards was found by applying the temperature limits as constraints in a simple dynamic model of the globally averaged enhanced greenhouse effect, derived from the first version of the model IMAGE (Rotmans, 1990); described by De Boer (2003). This model was simplified by using a static approximation of the fast kinetics of methane and its reaction products. This enabled calculation of global warming on a yearly instead of an hourly basis.

With this model, a solution with the least total elimination costs over the period 1990 - 3000 had to be found. Although optimal control theory was not applied, it provided a rough approximation of the optimal relative rate of the removal of each global greenhouse gas emission by the 'rate coefficient' of the slowest process facilitating the decline.

The costs of the reductions of the greenhouse gas emissions were calculated by applying total cost curves for the elimination of greenhouse gas emissions in each year. These were the same cost curves that were to be used later, in the final calculation of eSNI in the year of investigation, in this case 1990, except that direct shifts between production sectors were roughly included by simple linear extrapolations of the curves. Each 'trial' calculation delivered, for each year from 1990 on to the year 3000:

- the reductions of the global greenhouse gas emissions,
- the resulting developments of the globally averaged concentrations of these gases in the atmosphere during this period, and
- the effect of these concentrations on the global average of the temperature of the atmosphere during this period.

These trials were repeated until a set of *emissions of the greenhouse gases* were found that complied with the temperature standards at the least total elimination costs over the whole period. After an adaptation period of 30 years or so, all emissions in this set gradually approached apparent equilibrium levels. These final levels were interpreted as the standards for the global greenhouse gas emissions.

The globally and yearly averaged temperature of the atmosphere resulting solution showed a gradual asymptotical rise of the to 1.5 °C standard indeed, the major part occurring in the 21st century. The goal to limit the increase of this temperature to 0.01 °C per year was already violated in the past, but in the calculated sustainable scenario it would be satisfied from 2080 on.

The thus found set of global greenhouse gas emissions as functions of time was converted into one equivalent global CO_2 emission as function of time, by multiplying each emission with its Global Warming Potential (GWP) for the long run (1990-3000), and summing the results. These GWP's were calculated with the discussed model as well. The approximate equilibrium value of the equivalent CO_2 emission, reached in the last year of the calculation, 9220 billion kg $CO_{2\text{-eq}}$, was taken as the global sustainability standard. For comparison: the global equivalent emission of greenhouse gases in 1990, was calculated as 40065 billion kg $CO_{2\text{-eq}}$ (De Boer, 2003).

The *sustainability standard for the total equivalent emission of the greenhouse gases in the Netherlands* is found by multiplying the global standard with the ratio of the Dutch to the global equivalent CO_2 emission in the year of calculation, 1990. This standard is 53.3 billion kg $CO_{2\text{-eq}}$. This standard is used in the calculation of Dutch eSNI, shown in **Table 6.**

Reduction of the CO_2 emission by reforestation was included in the model completely as a global operation in the 21st and 22nd century. Its costs, however, were not included in the calculation, because reforestation was seen as a separate environmental problem to be included in future eSNI calculations.

The uncertainties in the input data and the model, as well as the sensitivity of the model outcomes to these, are hard to estimate. However, based on the calibration of the model output to measurement data, the relative error of the equivalent emission standard is roughly estimated as ± 20%.

All sustainability standards are dependent on our knowledge of the involved processes in the environment and should therefore be revisited each twenty years or so. The standard for climate changing emissions, like the standard for the use of fossil fuels (Section 9.9.2), however, depends on knowledge on the elimination technology as well. The standard should therefore be recalculated for each eSNI reporting year. However, regarding the time constants in the present model, a revision period for the climate change standards of 20 years might suffice.

21.4 *Dehydration*

'Dehydration' and 'desiccation' are terms for 'all effects of the lowering of the groundwater table on forest, nature and the landscape, both as a result of a water shortage and changes in the effects of seepage and precipitation' (V&W, 1985). Causes are drainage of agricultural area, groundwater extraction for drinking and industrial water production and other activities, related to about 60%, 30% and 10% of the total affected nature area surface (RIVM, 1996). The process is going on in the Netherlands for more than a century, but especially since the 1950's. Main effects are the impoverishment of natural vegetation and its sequential effects, particularly on fauna. Many typical ecosystems such as moist grassland, moist heath, moist dune valleys, high moorlands, fens, natural forests, brook dales and deciduous forest are declining rapidly. Several specific species have disappeared from these systems.

Following the principles discussed in Section 9.6.1, the sustainability standard would be that the species expected to occur in the Ecological Main Structure must be protected. However, the inventories of the effects and the measures needed to abate them are limited to the areas which the definition suggests, i.e. the existing nature areas (officially: the areas to which 'nature' has been assigned as main function or secondary function; in our reference system, these functions have to be understood as collective terms for the potential functions of these areas). As soon as urban nature areas are recognized as parts of the overall structure, for instance, the influence of urban and industrial drainage is expected to be greater than mentioned above. We conform ourselves to this data limitation, which should be removed in the second stage of the project.

Given this data limitation, De Boer (2004a) adapted the standard as to account for recovery of the original groundwater table in 100% of the dried out natural areas, measured as surface. It is expected, however, that not all ecosystems involved will fully recover (RIZA, 1996). RIZA estimates that the total affected area has not changed much since 1985. This concerns 3050 km^2 dried-out area with main function 'nature' and 2550 km^2 dried-out area with side function 'nature'. In the Milieubalans 1996 these areas are estimated 2990 and 3250 km^2, based on a new inventory (RIVM, 1996).

The second National Environment Policy Plan (VROM, 1994) includes as a goal for the year 2010 a 40% reduction of the area with drought damage compared to 1985, by the way.

21.5 *Depletion of the ozone layer*

Since the 1940's chlorofluorocarbons (CFC), halons and related volatile halogenated hydrocarbons have been produced in large quantities. These substances are used as propellants in spray cans, cooling fluids, cleansing agents et cetera. During or after their use, these substances evaporate and are transported through the troposphere, where they have long lifetimes. In the stratosphere they are broken down through the influence of high-energetic radiation and radicals. These reactions yield reactive forms of chlorine and bromine, which cause additional decomposition of stratospheric ozone, since 1978 roughly by 3% per year. This leads to increased intensities of ultraviolet radiation passed on to ground level.

The stronger ultraviolet-B radiation causes different kinds of damage to different species. Algae and plants suffer from increased damage to epidermal cells, and the photosynthesis systems, in both boreal and moderate zones, in alpine and aquatic ecosystems. Genetic damage occurs more often in various plant and animal species than before. Observations indicate that phyto- and zooplankton and larvae of fish and crustaceans are among the most vulnerable. Effects on the populations of these and other species cannot be excluded if the depletion of the ozone layer goes on (Van der Woerd and Slaper, 1992; UNEP, 1989 and 1991). The most sensitive species might have become or may become extinct.

Reviews by UNEP (1989, 1991) refer to marine research indicating that 9% ozone depletion, leading to 20% increase of ultraviolet-B, results in an 8%

reduction of the annual anchovy larvae population. With 16% ozone depletion 5% decrease in primary production and 6 - 9 % reduction of fish yield have been observed (Häder et al., 1989, 1991). Yet the organisms survive the natural longer lasting cycles of ultraviolet radiation, such as the 11 years' cycle caused by the sun's oscillation, which has an amplitude of ± 10% of the long run average. The standard for the avoidance of the extinction of the most sensitive marine species is therefore expected to lie between 1% and 10% ozone depletion, roughly estimated at 5% ± 2%.

More people suffer from sunburn more often and more seriously, which leads to a higher incidence of forms of skin cancer, that might lead to a higher mortality rate. Slaper et al. (1992) found a relation between the average lifetime dose of ultraviolet-B and the increase in death rate. However, a number of additional yearly deaths accepted in society is impossible to access.

A third limit to ozone depletion may be derived from the ozone depletion process itself. The total average concentrations of chlorine and bromine in the stratosphere amount to circa 4 ppbv chlorine equivalents at present. In order to close the 'holes' in the ozone layer, it is at least necessary to return to the concentrations occurring before the first detection of the Antarctic 'ozone hole', i.e. 1.5 to 2.0 ppbv (Van der Woerd and Slaper, 1991). Although the average natural background concentration of 0.6 ppbv would be the most fundamental sustainability standard in this respect, we regard 1.5 to 2.0 ppbv as a preliminary sustainability limit aimed at the prevention of 'ozone holes'.

A rough equilibrium analysis performed with the dynamic model of Slaper et al. coupling the following key variables as a chain: emissions of ozone depleting gases – equivalent chlorine concentration – ozone column – ultraviolet-B radiation – incidence of human skin cancers – skin cancer related deaths. It follows that the approximate standard of 3 to 7% ozone depletion for the protection of marine species boils down to a (equivalent) global emission of 80 to 186 million kg CFC11-eq/year. This standard entails a reduction of 84 to 93% of the 1990 emission of 1170 million kg CFC11-eq/year. This is stricter than standards for a limitation of skin cancer deaths and the prevention of the formation of 'ozone holes'. The equivalent emissions are calculated with ozone depletion potentials (ODPs) mainly taken from WMO (1999), Nimitz and Skaggs (1992) and Kindler et al. (1995).

The emission standard for the Netherlands is in the same proportion to the world emission standard as the Dutch emission to the global emission. The equivalent emission standard for ozone depleting gases in the Netherlands is therefore computed as 0.95 ± 0.45 million kg CFC11-eq/year. The equivalent emission in the Netherlands in 1990 was 10.4 million kg CFC11-eq/year, so the standard calls for an emission reduction of 87 to 95% in that year. This standard includes the types of use of these gases from which no emissions have been estimated. It is assumed that these emissions are not abated; therefore, the standard for the emission of abated gases in the Netherlands is set to 0.6 million kg CFC11-eq/year (De Boer, 2004b).

21.6 *Eutrophication*

Many human activities burden ecosystems with natural substances that are essential for all organisms, so-called nutrients. Generally, quickly growing algae and plants in an ecosystem profit most from this over-fertilisation or eutrophication, as well as 'more opportunistic' animals that graze plants and algae, the animals that prey upon them and so on, as well as the so-called scavengers. Less opportunistic species become less abundant or even disappear from the system, so the ecosystem changes. Roughly one third of the heaths in the Netherlands had turned to grass lands by 1990, while another third was on its way; the process has been going on since. Rare species typical for heath vegetation have disappeared in these areas. The most influential nutrients are phosphate, ammonium, nitrite and nitrate, and organic substances from which these ions can be formed by organisms. Standards for the emissions of nutrients to be used in this project were estimated by studying their inputs to ecosystems via processes in air, soil and surface water nation-wide; see De Boer (2004a).

21.6.1 *Air*

Erisman et al. (1996) made calculations in which local emissions of ammonia, nitrite and nitrate (expressed as nitrogen) into air are maximized under the constraint that the critical deposition levels of nitrogen on the soils and surface waters of nature areas may not be exceeded. The critical loads were calculated to prevent critical concentration levels from being exceeded, in order to prevent eutrophication (De Vries, 1993 and 1995). A linear and static model was used for the transport of the nitrogen nutrients through the atmosphere. Allowed emissions and depositions were calculated per grid cell on a map of the Netherlands, for the situation where the (then projected) *Ecological Main Structure* would be realized. Emissions and their locations were optimized; unrealistic emission densities were prevented. The total allowed nitrogen emissions thus found amounts to 105 million kg N/year, with confidence limits of 65 to 145 million kg N/year.

The total P emission into air amounts to only 0.5% of the total P emission in water, soil and air together. Therefore, the required *relative* reduction of the total P emission into air is assumed equal to the one for the total N emission into air.

21.6.2 *Soil*

For this study a simple model was made of the eutrophication of the Dutch agricultural areas in the years 1986 – 1994. Infiltration of surface water as a source of nutrients was neglected compared to the main sources, the applications of manure, artificial fertilisers, sewage treatment sludge and compost; see De Boer 2001. All agricultural soils together were represented by one compartment. The processes taken into account were uptake of nutrients by the crop, die-of of a fraction of the crop, evaporation of gases like ammonia, and seepage to the subsoil. The model was based on nutrient balances by the CBS (1989, 1992, and 1994) for unsaturated and saturated ground water in the Netherlands as a whole and approximates the average nutrient concentrations in the upper 10 meters of the ground water.

Sustainable fertilisation was originally approximated by the set of nutrient dosages that are just enough to alleviate the limitation of crop growth by nutrient shortage. On an annual basis, these nutrient quantities would then be equal to what the crop would need to fully develop during the growing season. Other growth factors such as the crop characteristics, the water table, additional infiltration and the amount of sunlight during the growing season would then determine the harvest. However, losses of nutrient cannot be fully excluded. Therefore, each reduction of the dosage of nutrients aimed at reduction of nutrient losses to the ground water will lead to a reduction of the crop yield. Environmentally sustainable dosages of N and P were supposed to occur if the crop loss by nutrient scarcity is about 15% of the yield in the situation of over-fertilisation. A consequence of this criterion is that the N and P dosages should occur in the optimal proportion for the average Dutch crop. This mass ratio N:P was roughly put at 7.5, because this resulted in a better fit to the national N and P budgets, and the national average N and P concentrations as well.

Life in the agricultural soil including the upper aquifer must not be disturbed so much that unsustainable effects on terrestrial life including soil ecosystems occur, such as the disappearance of species on a global scale, which includes local species in adjacent ecosystems. It was supposed that the simulated equilibrium fertilisation is a first line of defence for this goal. Additionally, however, the average nitrogen concentration in groundwater was limited to 5.6 mg/litre, a value proposed by RIVM (1997) to protect soil life in the long run. The simple model used here showed that this was practically reached *on average* at equilibrium fertilisation, as defined above.

The estimated environmentally sustainable emission to soil amounts to 128 million kilograms of phosphorus (or eutrophication equivalents, Eeq) per year. The uncertainties in the data and our experiences in calibrating the model lead us to expect a reliability interval of 100 to 150 million kg Eeq per year.

21.6.3 *Surface water*

CIW (1996) determined the national annual average of the local total nitrogen concentrations and the national average of the annual 90 percentiles of the local total phosphorus concentrations and tested these statistics to (temporary) limit values and (ultimate) goal values. Linear relations were assumed between these aggregates and, respectively, the total loads of phosphorus and nitrogen to surface waters in the Netherlands. The emission standards are then found by dividing the emissions by the factor by which the above mentioned concentration statistics exceed the goal values. These rough simplifications are judged acceptable because the nutrient emissions to surface waters are smaller than the emissions to air and soil; see **Table 10**. The derived standards for emissions in surface water appear to be at the lower end of the proposed range for the policy standard issued in the Second National Environmental Policy Plan (VROM, 1994).

21.6.4 *Total emissions and standards*

The emissions to water, soil and air are totalled in **Table 10.** This totalling can be done because transfers between these components of the environment are not incorporated in the emissions. Concretely: application of manure is counted as emissions of nitrogen and phosphorus to the soil. The resulting release of ammonia in the atmosphere is not counted as a part of the emission into air. This ammonia release and the emission of ammonia and nitrogen oxides into air are the main causes of the deposition of airborne nitrogen on soil. Again, this deposition is not counted as part of the emission of nitrogen in soil.

Table 10. Nutrient emissions and standards

	Emission in 1990	Sustainability standard
Total (million Eeq/year)	312	128
Nitrogen (million kg N/year)	1436	611
Air	420	90
Soil	956	500
Surface water	60	21
Phosphorus (million kg P/year)	169	67
Air	0.6	0.1
Soil	147	64
Surface water	21	3

1 Eeq = 1 eutrophication equivalent = 1 kg P = 0.1 kg N

21.7 *Fine particles in air*

The effects of fine particles occurring in the air depend on their size and composition. Irritation of mucous membranes may occur at high dosages. Dust from sources like road traffic has carcinogenic components such as polycyclic aromatic carbohydrates (PAC) and asbestos. The smaller the particles are, the higher amounts of these compounds they carry and the easier they are inhaled into the lungs. Therefore, a standard is chosen for particles sizing up to 10 µm (PM-10). The presence this 'fine dust' jeopardises a number of functions of air.

Limit values to the concentrations of fine dust in air have been proposed, aiming to reduce the health risks (Eerens, 1992). The limit for the yearly average of the PM-10 concentration given by RIVM (1995, 1996) is 40 µg/m^3. The concentration in a town like Amsterdam was estimated to be about 50 µg/m^3 in the years 1990 and 1992, from which 30 to 40 µg/m^3 would be of external origin. More than half of the fine dust concentration is formed by chemical conversions of acidifying gases. Say that 50% (25 µg/m^3) will be reduced due to abatement of acidifying emissions up to the sustainability standard. Then the goal would already be reached.

European guidelines (Eerens, 1992) propose a stricter standard: a concentration limit of 20 µg/m^3 leading to an emission standard for the Netherlands of 20 million kg/year have been proposed. This standard is used In the eSNI calculation, despite lacking background information. Improved emission figures are applied in the present study as well, summing up to 44 million kg PM10 in 1990. The necessary emission reduction in that year would then amount to 24 million kg (De Boer, 2004c).

21.8 *Fossil fuel depletion*

The issue of non-renewables is discussed in **Section 9.9.2**. The discussion there refers to the application by Bosch (1994) resulting in a sustainability standard for the use of fossil fuels in the Netherlands.

21.9 *Photochemical smog formation*

Photochemical smog is a kind of air pollution in which oxidants are formed that may have a negative effects on life. This smog type often occurs on sunny summer days with low wind velocities; the conditions worsen when a natural condition occurs in the troposphere that is known as an inversion layer. These conditions become problematic in regions where volatile organic substances (VOS, including methane, CH_4), carbon monoxide (CO) and nitrogen oxides (NO_x) are emitted. A complex of reactions can occur, in which NO and NO_2 are essential catalysts, VOS and CO are oxidised and oxidants are formed; of which ozone is the most damaging. Quick oxidation of volatile organic substances other than methane (non-methane VOS) dominates and high oxidant concentrations may be reached (De Leeuw, 1991).

Steadily increased ozone concentrations damage natural and agricultural vegetation. The peak levels occurring at summer smog conditions have a negative effects on the respiratory organs, irritate the mucous membranes of eyes, nose and throat of humans and many animals, and cause visual damage to plants. Loss of function is apparent; physiological effects on humans and plant and animal species play a key role. The Dutch standard for the average of the 98 percentiles of the ozone concentration at ground level over the growing season, from April to September, designed for the protection of ecosystems is exceeded by 13% in 1990, while the standard for this variable aimed at the protection of human health is exceeded by 3.5% in this period (RIVM, 1995).

Applications of a detailed model on continental scale (De Leeuw en Van Rheineck Leyssius, 1991) to the summer of 1980 allow us to set up a rough emission standard. It appears that the combinations of the total continental emissions of NO_x and NMVOS must stay below a certain curve to reach a 13% reduction of the growth-seasonal average of the ozone peak concentration in that year. We use this curve as the sustainability standard for the annual NO_x and NMVOS emissions.

This rough standard curve requires that at least one of the emissions be reduced each year. As the NO_x emission will be limited in order to limit eutrophication, a reduction of the NMVOS emission is probably not be required. For certainty, the sustainability standard for the NMVOS emission is set independent from this condition to 240 million kg/year (De Boer, 2004c).

21.10 *Soil contamination*

In principle, the sustainability limit for concentrations of contaminants in soil can be assessed following the procedure described in **Section 9.6.1**. These values would be the negligible risk levels (NRs) for these substances, which would have to be respected in 90 percent of all locations. In practice only information is available on concentrations in isolated measurement spots in several natural and agricultural areas and within a number of severely polluted locations. Considering even the large number of these polluted locations, the total surface of these areas is definitely smaller than the 10% where we allow the concentration limits to be breached. It would however be cynical to include the problematic soil pollution locations in the 10% exception area of our procedure. As experts have not yet corroborated this percentage to some extent, it seems more practical to use concentration levels up to which the severely polluted locations have to be cleaned-up in order to reach a minimum safety level.

Choice of 'multifunctional use' as a goal for all locations would aim too high. In the first place, the eSNI approach aims at minimal levels for the functions that the ecosystems somewhere in the region (ca. 100 km, see De Boer 2005c) can sustain for future generations, not for as many functions the location itself reasonably can get by cleaning it up. Secondly, it would in many cases be technically impossible to purify the soil up to the required concentration levels. Alternatives would be to dump the polluted or partially purified soil in controlled deposits, with doubtful advantages for the environment.

A less ambitious approach from an environmental point of view would be to let the concentration standards depend on the original functions of the area. Though this approach is closer to the eSNI approach than the multifunctional approach, it may still aim too high. This is because the original function levels may be (but do not need to be) higher than the minimally required function levels for sustainability, while moreover the latter need not be necessarily supplied at the polluted location.

In the second *National Environment Policy Plan* (VROM, 1994) a more modest approach is chosen. Lightly polluted locations are isolated and managed ("secured"), minimising the risk for people and the adjacent environment, at least on the middle long run. On the time scale of many future generations (sustainability) it is uncertain if the management can be maintained. Heavily polluted locations, which mostly form an urgent problem, are cleaning-up or "secured"; the extent of the local pollution determines the measures that are taken. This approach might be the closest to the eSNI approach, except that the precautionary principle may be lost out of sight in some occasions.

Within this study, the multifunctional approach is therefore followed wherever possible. It entails that not only the location, but also the extracted soil must be purified up to the required level. Only in cases where this approach seems impossible, the approach advocated by VROM (1994) is followed. We are aware of the inconsistency of this combination; however, the subsequent cost estimation is just as rough, or worse.

21.11 *Toxic substances in surface water*

As mentioned above, a system of concentration limits for hazardous substances in soil and surface water has been developed in the Netherlands, with the goal to avoid risks for the existence of species and human health. The system consists of three basic concentration levels and two policy levels, the latter of which are not used here. At the *maximum allowable risk level* of a substance (MAR), 95% of the existing species *potentially* present in the Dutch ecosystems are protected against potential hazardous effects of the substance, in absence of other hazardous substances. The limit value is based on data on species that function at high trophic levels, as these species are more vulnerable than other ones. The *negligible risk level* of a substance (NR) is intended to prevent risks that arise when the substance occurs together with other potentially dangerous substances (synergism). The NR limits for all potentially hazardous substances must be respected simultaneously at all time in order to avoid the risk of these substances to ecosystems. Both the MAR and the NR of a substance must be greater than its average *natural background concentration*, the third basic level. The NR of a substance is simply determined such that its distance to the background level is one hundredth of the distance between the MAR and the background level. The NRs are therefore scientifically less well underpinned and less certain than the MARs.

It may be inferred that the NRs are designed to warrant that 95% of the species potentially present in a subsystem of the environment may maintain themselves in the subsystem if all NRs are respected in the subsystem. It would be safe to expect that all still existing species would be protected against extinction on a global scale if all NR limits were respected "everywhere in the world". However, this goal could perhaps also be achieved if all NRs would be satisfied in a system of preferably linked areas that occupy only a part of the earth's surface. Say that these areas are the oceans and a system of interlinked fresh water ecosystems such as brooks, rivers and wetlands and terrestrial ecosystems such as forests and smaller 'nature' areas. In the Netherlands, such a system is the *Ecological Main Structure* (EMS), which is adopted by De Boer (2005c) as the standard for sustainable land use. The application of the NRs to the ecosystems within this structure, including the oceans and the MARs to the other ecosystems could be sufficient for the prevention of the extinction of species on the global scale.

The system of NRs seems overly safe. We suspect the sustainability limits to the concentrations of hazardous substances in protected areas like the EMS to lie somewhere between the NRs and the MARs. For instance, many species seem to be protected sufficiently against the effects of heavy metals dosages if their concentrations approach the MARs instead of the NRs, because of a stimulating effect of the presence of (other) metals on the defence system of many species (Reijnders, personal communication). We opt for the MARs for the concentrations of heavy metals in water and the NRs for the concentrations of other substances in water as sustainability limits within the structure of nature areas and, as said, for their MARs outside that structure. Sustainability moreover requires that these conditions be satisfied in equilibrium.

These conditions demand statistic information that can only be provided by fitting a spatial dynamic model for the considered substances in surface water and sediment to available data. The model's equilibrium solution belonging to a certain total emission of the substance must then calculated. It is a pattern of equilibrium concentrations on different locations in the country, in this case in the national surface water system. Running the model with different total emissions of a substance while keeping the proportions between the local emissions equal should lead to the total national emission with which the locally valid limits to the concentrations are satisfied at all locations; this is the emission standard for the substance.

A model fit for the job is RIZA's model Horizon for a network of surface waters including their sediments. The readily available first version (De Boer en Van der Meijden, 1990) could not distinguish between the 'more natural' waters and the other ones in sufficient detail and was not fit to more recent data. It did provide a first insight in the spatial dispersion of the concentrations, however. In second instance, a simple box (or completely stirred reactor) type of model of all Dutch fresh waters was used. The condition that the MARs of the metals and the NRs of other compounds had to be complied with within 'nature area waters' could not be maintained. Instead, it was demanded that these limits were respected in the whole box, representing about 50% of all Dutch fresh waters.

The hazardous substances incorporated in the eSNI calculation consists of eight heavy metals, a metalloid (arsenic) and eight polycyclic aromatic hydrocarbons (PAHs). These substances were chosen for a pragmatic reason: emission data and a joint cost effectiveness data were available, although the latter concern only the emissions through sewer systems and sewage water treatment systems. Aggregating the emissions with the aid of aquatic environmental toxicity potentials (AETPs) yielded a joint cost effectiveness curve that could be used in the applied general equilibrium model. The data and the approach have been explored by Van der Woerd et al. (2000). The advantage of this procedure is that technical measures with effects on several substances can be properly accounted for, i.e. with a single expenditure for each measure, but the risk of connecting substances to improper measures also exists.

After calibration of the box-type model to data for zinc in Dutch surface waters, it was applied using a maximum allowable risk concentration (MAR) equal to 7.9 μg/l and a background concentration of 2.8 μg/l. The model prescribed a sustainable zinc emission to Dutch surface waters of 190 tonnes per year, 62.2% lower than the emission in 1990, 502 tonnes. Standards for other heavy metals and PAHs were not yet calculated this way, mainly due to lack of time. Therefore, the relative reduction obtained for emissions of zinc in Dutch fresh waters was simply used for the equivalent emission of the whole group of considered heavy metals and PAHs in Dutch fresh waters, measuring up to 194.3 billion kg 1,4-dichlorobenzene in 1990. The standard is thus set to 73.5 billion kg 1,4-dichlorobenzene per year (De Boer, 2005c). Moreover, this standard was also supposed to warrant compliance with the relevant MARs and NRs (see above) in the oceans. Both assumptions are obviously wrong. This has to be improved in future eSNI calculations.

References

Some references in footnotes have not been included here.
The Appendices may have their own literature section.

22. *Literature: Hueting as first author*

This gives works by Hueting as first author. References are labelled in consistency with the online lists [80] [81] and Goodland (2001) except for some mixture of English and Dutch. These lists themselves provide only selected writings. The following gives a mixture of mostly English and some Dutch. More recent works tend to be available in PDF at www.sni-hueting.info. Also Hueting (1974a, 1980) *New Scarcity* is available online.

– (1967), "Welvaartsparadoxen", paper prepared for the National Centre of Administrative Studies, The Hague; a version published as (1968), "Welvaartsparadoxen", ESB 2636, p. 263-264

– (1969a), "Functions of Nature: Should Nature be Quantified?", London, World Wildlife Fund

– (1969b), "The Concept of Economic Growth", Note for dr. M.J.J.A. Imkamp, member of Parliament

– (1970a), "Propositions and Introduction", The Netherlands Congress for Public Health, 12th November, "The Price of a Livable Environment", Den Haag

– (1970b), "Wat is de Natuur ons Waard?", Baarn

– (1971), "A Statistical System for Estimating the Deterioration of the Human Environment", in: Pratt, J.W. (ed.), "Statistical and Mathematical Aspects of Pollution Problems", Symposium of the International Association for Statistics in Physical Sciences (IASPS) at Harvard University, August 10-20, also published in: J. W. Pratt (ed.), "Statistical and Mathematical Aspects of Pollution Problems", Marcel Dekker, New York 1974

– (1972), "The Set-up of the Statistical System Within Which the Deterioration of the Human Environment Will Be Estimated", in: Problems of Environmental Economics, Organization for Economic Co-Operation and Development, Paris: 7p

– (1973a), "A Statistical System for Estimating the Deterioration of the Human Environment", UN Seminar on Environmental Statistics (Statistical Commission and Economic Commission for Europe). Warsaw, October 15-19

– (1973b), "The Economic Quantification of the Environment", in: Planning and Development in the Netherlands, A Periodical of the Netherlands Universities Foundation for International Cod Operation, VII (2)

– (1974a, 1980), "New Scarcity and Economic Growth: More Welfare Through Less Production?", Dutch edition: Agon Elsevier, Amsterdam 285 p. English edition: North-Holland Publishing Company, Amsterdam, New York, Oxford 269 p. 1980

– (1974b), "Environment and Statistics", General Meeting of the International Association of Municipal Statisticians (IAMS), Zürich, 15-17 May

– (1974c), "Environmental Statistics in the Netherlands", U.N. World Health Organization, Seminar on Health Statistics, 5-14 June

– (1975), "Environmental Deterioration, Economic Growth and National Income", 14th General Conference of the International Association for Research in Income and Wealth (IARIW). Aulanko, Finland, August 18-23

– (1976a), "Possibilities for Environmental Improvements in the Face of Limited Availability of National and Local Means", in: Papers and Proceedings. Volume II. Hyogo International Conference of the International Federation for Housing and Planning, Kobe, Japan, May 18- 22

[80] http://www.sni-hueting.info/EN/SelectedPublications.pdf

[81] http://www.sni-hueting.info/NL/Publicaties/NederlandsePublicatiesHueting.pdf

– (1976b), "Loss and Damage in Transport", Introduction for the Conference of the International Cargo Handling Co-Ordination Association (ICHCA), Amsterdam, 28-29 October
– (1977a), "Socio-Economic Effects of Environmental Policy", Symposium: "Quality of Life". Universidad de Deusto, Bilbao, 21-23 September
– (1977b), "The Economy and the Ecology in the Perspective of the Motorcar", VIth Congress on Leisure and Touring, "The Motorist and the Environment", Theme A, "Ecology, the Motorcar and the Future", Manila, 5-9 December
– (1978) 'Economic Aspects of Pollution of the Rhine", in (H.U. Jessurun d'Oliveira (ed)), "Rhine Pollution: Legal, Economical and Technical Aspects", Nederlands Juristen Blad, series 5, Tjeenk Willink, Zwolle, The Netherlands, 127 p
– (1980a), "Environment and Growth, Expectations and Scenarios", in SK Kuipers and GJ Lanjouw (eds), "Prospects of Economic Growth", Amsterdam, New York, Oxford: North-Holland Publishing Company
– (1980b), "Scenarios as Information for Social Choice about the Environment", in Sensing the Environment, International Colloquy, 3-6 June, Council of Europe, Strasbourg.
– (1980c), "The Use of Environmental Data in the Economic Decision-Making Process", Seminar on Methodological Problems of Environmental Statistics, Conference of European Statisticians of the Economic Commission for Europe (ECE) of the United Nations, and the Senior Advisors to ECE Governments on Environmental Problems, Warsaw, 16-19 September: 17 p
– (1980d), "Comments on Orio Giarini's paper on Welfare and Wealth", Seminar: "Towards an Ecological Economy", Ecoropa, Kassel (BRD), 18-20 September
– (1981a), "Aspecten van welvaart op lange termijn", ESB, 3294: 180-185
– (1981b), "De relatie tussen produktiegroei en energieverbruik, maakt groeifanatisme blind?", ESB, nr. 3310, p. 609-611
– (1981c), "Some comments on the report "A Low Energy Strategy for the United Kingdom", compiled by G. Leach et al. for The International Institute for the Environment and Development (IIED)", Paper prepared for the Working Party on Integral Energy Scenarios, The Hague, 20 May
– (1982), "The Context of Environmental Data When Used in Making Decisions on the Environment", OECD Group: "The State of the Environment", Stockholm, 1-4 June.
– (1983), "Environment-saving Economy Is Feasible", introduction for the International Water Tribunal, Rotterdam, 4 October
– (1984a), "Note on the Acquisition of Statistical Material for Projections of Environmental Burdening and Environmental Costs", OECD Group "The State of the Environment", Paris, May
– (1984b), "Economic Aspects of Environmental Accounting", Environmental Accounting Workshop, UNEP & World Bank, Washington, D.C., November
– (1984c) 'Results of an Economic Scenario That Gives Top Priority to Saving the Environment and Energy Instead of Encouraging Production Growth", in (Sören Bergström (ed.)), Economic Growth and the Role of Science, Edsbruk, Holms Gårds Tryckeri, Sweden
– (1985a), "Energy, the Environment and Employment: the New Scenario", in (Centre for Energy Studies), The Future of the Electricity Supply Industry, Polytechnic of the South Bank, London, 25-27 June
– (1985b), "An Economic Scenario That Gives Top Priority to Saving the Environment Rather than Encouraging Production Growth", The Environmentalist 5 (4) p. 253-262.
– (1986a), "An Economic Scenario for a Conserver-Economy, in (Paul Ekins (ed.)), The Living Economy, A New Economics in the Making, London, Routledge
– (1986b), "A Note on the Construction of an Environmental Indicator in Monetary Terms as a Supplement to National Income with the Aid of Basic Environmental Statistics",

Report to Prof. Dr. E. Salim, Minister of Population and Environment, Indonesia. Jakarta, March
– (1986c), "Framework for a Cost-Benefit Analysis for Different Uses of a Humid Tropical Forest Area", Tropenbos, 22-24 September, Baarn, Netherlands
– (1987a), "The Use of Environmental Data in the Decision-Making Process", CBS Statistics Netherlands, Voorburg
– (1987b), "Economic Aspects of Environmental Accounting", Journal of Interdisciplinary Economics 2(1). Also published in: Societat Catalana d'Economia, Anuari 7, Barcelona, 1989
– (1987c), "Energy, the Environment and Employment: A New Scenario", Futures – (19 (3): 343-345
– (1987d), "An Economic Scenario That Gives Top Priority to Saving the Environment", Ecological Modelling 38 (1/2): 123-140
– (1988), "Collective Survival and the Fallacy of National Income as a Measure for Economic Growth", 19th World Conference, Society for International Development, "Poverty, Development and Collective Survival, Public and Private Responsibilities", New Delhi, 25-28 March
– (1989a), "The Implications for the Taiwan 2000 Study of the Netherlands Scenario Study 1980-2000", in (The Steering Committee Taiwan 2000 Study (ed.)), Taiwan 2000. Balancing Economic Growth and Environmental Protection, Taipei
– (1989b), "Correcting National Income for Environmental Losses: Towards a Practical Solution", in (Y. Ahmad et al. (eds))
– (1989c), "Design of the Cost-Benefit Analysis of the Lower Guayas Flood Control Project. Economic Evaluation of Environmental Impact", HASKONING Royal Dutch Consulting Engineers and Architects, Guayaquil, Ecuador, September 1989. Also published in (P.C. van den Noort (ed.)), Costs and Benefits of Agricultural Policies and Projects, Wissenschaftsverlag Vauk Kiel K.G., 1990
– (1990b), "The Fallacy of the Growth of Consumption", Introduction for the conference on the occasion of the thirtieth anniversary of the International Organization of Consumers Unions, Oegstgeest, May 2nd
– (1990c), "The Brundtland Report: A Matter of Conflicting Goals", Ecological Economics 2: 109-117
– (1991a), "The Use of the Discount Rate in a Cost-Benefit Analysis for Different Uses of a Humid Tropical Forest Area", Ecological Economics 3 (1): 43-57
– (1991b), "An Economic Scenario for the Netherlands: Shifting Priority from Production Growth to Environmental Preservation", in (M.J. Garrett et al. (eds)), Studies for the 21st Century, Institute for 21stCentury Studies, Arlington, Virginia, U.S.A.
– (1991f), "Correcting National Income for Environmental Losses: A Practical Solution for a Theoretical Dilemma", (194-213) In (R. Costanza (ed)), Ecological Economics, The Science and Management of Sustainability, Columbia University Press, New York
– (1991g), "Calculating a Sustainable National Income: A Practical Solution for a Theoretical Dilemma", CBS Statistics Netherlands, Voorburg
– (1991h), "Calculating a Sustainable National Income: A Practical Solution for a Theoretical Dilemma", in (Alfred Franz and Carsten Stahmer (eds)), Approaches to Environmental Accounting. Proceedings of the IARIW Conference on Environmental Accounting, Baden, Austria, 27-29 May 1991, Physica-Verlag, Heidelberg, 1993.
– (1992a), "The Economic Functions of the Environment", p61-69 in (P. Ekins and M. Max-Neef (eds)), Real-Life Economics: understanding wealth creation, Routledge, London. Also published in (L.L. Boyer (ed)), Proceedings of the 5thInternational Conference on Underground Space and Earth Sheltered Structures, Delft University Press, Delft, 1992
– (1992b), "Theoretical Problems around Growth, Environment and National Income: A Practical Solution", in (P.Ekins and M. Max-Neef (eds)), Real-Life Economics, Routledge, London, pp. 255-265

– (1992c), " Economic Evaluation of the Environmental Impacts: Design of a Cost Benefit Analysis of the Lower Guayas Flood Control Project, Equador", The Environmentalist 12: (2): 93-100
– (1992f), "Correcting National Income for Environmental Losses: a practical solution for a theoretical dilemma", p23-47 in (J.J. Krabbe and W.J.M. Heijman (eds)), National Income and Nature: Externalities, Growth and Steady State, Kluwer Academic, Dordrecht
– (1993b), "Calculating a Sustainable National Income: A Practical Solution for a Theoretical Dilemma", p322-343 in (J.C. Dragan, E.K. Seifert and M.C. Demetrescu (eds)), Entropy and Bioeconomics: Proceedings of the First International Conference of the European Association for Bioeconomic Studies - E.A.B.S., Rome 28-30 November 1991, Milan, Italy
– (1994), "Sustainable National Income in the Netherlands: The Calculation of Environmental Losses in Money Terms", p43-56 in (D. Pearce and S. Faucheux (eds)), Models of Sustainable Development: Exclusive or Complementary Approaches of Sustainability? Volume I. International Symposium, Paris, March 16-18, Université Panthéon-Sorbonne C3E and AFCET, Paris
– (1995b), "The Economic Functions of the Environment - valuation of environmental effects", in Evaluation of Environmental Effects of Transport, Report of an International Roundtable organised by PTRC Education and Research Services Ltd., The Hague, (19-20 June) & London
– (1996), "Three Persistent Myths in the Environmental Debate", Ecological Economics 18(2): 81-88, reprinted in Van Ierland et al. (2001:78-89)
– (1997), "Groei van de produktie is gevaar voor milieu", NRC Handelsblad, 2 August
– (2001c), "Three persistent myths in the environmental debate", p 78-89 in (E.C. van Ierland, J. van der Straaten and H.R.J. Vollebergh (eds)), Economic growth and valuation of the environment, A debate, Edward Elgar, Cheltenham, UK - Northhampton, MA, USA
– (2001d), "Rejoinders to symposium authors: Ekins, Daly, Norgaard et al., Beckerman, El Serafy, Pearce et al., Faucheux and O'Connor, Verbruggen et al., Goodland and Mäler", pp 333-378 in Van Ierland et al.
– (2001e), "The Theoretical Basis for Estimating SNI. Speech for the World Bank Seminar", October 1, sni-hueting.info
– (2002a), "The theoretical basis for estimating sustainable national income", pp. 15-20, in: Report on the World Bank seminar "A debate on sustainable national income", Economenblad, Memorandum nr. 1, The Hague
– (2002b), "SNI: A Macro Indicator for Sustainability", WSSD conference 'Perspectives on a Sustainable Future", 2ndSeptember 2002, Johannesburg
– (2003a), "Sustainable National Income: A Prerequisite for Sustainability", p 40-58 in (Van der Zwaan & Petersen (eds)), Sharing the Planet: Population-Consumption-Species, Eburon Publishers
– (2003b), "Ter overpeinzing op het wijde water. Voor Henk van Tuinen bij zijn afscheid van het CBS, van een vriend", ("To think about while sailing the seas. For Henk van Tuinen at his departure, from a friend") April, http://www.sni-hueting.info/NL/index.html
– (2006), "Het DNI & politieke belemmeringen", ("eSNI and political impediments") http://www.managementissues.com/index.php/duurzame-ontwikkeling/100-duurzame-ontwikkeling/373-het-dni-a-politieke-belemmeringen
– (2007a), "Introduction to the Theory of eSNI, a Macro Indicator for Sustainable Development", OECD World Forum on Statistics, Knowledge, and Policy "Measuring the Progress of Societies", Istanbul, 27-30 June 2007
– (2007b), "Environmentally Sustainable National Income (eSNI)", contribution to the "Virtual Indicator Expo" of the International Conference "Beyond GDP, Measuring

progress, true wealth, and the well-being of nations", European Union, Brussels, 19-20 November 2007
– (2008), "Why environmental sustainability can most probably not be attained with growing production", Conference on "Economic de-growth for ecological sustainability and social equity", Paris, 18-19 April
– (2010a), "Why environmental sustainability can most probably not be attained with growing production", in: Journal of Cleaner Production. Volume 19, Issue April 2010, p 525-530. Based on the paper with the same title for the "Conference on economic de-growth", Paris, 18- 19 April 2008
– (2010b), "How to correct wrong information about economic growth", "2nd Conference on economic de-growth", 26th - 29th March 2010, Conference Proceedings, Universitat Autónoma de Barcelona
– (2010c), "A Rejoinder to Wilfred Beckerman and Herman Daly", in (J.Boersema and L.Reijnders (eds)), Principles of Environmental Sciences, Springer, Dordrecht, Heidelberg, London, New York, p 491-501
– (2011a), "Environmentally Sustainable National Income and Other Ways to Improve Information About Growth", In: Problems of Sustainable Development, Volume 6, No 1, European Academy of Science and Art, Salzburg
– (2011b), "Five ways to combat misleading information about economic growth", in: Richard L. Bertrand (ed), "Theories and Effects of Economic Growth", Nova Publishers, New York
– (2011c), Environmentally Sustainable National Income (eSNI), asymmetric entries and other ways to improve information about economic growth. European Union, Beyond GDP, Measuring progress, true wealth, and the well-being of nations. http./.www.beyond gdp.eu
– (2011d), "Sustainable national income: information for attaining sustainability", in: Management Research Review, Volume 34, number 11, p 1190-1201. Based on the paper 'Environmentally Sustainable National Income: Indispensable Information for Attaining Sustainability", that won the Best Paper Award at the First Annual Kent State International Symposium on Green Supply Chains, Kent University, Ohio June 2010
– (2011e), "The future of the Environmentally sustainable national income", in: Ökologisches Wirtschaften, no 4, 2011. Based on the speech 'Our planet is threatened by a wrong belief in a wrongly formulated growth", Congress Jenseits des Wachstums, Berlin, 20th- 22th May 2011 (www.jenseits-des-wachstums.de; Documentation link; Übersichtskurs; Speech Degrowth)
– (2011f), "Milieuduurzaamheid en economische groei, asymmetrische boekingen", ESB 13 mei, no 96 (4610), pag 310-313
– (2013), "Environmentally Sustainable National Income: Indispensable Information for Attaining Environmental Sustainability", in: Environmental Values, volume 22, number 1, pp. 81-100
– , Boer B de, Bosch PR, Soest JP van (1995a), "Estimating Sustainable National Income", pp. 206-230 in (Wouter van Dieren (ed)), Taking Nature into Account: A report to the Club of Rome, Springer-Verlag, New York
–, Boer B de (2001a), "The Parable of the Carpenter", International Journal of Environment and Pollution, 15(1), pp. 42-50
–, Boer B de (2001b), "Environmental valuation and sustainable national income according to Hueting", p17-77 in (E.C. van Ierland, J. van der Straaten and H.R.J. Vollebergh (eds)), Economic growth and valuation of the environment, A debate, Edward Elgar, Cheltenham, UK - Northhampton, MA, USA
–, Boer B de (2002c), "Theory of SNI, a Macro Indicator for Sustainability", OECD Seminar on Sustainable National Income, 17th October, Paris

–, Boer B de (2004b), "Sustainable National Income and Multiple Indicators for Sustainable Development", p 39-52 in Measuring Sustainable Development: Integrated Economic, Environmental and Social Frameworks, OECD
–, Boer B de (2014), "Kosten en baten van groene welvaart", TvOF 46 no 2, Wim Drees Stichting voor Openbare Financiën
–, Boer B de (2018, 2019), "Milieuduurzaam Nationaal Inkomen, grondslagen en schatting voor 2015", cited in the Monitor Brede Welvaart 2018, with a correction in 2019, https://www.cbs.nl/nl-nl/achtergrond/2018/20/toelichting-mdni
–, Boer B de, Haan M de (1999b), "Green Accounting and Sustainable National Income Calculation in the Netherlands", In: From Research to Implementation: Policy-Driven Methods for Evaluating Macro-Economic Environmental Performance. Proceedings from a workshop, Luxembourg, 28-29 September 1998. European Commission, EU RTD in Human Dimensions of Environmental Change, Report Series 1999/1
–, Bosch PR (1990d), "On the Correction of National Income for Environmental Losses", Statistical Journal of the United Nations Economic Commission for Europe, 7(2): 75-83.
–, Bosch PR (1991e), "Note on the correction of National Income for Environmental Losses", in O. Kuik and H. Verbruggen (eds), In Search of Indicators of Sustainable Development, Kluwer Academic Publishers, Dordrecht
–, Bosch PR (1992e), "The Calculation of a Sustainable National Income in the Netherlands, Environment Statistics and Other Information Requirements", Work Session on Specific Methodological Issues in Environment Statistics, Conference of European Statisticians (Statistical Commission and Economic Commission for Europe), and Eurostat (Commission of the European Communities). Lisbon, 14-17 September
–, Bosch PR (1994), "Sustainable National Income in the Netherlands: The Calculation of Environmental Losses in Money Terms", p43-56 in (D. Pearce and S. Faucheux (eds), "Models of Sustainable Development: Exclusive or Complementary Approaches of Sustainability?", Volume I. International Symposium, Paris, March 16-18, Université Panthéon-Sorbonne C3E and AFCET, Paris
–, Bosch PR, Boer B de (1992d), "Methodology for the Calculation of Sustainable National Income", Statistical Essays, M44, CBS Statistics Netherlands, SDU Publishers, The Hague 64 p. Also published as WWF International report, Gland, Switzerland, June 1992
–, Bosch PR, Boer B de (1993a), "Methodology for the Calculation of Sustainable National Income", in (A. Markandya and C. Costanza (eds)), Environmental Accounting: A Review of the Current Debate, Harvard Institute for International Development, the United Nations Environment Programme, Environmental Economics Series, Paper No. 8, p. 59-63
–, Bosch PR, Boer B de (1995c), "The Calculation of Sustainable National Income", Occasional Papers and Reprints, IDPAD OP&R 1995(2), Indo-Dutch Programme on Alternatives in Development IDPAD, New Delhi & The Hague
–, Leipert C (1990a), "Economic Growth, National Income and the Blocked Choices for the Environment", The Environmentalist 10 (1): 25-38
–, Leipert C (1991c), "National Income and Economic Growth and the Concept of Defensive Expenditures", in (S. Busuttil and B. Rhode (eds)), Sourcebook: Ecological Economics, European Coordination Centre for Research and Documentation in Social Sciences and Foundation for International Studies, UNESCO, Vienna
–, Reijnders L (1996a), "Duurzaamheid is een objectief begrip", ESB 4057, p. 425-427
–, Reijnders L (1996b), "Duurzaamheid and preferenties", ESB 4062, p. 537-539
–, Reijnders L (1998b), "Sustainability is an Objective Concept", Ecological Economics 27 (2): 139-147
–, Reijnders L (1999a), "Uncertainty and Sustainability", Ecological Economics 29(1): 9-11
–, Reijnders L (2004a), "Broad Sustainability contra Sustainability: The proper Construction of Sustainability Indicators", Ecological Economics 50, 249-260.

–, Reijnders L, Boer B de, Lambooy J, Jansen H (1998a), "The Concept of Environmental Function and its Valuation, Ecological Economics 25(1): 31-35

23. *Literature: other authors*

The UNEP Global 500 Award. [82]

Ahmad Y, Serafy S el, Lutz E (eds.)) (1989), Environmental Accounting for Sustainable Development, The World Bank, Washington, D.C., 100 p
Arthur D et al. (1972), "A blueprint for survival", The Ecologist 2, No. 1.
Ayres RU, Kneese AV (1969), "Production, consumption and extemalities", American Economic Review, June
Bergh JCJM van den (2005), "BNP, weg ermee!", ESB 18-11-2005, p502-505
Bergh JCJM van den (2007), "Abolishing GDP. The Largest Information Failure in the World", TI 2007-019/3 Tinbergen Institute Discussion Paper
Bergh JCJM van den (2015), "Green Agrowth as a Third Option: Removing the GDP-Growth Constraint on Human Progress", WWWforEurope, Vienna, Policy Paper no 19 (paper cover date: December 2014), http://hdl.handle.net/10419/125646
Bergh JCJM van den (2017a), "A third option for climate policy within potential limits to growth", Nature Climate Change, Vol 7 p 107-112
Bergh JCJM van den (2017b), "Green agrowth: removing the GDP-growth constraint on human progress", p181-210, in Peter A. Victor and Brett Dolter, "Handbook of Growth and Sustainability", Edward Elgar
Bergh JCJM van den (2019), "Het bbp vervangen door een brede-welvaartsmaat is moeilijk en onnodig", ESB 104 (4772S) April 11 p62-66
Bergh JCJM van den, Verbruggen H (1999), "Spatial sustainability, trade and indicators: an evaluation of the 'ecological footprint'", Ecological Economics, Vol 29-1, April, p61-72
Boer B de (2003) "Klimaatverandering", draft report, CBS Statistics Netherlands, Voorburg, The Netherlands
Boer B de (2004a), "Ruimtegebruik, verzuring, overbemesting en verdroging", draft report, CBS Statistics Netherlands, Voorburg, The Netherlands
Boer B de (2004b), "Aantasting van de ozonlaag", draft report, CBS Statistics Netherlands, Voorburg, The Netherlands
Boer B de (2004c), "Verspreiding van milieugevaarlijke stoffen in lucht, water en bodem", draft report, CBS Statistics Netherlands, Voorburg, The Netherlands
Boer B de, Bosch PR (1995), "The greenhouse effect: an example of the prevention cost approach", Paper prepared for the 2nd meeting of the London group on national accounts and the environment, Washington, March 15 – 17, 1995
Boer B de, Bosch RA, Hueting R (2013), "De monetaire meetbaarheid van duurzame ontwikkeling",http://www.sni-hueting.info/NL/Documentatie/2013-11-02-EZ-Monetaire-meetbaarheid-duurzaamheid.pdf
Boer B de, Hueting R (2010), "Relatie NI ex asyms en mDNI", http://www.sni-hueting.info/NL/Documentatie/2010-07-10-Hueting-DeBoer-Asymmetrische-Boekingen.pdf
Boer B de, Hueting R, Sigmond T (2008), "Annotaties bij 'Aan schaarste geen gebrek', gebaseerd op het werk van Hueting en De Boer", http://www.sni-hueting.info/NL/Documentatie/2008-08-Annotaties-AanSchaarsteGeenGebrek.pdf

[82] http://www.global500.org/index.php/thelaureates/online-directory/item/208-roelof-hueting
http://www.sni-hueting.info/EN/Others/2019-05-02-Tinbergen-1990-UNEP-Sasakawa-Hueting.pdf

Boer B de, Meijden AM van der (1990), "Prognose van de waterbodemkwaliteit", DHV Raadgevend Ingenieursbureau BV, Amersfoort, rapport in opdracht van Dienst Binnenwateren RIZA, Lelystad,1990
Boer PJ den (1979), "Het overleven van soorten", Intermediair 15(48):7-13
Bosch PR (1994), "Energiedragers", draft report, CBS Statistics Netherlands, Voorburg, The Netherlands
Boulding KE (1966) "The economics of the coming spaceship earth" In: Environmental Quality in a Growing Economy, Baltimore, 1966
Boulding KE (1970), "Fun and games with the gross national product - the role of misleading indicators in social policy", in: "The Environmental Crisis", London
Boulding KE (1971), "Environment and economies". In: "Environment, Resources, Pollution and Society". Stanford (Cal.)
Brown LR, Flavin C, French H (1998), "State of the World 1998", W.W. Norton, New York
CBS (1989, 1992, 1994), "Mineralen in de landbouw", Centraal Bureau voor de Statistiek, Voorburg/Heerlen
CBS Statistics Netherlands (1990), "Tax incidence in the Netherlands: accounting and simulations", Statistics Netherlands report M42, SDU Publishers
CBS, CPB, MNP, SCP (2009), Monitor Duurzaam Nederland 2009", CBS Voorburg
Central Bureau of Statistics (1972), "Waterverontreiniging met Afbreekbaar Organisch en Eutrofiërend Materiaal", The Hague
Central Bureau of Statistics (1975), "Luchtverontreiniging door Verbranding van Fossiele Brandstoffen 1960-1972", The Hague
Central Bureau of Statistics (2018), "Monitor Brede Welvaart 2018)", The Hague
Central Bureau of Statistics (2019), "Monitor Brede Welvaart 2019)", The Hague
Central Planning Bureau (CPB) (1972), "Economische gevolgen van de bestrijding van waterverontreiniging met afbreekbaar organisch materiaal", Monograph 16, The Hague ("Economic consequences of the abatement of water pollution with decomposable organic materials")
Central Planning Bureau (CPB) (1975), "Economische Gevolgen van Bestrijding van Milieuverontreiniging", Monografie No. 20. The Hague, 1975
CIW (1996), "Voortgangsrapportage integraal waterbeheer en Noordzee-aangelegenheden 1996", Commissie Integraal Waterbeheer (CIW-CUWVO)
Colignatus T (2000a), "The seminal contribution of Roefie Hueting to economic science: Theory and measurement of (environmentally) Sustainable National Income", website, included in (2009b, 2015, 2019)
Colignatus T (2001), "Roefie Hueting and Sustainable National Income", translation of ESB, August 24, p652-653, available at www.sni-hueting.info
Colignatus T (2008, 2009a), "The Old Man and the SNI: A review of advance and adversity in Hueting's research in economic growth and the new scarcity from the environment and sustainable national income (SNI)", in Colignatus (2009b, 2015, 2019)
Colignatus T (2009b, 2015, 2019), "The Tinbergen & Hueting Approach in the Economics and National Accounts of Ecological Survival", https://mpra.ub.uni-muenchen.de/63904/ and update in 2019
Colignatus T (2019c), "The Old Man and the eSNI. A review of advance and adversity in Hueting's research in economic growth and the new scarcity in the environment and environmentally sustainable national income (eSNI)", update of (2009a)
Commoner B (1972), "The Closing Circle", London
Conference of European Statisticians (CES) (2013), "Recommendations on measuring sustainable development", UNECE – Eurostat – OECD
Crommentuin T, Polder MD, Plassche EJ van de (1997), "Maximum Permissible Concentrations and Negligible Concentrations for metals, taking background concentrations into account", Rijksinstituut voor Volksgezondheid en Milieu, Bilthoven, The Netherlands, Report no. 601501001

Daly H (2001), “Roefie Hueting's perpendicular ‘demand curve’ and the issue of objective value”, in Van Ierland et al. (2001) p137-150
Daly HE, Cobb JB Jr (1989, 1994) “For the Common Good: Redirecting the Economy toward Community, the Environment, and a Sustainable Future”, (2nd updated and expanded ed.), Boston: Beacon Press
Daly H (2007), “Ecological Economics and Sustainable Development, Selected Essays of Herman Daly”, Edward Elgar
Dasgupta PS, Heal GM (1979), “Economic theory and exhaustible resources”, Nisbet/Cambridge University Press, Welwyn/Cambridge
Dellink RB (2000), "Dynamics in an applied general equilibrium model with pollution and abatement", May 16, Draft, Wageningen University, https://www.copsmodels.com/2000gtapconf/5dellink.pdf
Dellink RB and Hofkes MW (2008), “Sustainable National Income 2005: analysis for The Netherlands”, Institute for Environmental Studies, Vrije Universiteit, Amsterdam, R-08/06.
Dellink RB, Ierland E van (2004), "Pollution Abatement in the Netherlands: A Dynamic Applied General Equilibrium Assessment", CCMP – Climate Change Modelling and Policy
Dellink RB, Woerd KF van der (1997), “Kosteneffectiviteit van milieuthema's”. IVM-R97/10, Institute for Environmental Studies, Vrije Universiteit, Amsterdam
Easterlin RA (1972), “Does Economic Growth improve the Human Lot?”, Mim. paper, University of Pennsylvania
Easterlin RA (2003), “Income and happiness: towards a unified theory”,Economic Journal 111, pp. 465-484
Eerens HC (1992), “The limit for the yearly average of the PM-10 concentration given by RIVM (1995, 1996)”, RIVM
Ensing B (1995) “Sustainability costs of imported products”, CBS Statistics Netherlands
Erisman JW, Bleeker A, Heuberger PSC, Bakema AH, Makaske GB, Bouwman AF (1996), “Emissieplafinds voor ammoniak en maximale stikstofgiften per gemeente in Nederland. Een eerste orde benadering”, RIVM, Bilthoven, rapport nummer 722108019
EU (1996), “Council Regulation 2223/96”, June 25th
Forrester W (1971) “World Dynamics”, Cambridge (Mass)
Foundation for research of sustainable national income (FSNI) (2001), “Report on the World Bank seminar on economic growth and valuation of the environment, A debate on sustainable national income”, Delft, http://www.sni-hueting.info
Gerlagh R, Dellink RB, Hofkes MW, Verbruggen H (2000), “An applied general equilibrium model to calculate a Sustainable National Income for the Netherlands”, chapter 5 in Verbruggen (ed) (2000), p97-132
Gerlagh R, Dellink RB, Hofkes MW, Verbruggen H (2002), “A measure of sustainable national income for the Netherlands”, Ecological Economics, 41-1, April, p 157-174
Goodland R (1995), “The concept of environmental sustainability”, Annual Review of Ecology and Systematics 26:1-24
Goodland R (2001), “An appreciation of Dr Roefie Hueting's ecological work”, in Van Ierland et al. (ed), p315-332
Haan M de (2004), “Accounting for goods and for bads. Measuring environmental pressure in a national accounts framework”, thesis TU Twente, also CBS Statistics Netherlands
Haan M de, Boer B de, Keuning SJ (2001), "Econologische statistiek", ESB, 86e jaargang, nr. 4299, pagina D14, 15 maart, Vernieuwende Statistiek
Häder D-P, Worrest RC, Kumar HD (1989), “Aquatic ecosystems”, In: UNEP (1989)
Häder D-P, Worrest RC, Kumar HD (1991), “Aquatic ecosystems”, In: UNEP (1991)
Hamilton K (1994), "Green Adjustments to GDP," Resources Policy 20: 155-68
Hartwick JM (1977), “Intergenerational equity and the investing of rents from exhaustible resources”, American Economic Review 66: 972-974

Hartwick JM (1978), "Investing returns from depleting renewable resource stocks and intergenerational equity", Economics Letters 1: 85-88
Hawksworth DL (ed.), (1995), "Biodiversity, Measurement and Estimation", Chapman & Hall, London
Hecht JE (2007), "Report on the World Bank Seminar on Economic Growth and Valuation of the Environment", 3rd edition, FSNI, sni-hueting.info
Heertje A. (2006), "Echte economie", Nijmegen: Valkhof Pers, p. 138
Heertje A. (2014), "Economie", Prometheus ebook
Hennipman P (1940), "Economisch motief en economisch principe", thesis Amsterdam
Hennipman P (1962), "Doeleinden en criteria", in Andriessen JE, Meerhaeghe MAG, editors, "Theorie van de economische politiek", Leiden: Stenfert Kroese
Hennipman P (1995), "Welfare economics and the theory of economic policy", Bodmin, Cornwall: Edward Elgar
Hofkes MW, Gerlagh R, Lise W, Verbruggen H (2002), "Sustainable National Income: A Trend Analysis for the Netherlands for 1990 - 1995", R-02/02 March
Hofkes MW, Gerlagh R, Linderhof V (2004), "Sustainable National Income: A Trend Analysis for the Netherlands for 1990-2000", June 8, available at SSRN – a report commissioned by RIVM
Hofkes MW, Verbruggen H (2008), "De Nederlandse zoektocht naar een Groen BNP", p71-82 in Oosterhuis (ed) (2008)
Hofkes MW, Verbruggen H (2012), "Van groene welvaartsmaten tot een nationale maatschappelijke kosten-batenanalyse", TvOF 44 no 4, Wim Drees Stichting voor Openbare Financiën
Houghton JT, Jenkins GJ, Ephraums JJ (1992), "Climate Change; the IPCC Scientific assessment", CUP
Ierland EC van, Straaten J van der, Vollebergh HRJ (2001), "Economic growth and valuation of the environment: a debate", Edward Elgar
Isard W (1969), "Some notes on the linkage of the ecologic and economic systems", Regional Science Association: Papers 22
Isard W et al. (1968), "On the linkage of socio-economic and ecological systems", The Regional Science Association: Papers 21
IUCN, UNEP and WWF (1980), "World Conservation Strategy: Living Resource Conservation for Sustainable Development", Gland, Switzerland
IUCN, UNEP and WWF (1991), "Caring for the Earth. A Strategy for Sustainable Living", Gland, Switzerland
Jäger, J (1988), "Developing policies for responding to climatic change; a summary of the discussions and recommendations of the workshops held in Villach (28 September-2 October 1987) and Bellagio (9-13 November 1987) under the auspices of the Beijer Institute", Stockholm / World Meteorological Organization / UN Environment Programme, World Climate Programme Impact Studies
Kapp KW (1950), "The Social Costs of Private Enterprise", Cambridge (Mass)
Kapp KW (1963), "Social Costs of Business Enterprise", London
Keller WJ (1980), "Tax incidence", North-Holland
Kindler TP, Chameides WL, Wine PH, Cunnold DM, Alyea FN, Franklin JA (1995), "The fate of atmospheric phosgene and the stratospheric chlorine loadings of its parent compounds: CCl4, C2Cl4, C2HCl3, CH3CCl3, and CHCl3", Journal of Geophysical Research 100 (1): 1235-1252, paper no. 94JD02518
Kneese AV (1970), "Economic responsibility for the by-products of production", The Annals of the American Academy ofPolitical and Social Science 389, May
Kneese AV, d'Arge AC (1969), "Pervasive external costs and the response of society", in: "The Analysis and Evaluation of Public Expenditures: The PPB System", A compendium of papers submitted to the Subcommittee on Economy in Government of the Joint Economic Committee, 91 Congr., 1 sess.

Kuik O (2006), “Sustainable National Income”. In: “Overview of Advanced Tools for Sustainability Assessment”, Institute for Environmental Studies (VU, Amst erdam), Sustainability A-Test project, European Union, DG Research
Lange GM, Wodon Q, Carey K (2018), “The Changing Wealth of Nations 2018 : Building a Sustainable Future” Washington, DC: World Bank http://hdl.handle.net/10986/29001
Layard R (2005), “Happiness”, Allen Lane, London
Leeuw FAAM de (1991), “Ozon op leefniveau”, In: “Nationale Milieuverkenning 2, 1990-2010”, RIVM, Samson H.D Tjeenk Willink BV, Alphen aan den Rijn
Leeuw FAAM de, Rheineck Leyssius HJ van (1991), “Calculation of long-term averaged and episodic oxydantconcentrations for the Netherlands”, Atmospheric Environmnet 25A (1991):1809-1818
Leontief WW (1970), “Environmental repercussions and the economic structure: an input-output approach”, The Review of Economics and Statistics, August
Lintsen H, Veraart F, Smits J-P, Grin J (2018), “Well-being, Sustainability and Social Development. The Netherlands 1850–2050”, Springer Open Access, https://link.springer.com/book/10.1007%2F978-3-319-76696-6
Lovelock JE (1979), “Gaia, A New Look at Life on Earth”, Oxford University Press, Oxford
Marcuse H (1964), “One Dimensional Man, the Ideology of Industrial Society”, Beacon Press, London
Marshall A (1890, 1969), “Principles of Economics”, 8th ed. London, 1969, p. 221 et seq.
Mazijn B (ed) (2000), "Duurzame ontwikkeling meervoudig bekeken", Academia Press, Gent
Meadows DH, Meadows DL, Randers J, Behrens III WW (1972), “The limits to growth, A report for the Club of Rome Project on the Predicament of Mankind”, Universe Books, New York.
Mesarovic M, Pestel E (1974a), “Mankind at the Turning Point”, New York
Mesarovic M, Pestel E (1974b), “Multilevel Computer Model of the World Development system”, IIASA Report SP-74-1. Luxembourg
Milieu- en Natuurplanbureau (MNP) (2006), “Milieubalans”, p. 21
Mill JS (1862, 1876), “Principles of political economy”, London
Ministry of VROM (2002), “Nationale strategie voor duurzame ontwikkeling. Verkenning van het Rijksoverheidsbeleid”, The Hague. Preface by minister J.P. Pronk
Mishan EJ (1967), “The Costs of Economic Growth”, London
Nimitz JS, Skaggs RS (1992), “Estimating troposheric lifetimes and ozone depletion potentials of one and two carbon hydrofluorocarbons andhydrochlorofluorocarbons”, Environmental Science and Technology 26: 739-744
Nordhaus W, Tobin J (1972), "Is Growth Obsolete?", in "Economic Research: Retrospect and Prospect", Volume 5, Economic Growth, NBER 7620
NRC Handelsblad (2014), “Wij doen niet aan politieke inkleuring. Interview met Tjark Tjin-A-Tsoi”, July 19
O'Connor, J. et al. (1995), "Monitoring environmental progress. A report on work in progress", World Bank, Environmental Sustainable Development Series (Chapter 7 "Are We Saving Enough for the Future?", p 53-56; Chapter 8, "Where Is the Wealth of Nations?", p57-66), https://invenio.unidep.org/invenio//record/1584/files/environmental.pdf
Odum EP (1971), Fundamentals of Ecology”, 3rd edn, Philadelphia (Penn.), p.223 et seq.
OECD (2004), "Measuring Sustainable Development. Integrated economic, environmental and social frameworks", Paris
Oosterhuis FH (ed) (2008), "Aan schaarste geen gebrek - 21 jaar milieueconomie in Nederland", VU, ISBN 9789090229416
Oosterhuis FH, Esch S van der, Hoogervorst N (2016), "From statistics to policy. The development and application of environmental statistics and environmental accounts in the Netherlands", report developed in support of the World Bank’s programme ‘Wealth

Accounting and the Valuation of Ecosystem Services' (WAVES), PBL Netherlands Environmental Assessment Agency, publication number: 2433, The Hague, https://www.wavespartnership.org/sites/waves/files/kc/pbl-2016-from-statistics-to-policy-2433.pdf
Opschoor JB (1987), "Duurzaamheid en verandering: over ecologische inpasbaarheid van economische ontwikkelingen", inaugurele rede, VU Boekhandel/Uitgeverij
Opschoor JB (1995), "Ecospace and the fall and rise of throughput intensity", Ecological Economics Volume 15, Issue 2, Pages 137-140
Pearce DW (1998), "Auditing the Earth: The Value of the World's Ecosystem Services and Natural Capital", Environment, vol. 40, no. 2 (March)
Pearce DW, Atkinson G (1993), "Capital Theory and the Measurement of Sustainable Development: An Indicator of Weak Sustainability," Ecological Economics 8 (1993) 103-108
Pearce DW, Hamilton K, Atkinson G (2001), "Valuing nature", in Van Ierland et al. pp 211-224
Pearce DW, Markandya A, Barbier EB (1989), "Blueprint for a Green Economy", Taylor & Francis
Pen J, Berg WJ van den, Haan H de, Janssen R (2006), "Bnp, weg ermee?", ESB 10-3-2006 p116-117
Pethig R (1994), "Valuing the environment: methodological and measurement issues", Kluwer Academic Publishers, Dordrecht/Boston/London
Pezzey JCV (1994), "Theoretical essay on sustainability and environmental policy", University of Bristol, United Kingdom
Pigou AC (1920, 1962), "The Economics of Welfare" New York, 1962
Raup DM (1986), "Biological Extinction in Earth History", Science 231:1528-33
Reijnders L (1996), "Environmentally Improved Production Processes and Products", Kluwer Scientific Publishers, Dordtrecht.
RIVM (1991), "Nationale Milieuverkenning 2, 1990-2010", RIVM, Bilthoven, Samson H.D. Tjeenk Willink BV, Alphen aan den Rijn
RIVM (1992), "National Environmental Outlook 1990-2010", RIVM, Bilthoven, Samson H.D. Tjeenk Willink BV, Alphen aan den Rijn.
RIVM (1993), "Nationale Milieuverkenning 3, 1993-2015", RIVM, Bilthoven, Samson H.D. Tjeenk Willink BV, Alphen aan den Rijn
RIVM (1994), "Milieurendement van het NMP-2: Bijlage E-H", RIVM-rapport 251701013.
RIVM (1995), "Achergronden bij: Milieubalans 95", RIVM, Bilthoven, Samson H.D. Tjeenk Willink BV, Alphen aan den Rijn
RIVM (1996), "Milieubalans 1996", RIVM, Bilthoven, Samson H.D. Tjeenk Willink BV, Alphen aan den Rijn
RIVM (1997), "Nationale Milieuverkenning 4 1997-2020", RIVM, Bilthoven, Samson H.D. Tjeenk Willink BV, Alphen aan den Rijn
RIVM (2004), "Milieubalans 2004", Bilthoven
RIVM et al. (1997), "Natuurverkenning 97", RIVM, Informatie- en KennisCentrum Natuurbeheer, DLO-Instituut voor Bos- en Natuuronderzoek, DLO-Staring centrum, Samson H.D. Tjeenk Willink BV, Alphen aan den Rijn
RIZA (1996), "WaterSysteemVerkenningen", concept
Robbins L (1932, 1935), "An essay on the nature and significance of economic science," 2nd ed. London: MacMillan (1st edition 1932)
Robbins L (1939), "The economic causes of war", London
Roberts F (1988), "Modern Cassandras", Resource Policy, 14: 306-7
Røpke I (2004), "The early history of modern ecological economics", Ecological Economics 50, p293– 314
Rosenstein-Rodan PN (1927), "Grenznutzen", in "Handwörterbuch der Staatswissenschaften" 4. Auflage. Jena: Vierter Band; 1927. p. 1195.et seq.

Rotmans J (1990), “IMAGE: an integrated model to assess the greenhouse effect”, Kluwer Academic Publishers, Dordrecht etc.
Serafy S el (1998), "Pricing the invaluable: the value of the world’s ecosystem services and natural capital", Ecological Economics 25 (1998) 25 – 27
Serafy S el (2001a), “Steering by the right compass: the quest for a better assessment of the national product”, in p189-210 in Van Ierland et al.
Serafy S el (2001b), “Summary of article by Salah El Serafy: Green Accounting and Economic Policy” in “Frontier Issues in Economic Thought, Volume 6: A Survey of Sustainable Development”, Island Press: Washington DC, pp. 33-36
Serafy S el (2013), “Macroeconomics and the environment”, Edward Elgar
Serafy S el (2014), “Shouldn’t economists get involved in the making of the national accounts?”, Newsletter of the Royal Economic Society, no 167, October, p14-15. Also included in Colignatus (2009b, 2015, 2019)
Siebert H (1982), "Nature as a Life Support System: Renewable Resources and Environmental Disruption". Journal of Economics Vol. 42 No 2:133-142
Slaper H, Elzen MGJ den, Woerd HJ van der, Greef J de (1992), “Ozone depletion and skin cancer incidence: an integrated model approach”, RIVM, Bilthoven, rapport nr. 749202001.
Solow RM (1974), “Intergenerational equity and exhaustible resources”, Review of Economic Studies, symposium, 29-45
Sprengers SA, Slager LK, Aiking H (1994), “Biodiversity and climate change, Part I: Establishment of ecological goals for the climate convention”, Institute for Environmental Studies, Vrije Universiteit, Amsterdam, report R-94/09
Stauverman P (2007), “Frequently Asked Questions on Hueting’s SNI concept”, http://www.sni-hueting.info/EN/2007-05-Stauvermann-FAQ.pdf
Stern N (2006), “Stern Review on the Economics of Climate Change”, HM Treasury, London
Tinbergen J (1985), “Production, income and welfare. In search for an optimal social order”, Wheatsheaf Books, Univ. of Nebraska Press
Tinbergen J (1990), “Bepalen van omslagpunt is van essentieel belang”, NRC-Handelsblad, 16 October
Tinbergen J (1993), “Origin of national accounts and relation to economic theory”, in WFM de Vries e.a. (1993), p13-17
Tinbergen J, Hueting R (1991), “GNP and market prices: wrong signals for sustainable economic success that mask environmental destruction”, in: Goodland R, Daly H, El Serafy S, Von Droste B, editors. Environmentally sustainable economic development: building on Brundtland. Ch 4: 51-57, United Nations Educational, Scientific and Cultural Organization, Paris, 1991. Also published in (R. Goodland et al. (eds)), Population, Technology and Lifestyle: The Transition to Sustainability, Ch. 4: 52-62. Island Press, The International Bank for Reconstruction and Development and UNESCO, Washington, D.C., 1992. Also published in (R. Goodland et al. (eds)), Environmentally Sustainable Economic Development: Building on Brundtland, Environment Working Paper 46, The World Bank, Washington, D.C.1991
Tuinen HK van (1975), “Het begrip nationaal inkomen: corrigeren of niet?”, ESB 5-3-1975 p221-224
Tuinen HK van (1993), “Issues in Dutch national accounting 1970-1985”, in WFM de Vries e.a. (1993) p19-31
Tuinen HK van (2009), “Innovative Statistics to Improve Our Notion of Reality”, Journal of Official Statistics, Vol. 25, No. 4, 2009, pp. 431–465
UNEP (1989), “Environmental effects panel report pursuant to article 6 of the Montreal Protocol on substances that deplete the ozone layer under the auspices of the United Nations Environment Programme”, UNEP, Nairobi, Kenya

UNEP (1991), “Environmental effects of ozone depletion: 1991 update, Panel report pursuant to article 6 of the Montreal Protocol on substances that deplete the ozone layer under the auspices of the United Nations Environment Programme”, UNEP, Nairobi, Kenya.
UNEP (2002), “Global Environmental Outlook 3”, London: Earthscan
United Nations (UN), European Commission (EU-EC), International Monetary Fund (IMF), Organisation for Economic Co-operation and Development (OECD), World Bank (2003), “Handbook of National Accounting – Integrated Environmental and Economic Accounting 2003 (SEEA)”, New York
Vellinga P, Swart RJ (1991), “The greenhouse marathon: A proposal for a global strategy”, Climatic Change, 18:vii-xii
Ven P van de (2006), “In memoriam: Kees Oomens (1917-2005). A self-made man and a great visionary statistician”, The review of income and wealth, Volume 52, Issue 2, June 2006, pages 341-342
Verbruggen H (ed) (2000), “Final report on calculations of a sustainable national income according to Hueting’s methodology”, Institute for Environmental Studies, Vrije Universiteit, Amsterdam, O-00/10
Verbruggen H, Dellink RB, Gerlach R, Hofkes MW, Jansen HMA (2001), “Alternative calculations of a sustainable National Income for the Netherlands according to Hueting”, in: Van Ierland et al., p. 275–312
Verbruggen H (2018), “Duurzaamheid tussen overheid en markt”, TPE-digitaal (12) 1, p87-99
Vries W de (1993), “Average critical loads for nitrogen and sulphur and its use in acidification abatement policy in the Netherlands”, Water, Air and Soil Pollution 68 (1993): 399-434
Vries W de (1995), “Kritische depositieniveaus voor totaal zuur en stikstof op bossen”, Actieprogramma Verzuring III, Appendix 1, draft
Vries W de (1996), “Critical loads for acidity and nitrogen for Dutch forests on a 1 km x 1 km grid”, DLO-Winand Staring Centre for Integrated Land, Soil and Water Research, Wageningen, SC-DLO report 113. (bodem)
Vries WFM de, et al. (eds) (1993), “The Value Added of National Accounting: Commemorating 50 years of national accounts in the Netherlands”, CBS Statistics Netherlands
VROM (1994), “Second National Environment Policy Plan for the Netherlands”, Ministry of VROM
Wackernagel M, Rees WE (1996), “Our Ecological Footprint”, New Society Publishers, Gabriola Island, Canada
Wilson CL et al. (1970), “Man’s Impact on the Global Environment. Assessment and Recommendations for Action”, Cambridge, Mass.
WMO (1999), “Scientific assessment of ozone depletion: 1998”, World Meteorological Organization, Geneva, 1999, Global Ozone Monitoring Project, Report no. 44
Woerd H van der, Slaper H (1991), “Aantasting van de ozonlaag”, in: Nationale Milieuverkenning 2, 1990-2010, rapport van het RIVM, Samson H.D. Tjeenk Willink bv, Alphen aan den Rijn
World Bank (1972), “Report on the Limits to Growth, A Study by the World Bank”, Washington DC
World Bank (2006), "Where is the Wealth of Nations? Measuring Capital for the 21st Century", Washington
World Commission on Environment and Development (WCED) (1987), “Our Common Future”, United Nations
Zeelenberg K, Boer B de, Brouwer R (1997), “Sustainability in Growth Models”, Report LMI-20070, CBS Statistics Netherlands

24. *Index*

N

O

P

R

S

Made in United States
Orlando, FL
04 November 2026

90206773R00122